ENEMIES OF SOCIETY

BOOKS BY PAUL JOHNSON

Contents

ENEMIES OF SOCIETY

Hell is truth seen too late
Thomas Hobbes

CHAPTER 1

The Escape from Archaism

One characteristic of the 1970s in the West has been a new and sombre mood of introspection. The exhilaration of the long, post-war boom is over and we now harbour a growing number of doubts about the future of our societies, and the civilization which embraces them. It is true, as the more pessimistic among us warn, that our familiar culture, in its political, social, economic and creative aspects, is soon to perish, from a combination of external assault and internal decay? Is it likewise true, as our more savage critics claim, that the presumptions and performance of the western world economy are themselves intrinsically evil and wasteful, and so will contribute to the approaching catastrophe? The Cassandras of our time are divided between those who struggle to save the civilization of the West from itself and its enemies, and those who deny it is worth saving. Where does the truth lie? Or, rather, is there any substance in the debate itself, or are the fears so widely expressed mere fantasies – collective nightmares of a kind which afflict even the most healthy and soundly based societies?

This book is an attempt to answer such questions, and many others which are relevant to the well-being of humanity. We shall start the quest at the beginning, not by analysing the ills, real or imaginary, of our present-day civilization, but by inspecting its roots, the forces and factors which brought it into being over many centuries and gave it its peculiar flavour and virtue. We shall, in the first instance, try to isolate the matrices, whether political, economic or cultural, of a progressive civilization, and then to examine whether, and if so how, such a civilization can decline and disappear. Then, having established our historical model, we shall be ready to investigate the origins and development of western society and to weigh its current strengths and weaknesses, and its prospects of survival. Let us then start by turning to the ancient world.

*

It is a matter of argument whether we should wonder at the speed with which human kind has mastered a hostile environment, and so created the industrialized world we now inhabit, or, alternatively, despair at the almost agonizing slowness with which primitive man hoisted himself from degradation to comparative plenty. The 'take-off' to self-sustaining industrial growth was achieved towards the end of the eighteenth century. Yet the initial take-off to settled societies, when *Homo sapiens* first began to exploit his physiological resources as a rational creature, took place as long ago as the Neolithic Age. It was then that the key discoveries were made, or rather came into widespread use: how to grow crops, how to herd, breed and exploit animals; how to use tools; how to pass from mere defence against nature to attack, and in particular how to organize the collective power of the group. These gigantic intellectual leaps, which involved the concept of planning and the development of a sense of time, were more difficult than anything we have performed since. Hence our wonder. But we are also bound to ask why it was that Stone-Age man, having broken through the prison of his environment at a number of related points, took such a long time to capitalize on his victories. Should not the process of continuous acceleration have begun thousands of years ago, instead of a mere two hundred? What were the inhibiting or frictional factors? Were they intrinsic or man-made? Or, to put it another way, were they technical or political?

The truth is that the history of the ancient world is to a great extent the history of lost opportunities. Once the Neolithic breakthrough had been achieved there was no invincible reason why man should not have progressed fairly rapidly towards an advanced industrial society. Yet archaic societies are notable not only for stagnation but retrogression. Decades and centuries rolled by without specific progress; often technology deteriorated, as the adventurism behind its discovery was lost to sight. Archaic technology was empirical: that is, discovered by trial and error rather than by analytical reasoning. Granted the enormous natural curiosity of man, or rather some men, it is hard to escape the conclusion that the wisdom of the individual was suppressed by the conservative folly of the collective. Thus old processes were retained even after better ones were discovered: it is a curious fact that the significance of inventions originating in the Near East were only realized when they were adopted by other societies. Why was this?

From what we know of archaic science, that is the attempt to record and describe techniques, it limited itself essentially to classification. It did not formulate concepts or apply logic. The mental operations behind it are concrete, non-abstract, non-analytical. The surviving mathematical texts work out sets of examples, but do not generalize or prove propositions. Precious papyri from Egypt, some of them over four thousand years old, describe to medical students specific treatments for particular maladies, but show no interest in how the body works or why it becomes ill. Always there is one 'right' way of doing things, the time-honoured one, based on inescapable precedents. In fact technology in archaic times was not even truly empirical, since experiment, novelty, might be dangerous. What might be termed the 'Galileo Principle' acted as a warning at all times in antiquity. In fifth-century Athens, the philosopher Anaxagoras declared the sun to be nothing more than a ball of brazen matter; he was saved from death for impiety only by his powerful pupil, Pericles. The point of the story is not the illiberalism of Periclean Athens but the fact that Anaxagoras was spared. In earlier societies (and sometimes in later ones) death would have been inescapable. In the archaic world all knowledge congealed into formulae, which then became part of a set of inflexible rules, religious and magical in origin. Technology and understanding were thus regarded as finite and proprietory. As a result, societies came to a full stop; then declined. The Mesopotamians believed they came into their country with their civilization already in perfect form. They had learnt to farm, use metals and to write; that was it, and 'since then no new inventions have been made'. Once precedent raised its absolutist head, science had to abdicate. In Egypt, for instance, it attained its fullest development under the Old Kingdom – thereafter there was stagnation and decay. Men accepted this decay since all believed, and were taught to believe, in a Golden Age, the ubiquitous myth of Eden.

Thus the obstacle to progress lay not in man's lack of ingenuity but in the obscurantism of unfree political systems. Indeed, in some cases we can see exactly how the state inhibited progress and change. In ancient India there was in some respects a relatively high degree of technology and even of organization. Thousands, even tens of thousands of peasants could be regimented into carefully planned collective efforts:

the building of dams, irrigation channels, highways, forts, temples and other public works. Artistic techniques were widely practised: vast numbers of villages maintained high traditions of handicrafts. But this was a mere storage economy, not a market one. The activities of the state inhibited developing technology. Surplus produce was collected for the use of the authorities, leaving none for investment. Villages had to be virtually self-sufficient; their artisans served the community and were often paid in kind, not cash. At harvest-time the grain was heaped up, then shared out, according to degree and profession. The king's share went to his store-house and was used to pay officials. Towns were centres of consumption rather than production, with limited markets. There was trade with the outside world but, as Gibbon put it, 'the objects of oriental traffic were splendid and trifling'. With few roads or wheeled vehicles, and untamed rivers, only lightweight luxury goods were transported; in any event, there was no middle class, the few merchants being strictly regulated and milked by government. Specialist artisans worked for the rich alone, and the few large workshops, plus mines and quarries, served the state, not the market. Thus there was, in effect, no market mechanism, which regulated itself. The caste system limited professional mobility and any technical improvement. If the state was authoritarian, society at the base was collectivized by the extended family; this minimized individual misfortune since the 'family' shared what it had, but it also destroyed the connection between reward and effort and subjected the individual to a paralysing degree of corporate control. The extended family also dissociated procreation from the responsibility to maintain offspring, and so produced ultra-high birthrates, the population being kept in check only by savage natural forces – appalling hygiene and malnutrition, leading to low physique and efficiency. Hence Indian philosophy, for perhaps four thousand years, commenting on the predicament produced by political and social factors, deprecated the physical desire for betterment and stressed ideologies which transcended matter. The pressure of population on limited natural resources made stagnation inevitable. Such societies slept for centuries, even millennia, under their despotic superstructures, until the incursion of the West awoke them.

If we turn to China we see even more clearly that it is the political and social structure, rather than technical capacity, which limits growth. The Chinese were responsible for some of the world's most basic inventions. They were the first to create an efficient harness for horse-driven carts, to convert circular into rectilinear motion (and vice versa), and to develop mechanical time. Above all, they produced gunpowder, the magnetic compass and printing, the magic trio, as Bacon called them, 'that have changed the whole face and state of things throughout the world'. But he meant the western world, for it was only when these three were taken out of their original setting and established in Europe that they combined to transform society. Chinese society was isolated, rich in many ways, but complacent and conservative – above all, rigid and ritualized in its political structure. The state was all, and the aggrandizement of its empire the sole object of its activities. There was no concept of freedom, or of a commonwealth: no one thought it the state's duty to act for the benefit of its people, and any such benefit which came about as a result of its actions was seen as pure coincidence. Society was almost wholly agricultural; villages were self-sufficient and static; for a peasant to leave the land, or his particular community, was a severely punished offence. Towns provided administration, not trade or markets. Artists, writers, innovators, where they existed at all, remained anonymous. Everyone had a prescribed and unchanging role in society, and its structure was fashioned with such skill and precision that there were no cracks through which the individual entrepreneur could slip. As a social structure, China was a monolithic artifact, and in all essentials remained unchanged for two thousand years. Before it could progress and modify itself, the imprisoning carapace had to be broken from outside, by force.

Hence there seems to have been an inherent tendency in all archaic societies to develop and refine the Neolithic discoveries only to a limited degree. This degree varied enormously but always at a certain point the iron curtain of political and social control slammed down, and the culture became static and non-innovatory. The closed political system was accompanied by a closed economic system, and we must assume it was the former which shaped the latter, since these tyrannies, which often controlled huge areas, could not have existed without constant interference with and exploitation of the basic producers. There was no such thing as freedom in these societies since even the rulers and the high priests were imprisoned in precedent, ritual and protocol. Men were encased, as it were, in a gigantic collective corpse, of which they formed part of the organs, each in his place; the corpse was not dead but in suspended animation. The archaic corporative state could expand, sometimes to grotesque size; and it could decay or implode. What it could not do was move. By about 1000 BC the development of man had reached a plateau.

Might we have remained on that plateau indefinitely? The route to escape, as we can now see clearly, lay through a combination of economic and political enterprise. Enterprise involves innovation, and innovation implies some element of freedom, the right to defy precedent. And men usually defy precedent only when they move some distance. In the land-locked areas men were imprisoned in their villages; elsewhere by oceans. But the Mediterranean is a natural theatre for experiment since its exploration involves no gigantic problems of long-distance sea-travel, and the unity of its climate and ecology invites cross-settlement. The first free-enterprise economies, very small in scale, began to develop about 1200 BC, radiating from the eastern Mediterranean and the Aegean, as first the Phoenicians, then the Greeks, were driven by the poverty of the land to trade at sea and to colonize. The Phoenicians had reached the outlet to the Atlantic soon after 1200 BC and soon had many small colonies; when Tyre was destroyed, the largest of the colonies, Carthage, took over the chief trading and expanding role. The Greek colonizing movement, from the eighth century BC, set up cities throughout a large area of the Mediterranean littoral, independent or semi-independent, bound together by ties that were primarily religious and moral.

What was important about these settlements, and the trading which took place between them, was that for the first time in history, as far as we are aware, the initiative for the ventures came not from the state or community but from individuals. Indeed, the Greeks, building on Phoenician precedents, slowly developed special categories of men who carried out various forms of trading activity: the *naukleros*, who traded in his own ship; the *emperos*, who merely shipped his wares as cargo; the *kapelos*, or resident trader. Herodotus says that the Lydians were the real retail traders, and they were also the first to use coins widely. The intellectual background to this mercantile flowering was made possible by the emergence of a large urban middle class. The improved production and use of iron allowed the cultivation of increasingly heavy soils, and so a denser population, which slowly concentrated in cities, fed by the new agricultural surpluses. As the city populaces became larger, they differentiated into classes, and forms of class-competition, very characteristic of free commercial economies, began to develop. In the Greek cities large landowners, or aristocrats, were obliged to relinquish their monopoly of political power, and share it with the middle class, the criterion of full citizenship being the mere ownership of land.

Thus for the first time we have organized political societies in which comparatively large numbers of the inhabitants are free men. It can be argued indefinitely whether trading enterprise created political rights, or whether the exercise of such rights made individual enterprise possible; what is important is the element of freedom common to both activities. The two developments advanced *pari passu*; in a sense they were indivisible. There was a third factor which might prove, if only we knew more, more important than either. Greek society, as it developed, was characterized by the drive to freedom and novelty, and by the desire to formulate general laws by a process of rational explanations. They were the first society which not only noted how nature worked, but sought earnestly to discover why. Behind this search, and making it possible, was a progressive simplification of the alphabet, leading to widespread literacy. Reading and writing ceased to be the arcane science of a priestly or scribe class, and became an acquisition of the innovatory section of the people, the traders, and later of an enlarged middle class.

Here we have the elements of a new take-off, the first since Neolithic times. The language link is the key one. Man was a social being long before he became human. What marked the dividing point was the creation and use of language. It seems very probable that it was the development of language which lay behind the intellectual discoveries of the Neolithic Age. For the next great leap forward man had to wait not so much for literacy itself but for its extension beyond its original hieratic limits. Once a society has a middle class freed from agricultural shackles and equipped with a script it understands, it is poised for cultural adventure.

What the Greeks in fact did was to develop the principle of criticism; that is, they first discovered it, and then, equally important, made it legitimate. This could be described as the most important event since the creation of language itself, since it allowed man to put to use whole new areas of his intellect and personality, hitherto dormant. To question received opinion had not, hitherto, been something that human beings did. But the taste, once acquired, became habitual; such pre-Socratic teachers as Thales, Anaximander and Anaximenes not only permitted their pupils to criticize but deliberately encouraged them. One might say that the cultivation of this technique not only enlarged human horizons but almost produced a new human being: alongside the Dogmatic Man of the archaic societies it placed a new creature – Critical Man. In one part of the world at least, and for a time, the dogmatic tradition of passing on received Truth unsullied by change was broken. It was the beginning of scientific method, and the blueprint for a continuously advancing society. At this turning point, man enormously strengthened his chances of survival. For Dogmatic Man is no more secure than the validity of his Truth, which after all is simply a theory based on limited evidence. The great power of Critical Man is not that he can avoid error but that he can turn it from disaster to advantage. He does not stand or fall by his theories because in a sense he has none, merely working hypotheses.

The Greek intellectual take-off was accompanied by the economic and cultural achievements of the classical world. We need not describe them. But it is important to note the scale of the classical trading system. By the third century BC the Greeks had extended their system of inter-locking manufacturing and trading cities to large areas of the Near and Middle East. These centres were huge. Apamea in Syria had half a million inhabitants. Antioch and Alexandria were probably as big. Cities of 100,000 were common. In the West the Italian middle class duplicated this achievement. It is possible that at one time Rome had over two million inhabitants, an urban size not reached again until the nineteenth century. In the Roman world-economy, the bulk of goods transported, and the distances involved, were both impressive by all but comparatively modern standards. Rome imported up to seventeen million bushels of corn a year, nearly all by ocean-going ships. Some of these vessels, based on Alexandria, could carry as much as 1,300 tons of food. Rome's trading routes stretched over 7,000 miles, from Britain to the Coromandel Coast, where a string of posts was maintained. The state postal service moved at the rate of forty miles a day, and even the goods traffic to the Coromandel, took, as a rule, no more than sixteen weeks – so close, said Pliny, had India been brought by greed. What is perhaps even more striking is that, under the Roman republic and the early empire, this massive trading system was essentially liberal. It is true that the Roman government organized the corn-trade, leasing out state shipping to private contractors; true, also, that it had a monopoly of Egyptian papyrus, and artificially restricted its production – though this was an alien inheritance from the Ptolemies. Rome also monopolized large-scale mining; though here again it often leased out production to private firms. In all essential respects, however, Rome in its prosperity ran a gigantic free-enterprise economy. The state acted as little more than the night-watchman for private owners and businessmen. In some ways, the Roman system in its prime appears immensely strong even to the modern economist; certainly it would have won the approval, or even the admiration of Adam Smith, as a tribute to the power of the 'invisible hand'. If, after the first take-off of the Neolithic Age, man had found himself struggling for millennia across an endless plateau of storage-economies, or into the blind alleys of dogmatic status-empires, in the fifth century BC he at last found himself swept along by another take-off, and by the time of Augustus it seemed to promise unlimited and permanent growth.

Yet it was all an illusion. As had occurred so often before in the archaic and classical world, the Graeco-Roman system first stagnated, then collapsed in total ruin. The novelty lay only in the magnitude of the disaster. So for man, all was to begin again, with the sombre knowledge that even the most impressive structure he creates is not invulnerable. How did it take place? Might it have been avoided? With our own confident but vulnerable society in mind, we shall now look at what exactly happens when a high civilization goes into irreversible decline.

CHAPTER 2

Cancers of the Ancient World

No event, or rather process, in human history has aroused more inconclusive discussion than the decline and disintegration of the Roman empire. For over a thousand years, what Gibbon called 'the awful revolution' was seen as the central event, or pivot, of history, astounding alike in its calamitous effects, in the gruesome contrast it provided between absolute security and total dissolution, and in the direful lessons it held for all mankind. For if Rome could fall, what system could ever be safe? The medieval and Renaissance world, well-versed in the Church Fathers, was familiar with a famous passage in Tertullian's *De Anima*, written around AD 200, celebrating the solidity of Rome's achievements:

The world is every day better known, better cultivated and more civilised than ever before. Everywhere roads have been built, the countryside explored and every part of it opened to commerce. Smiling fields have abolished the forest; flocks and herds have routed the wild beasts; the sands have been sown, the rocks broken up and cleared, the marshes drained. There are now as many towns and cities as once there were cottages. Reefs and shoals have lost their terrors. Wherever there is a trace of life, there are houses, buildings and well-ordered government.

How could such apparent certitudes be swept away?

Theologians studying Augustine's *City of God*, written early in the fifth century at the height of the tempest, had no doubt that the eclipse of Rome was a deliberate act of the Deity, to underline the transience of all human constructs; indeed, Augustine's whole theory of history was based on the determinist assumption that political and economic systems were doomed to perish as God's purpose unfolded. Why inquire further?

This, however, was precisely what more secular minds insisted on doing. Granted God's design was the ultimate cause, was it not possible to identify proximate causes? Writing in the fourteenth century, Petrarch pointed to the ambitions of Caesar, whose overthrow of the republic, by destroying popular liberties, fatally weakened the moral greatness of the Roman people. More than a century later, Machiavelli was clear that it was the barbarians who overthrew Rome, but it was the empire's constitutional and economic weakness which made their victory possible: he was the first historian since Polybius, in the second century BC, to analyse the internal process of decay within society. In 1599 Paolo Paruta, the Venetian, patriotically dated the decline from the abolition of the republic, and attributed this in turn to the class warfare between Senate and populace. Indeed, writers have always framed their answers to the problem in terms which satisfied their contemporary prejudices. Thus Voltaire: 'Two flails at last brought down this vast Colossus: the barbarians and religious disputes' – a formula more briefly echoed by Gibbon: 'The triumph of barbarism and religion.' In turn, more modern writers have isolated the central factor in accordance with their own preoccupations and special knowledge: the spread of plague, the scourge of the malarial mosquito, the exhaustion of the soil or a secular change in climate, vice or racial deterioration (or both). One widely held view today, put by the French historian André Piganiol in *L'Empire Chrétien*, is that Rome herself was successfully reshaping her society when the barbarians overthrew it by sheer force: 'Roman civilization did not die a natural death: it was murdered.' In the 1970s alone, half a dozen new and lengthy explanations have been published.

At the time, commentators and historians would certainly have endorsed Piganiol's verdict. Writing, for the most part, with an official audience in mind, they tended to stress the solidity of the Roman structure, and therefore were obliged, almost, to blame all on the ferocity and treachery of the savages. It is true that the more objective writers sought ancillary factors. Ammianus, the ablest of the later imperial historians, plays the moral card, listing the growing weaknesses of the Roman character, and in particular the appalling corruption in public life, and contrasting them with the stern rectitude of the ancients; but even he is adamant that the essential cause was a massive and irresistible movement of population. 'The people called the Huns,' he wrote, 'whom our ancestors had scarcely heard of . . . exhibit a degree of barbarism we have never come across before.' They were 'a new kind of human being, who had broken out of some hidden recess in the earth, ravaging and destroying everything around them, like a sudden tempest hurtling down from the mountains'. The image of the hateful but virile horde, the *diabolus ex machina*, was immovably implanted in the minds of the civilized ancients.

Yet even at the height of Rome's stability, the articulate few who were not wholly committed to the imperial concept were well aware that the civilization by its very nature and composition and attitudes was by no means as solid as it looked. Tertullian, in the passage quoted above, was portraying the *apparent* prosperity and permanence of the Roman 'miracle'. But being not only a Christian but a sectarian and an anti-nomian, he went on to point out, in his *Apologia* for his faith, that Rome was no stronger than the sum of its parts, and that its existence depended essentially on the extent to which those it ruled accorded it their loyalty or even acquiescence, itself conditional on Rome's respect for their culture. He was making the point that Rome ruled by the consent of 'the silent majority', that it was a coalition of compatible interests and beliefs. As he said, Rome endured on Christian sufferance:

We could take up the fight against you without arms and without riot merely by passive resistance and secession. With our numbers, the loss of so many citizens in the far corners of the earth would be enough to undermine your empire – our mere defection would hit you hard. Imagine the dread you would feel at finding yourself thus deserted, in the uncanny stillness and torpor of a dying world. You would look in vain for your subjects. The enemy at your gate would be more multitudinous than the population of your entire empire.

Without attributing too much prescience to Tertullian, one feels he here put his finger on the true line of argument. We have noted the essential part the concept of 'freedom' played in the Greek take-off; we have characterized its development into the Roman world-system as essentially a liberal economic process, presided over by a night-watch-man state. In a real sense, a degree of freedom was an essential element, perhaps the quintessential element, both in the relative prosperity and, still more, the relative acceptability of the Roman way. We must, of course, distinguish between types of freedom. Roman rule was not free in the sense that it accepted the principle of 'one man one vote'. It was, rather, free in the more fundamental sense as understood by Thomas Hobbes, when he wrote: 'The freedom of the subject is the absence of laws.' He meant by this that laws should be few, clear and simple. The

Romans had inherited from the Greeks, and expanded, the idea of an ethically based and rationally designed system of law, and the collateral notion of 'the rule of law'. The practice of such a concept is, of course, the real cement of civilization and the real guarantee of individual liberty. But the Romans, under the republic and early empire, observed the true Hobbesian forbearance: when the state could choose, its laws were silent (or unenforced). As in the British nineteenth-century empire, political power was vested in elite minorities; but there was freedom of movement and of trade, and, to a great degree, freedom of communication, speech, occupation and religion. One might say, for instance, that the late-first-century *Acts of the Apostles* is an unconscious and unsolicited tribute to Roman liberalism, and an explanation of why over seventy million people of innumerable races clung together under minimum restraint.

Yet there was a fatal flaw in the Roman formula; or, rather, a cancer eating at its heart and muscles. Along with other Greek concepts, the Romans inherited slavery. For, by a paradox more apparent than real, the Greeks not only invented freedom and institutionalized it; they also invented slavery and institutionalized that too. The pre-Greek world of the Sumerians, Babylonians, Egyptians, Assyrians and Mycenaeans was one which could not conceive of the existence of free men, and therefore one in which chattel slavery played no role of importance. In a sense, all men were slaves, and so it was not necessary to define or particularize one. The Greeks, by the very act of creating a free man, found themselves producing a servile class. There were a very large number of Greek words for slave, and servile status, and infinite gradations of servitude. But it is notable that the two concepts of freedom and slavery advanced hand in hand as Greek civilization developed, and that those cities where chattel slavery flourished were also those where freedom was most fully developed. Thus Greek society was, not accidentally but essentially, a slave society, and, since war and conquest were the most fertile providers of slaves, the triumph of the Greek culture meant the spread and intensification of slavery. Indeed, one must always bear in mind that Athenian democracy was wedded to imperialism: the Acropolis was built from the tributes of subject city-states, and the Athenian economy was underpinned by servile captives. Scholars argue about the number of slaves in the Athenian climax of the fourth to fifth centuries BC. Thus, Professor A. H. M. Jones calculates there were about 20,000 slaves to 60,000 free adults. Dr Moses Finley thinks this estimate is too low, and argues that a peak of 80,000–100,000 was reached, with three to four slaves (on average) in each free household. Certainly slaves were plentiful, and cheap: Demosthenes says that even peasant-farmers had a slave-maidservant in their houses, and the poorest teacher had his slaves.

Moreover, slavery was spreading both in numbers and geographically during the conquests of Alexander, the wars of his successors, and the rise of the Roman republic. The more territory changed hands, as the armies marched and countermarched, the more ordinary people were plunged, as it were, into the servile cauldron. Then the price of slaves fell. When peace came, it rose again. The Greeks found it highly profitable to employ crude slave labour in mines and industry, but skilled freemen could always undercut slaves: hence the free poor of the cities did not regard the institution as a threat to them, and slaves were little employed on the land. Slaves tended to be associated with barbarians; but there was no colour-line as such, indeed great fluidity in moving into slavery or out of it. Slaves enjoyed the advantage that they were exempt from military service and all civic duties, and we hear of no servile revolts in Greece. With the spread of the Roman republic through battle, great multitudes of slaves came on to the market and in the last century BC it became practicable to introduce gang-slavery in its most revolting form on the great Italian and Sicilian *latifundia*. But this was exceptional, as were the ferocious uprisings it provoked. With the long Augustan peace, the price rose rapidly, and did not fall again until the troubled times of the late empire.

At all times in the Graeco-Roman world slavery was accepted as inevitable. It was never effectively challenged. Greek culture drew a line between those who worked by hand, who were slaves, and those who worked with their minds, and were free. The distinction invaded society even above the servile line. Thus, in Plato's class republic, he drew the distinction between Guardians, with a 'golden' cast of mind, who governed; their 'silver' auxiliaries, who fought for and policed the state; and the workers, or 'base metals', who laboured and obeyed. Aristotle glossed the point in his *Politics:* 'Doubtless in ancient times the artisan class were slaves or foreigners, and therefore the majority of them are so now. The best type of state will not admit them to citizenship.' He added: 'From the hour of their birth, some are marked out for subjection, and some for rule.'

The Romans, elaborating the system, did not regard slavery as part of the natural law; it was, rather, a fact of life, a conventional institution universally practised. In Roman law, as Florentinus put it, 'Slavery is an institution of the *ius gentium*, whereby someone is subject to the dominion of another contrary to nature.' As such, its ramifications attracted the best legal minds, and slavery is so prominent in Roman legal digests that W. W. Buckland, the great Cambridge authority on the Roman law of slavery, called it 'the most characteristic part of the most characteristic intellectual product of Rome'. Slavery (as we shall see shortly) changed its relationship to the rest of society as the empire matured and decayed. Also, demand tended to outstrip supply, even if total numbers increased – thus we find the great fourth-century senator, Symmachus, St Ambrose's contemporary, asking a Danubian official to buy him twenty slave-boys, 'because on the frontier it is easy to find slaves and the price is usually tolerable'. But right until its eclipse, the ancient world endorsed the definition of Polybius: 'The necessities of life – cattle and slaves.'

The existence of slavery as a powerful and ubiquitous institution was all the more unfortunate, from an economic viewpoint, in that Graeco-Roman technology lacked dynamism. The civilizations of the Nile and Euphrates had come into existence because of their technical inventions, notably the plough and the wheeled cart, the sailing boat, the solar calendar, the smelting of copper ores, the use of oxen. But they did not systematically develop this repertoire; nor, essentially, did the Greeks, although it was the physical basis of their intellectual take-off. Compared to their striking advances in other directions, involving the critical method, their approach to technology was comatose and unadventurous. Why? Because slaves provided the muscle power. The quest for mechanical energy was thus to a large extent unnecessary: there was no market demand for technological advance. And this, in turn, tended to shift Greek rationalization in a metaphysical direction. Plato, so characteristic of the Greek approach, was an anti-empiricist. He argued that true science was teleological. It concentrated on the Mind. It was not the function of science to assist vulgar traders and suchlike; it was, rather, to help the soul to contemplate eternal truth.

After the fifth century the curve of Greek technological advance flattened out. The more enterprising elements tended to emigrate to overseas centres of Hellenism, and colonies, especially after the Alexandrine conquests, while in Greece itself there were destructive wars and class conflicts. Greek emigration transformed large areas of the orient;

great cities arose; but these were not enshrined by free societies. Greek language and culture remained urban and limited in their spread, dominating culture and trade but not permeating society as a whole. And, once the spread of Rome absorbed the Hellenized states, the recovery of orientalism was rapid and the original Greek spark soon extinguished.

For the Romans were less interested in technology than the Greeks, and more committed to the disciplined and highly-organized use of muscle-power. Rome was built on oceans of human sweat. Democracy in the Greek sense never really took root there; the wealth of the republic in its prime was a composite of forced provincial labour, war-loot and the agonies of innumerable slaves, working plantations owned by absentee aristocrats who lived in Rome. The coming of the empire pushed these tendencies even further in the same direction, so that its great cities were never centres of technical industry but rather, as the Russian economic historian Rostovtzeff put it, 'hives of drones'.

Roman intellectuals pushed the Platonic contempt for empiricism to its logical conclusions, and added an element of class-consciousness which was rigid, conservative and obscurantist. In his *De officiis*, Cicero summarized the prevailing view:

Public opinion divides the trades and professions into the liberal and the vulgar. We condemn the odious occupations of the collector of customs and the usurer, and the base and menial work of unskilled labourers; for the very wages the labourer receives are the badge of slavery. Equally contemptible, the business of the shopkeeper. . . . The work of the mechanic is also degrading. . . . The learned professions, such as medicine, architecture and higher education, from which society derives the greatest benefit, are considered honourable occupations. . . . But of all the sources of wealth, farming is the best, the most fitting, the most profitable, the most noble.

This analysis did not even have the redeeming merit that the Roman intelligentsia and aristocracy put their brains to work on improving agricultural technology. The treatise on scientific farming had been a feature of the republic, but even by Cicero's day such works were becoming rare, and inclined to be repetitive rather than innovatory. Here again the huge increase of slavery in the first century BC killed off the economic urge to explore new methods. As the empire progressed, interest in technology of any kind petered out. There were compilations of available knowledge, codes, digests, rearrangements: nothing creative. In the whole of the fourth century AD, for instance, there was no original work published (or even, to a great extent, any scholarly work) in the entire fields of science, agriculture, mathematics, engineering, architecture or any other technical subject. It is remarkable that the Romans did not explore possibilities even in matters which were of passionate importance to them. Thus they spent prodigies of effort building aqueducts but never developed even the most primitive pressurized water system. They consumed vast quantities of grain but made no attempt to develop water-mills, though the principles were actually described by Vitruvius. Devoted as they were to artificial light and illumination, they failed to devise even an improved oil lamp, simply turning out the old model in colossal quantities. Economies of scale meant nothing to them: if they wanted to construct a building twice as large as its prototype, they simply doubled the number of labourers employed. The biographer of the emperor Vespasian says that, when an inventor devised a new way of dragging huge columns of marble to the Capitol, Vespasian gave him money but declined to adopt his idea, saying that the poor must be allowed to earn their pittance. Most curious of all, the Romans showed little interest even in military technology, though their empire stood (and eventually fell) on the efficiency of its army. The only original military work during the whole period of the empire is an anonymous tract, *De rebus bellicis*, believed to have been written about AD 370. The author advocated the creation of a mechanized army, along with far-reaching administrative reforms to pay for and supply it. So far as we can see, no notice whatever was taken of the plan.

Granted the existence of a world market and, in late republican and early imperial times, a liberal economy, why did not purely market factors produce technical dynamism? The answer is that they might have done if wealth had been more evenly spread. But the fruits of conquest went into few hands. The consumption of the poorer classes remained low, and there was no economic base for industrialization. Hence, when the expanding empire brought new markets, production of basic goods like pottery soon decentralized itself. As production costs remained roughly equal all over the empire, trade remained local and tied to the prosperity simply of its area. Industry tended to export itself, rather than its products. Italy itself became more parasitical as the provinces made themselves self-sufficient in grain, oil, wine, salt and manufactures like pottery, brassware and textiles. From the end of the first century AD there is evidence that the population of Italy declined, along with its exports of agricultural and manufactured goods. No really large factories developed; indeed, they became smaller. Business organization was never other than individualistic. In fact under the later empire, manufacturing shifted from the town to the countryside in Italy (and not only in Italy). Country estates grew larger. In Nero's reign, says Pliny, six men owned half the province of Africa, and this process of concentration continued so long as the western empire had any meaning at all. These rural units were self-contained manufacturing centres, thus wrecking town industry, such as it was. The phenomenon had been a feature of the Bronze Age, and was to perpetuate itself well into the Middle Ages. In economic terms it was a disastrous regression, because it meant the end of the division of labour and specialization: the end of the free market economy, in fact.

Of course one reason why an industrial system was never created was the cost and uncertainty of transport. In theory, shipping costs were comparatively low, and the loans used to finance maritime trade carried with them an element of insurance, a comparatively advanced concept. But only during the first two centuries of the empire were regular naval forces effective in suppressing piracy. Where trade involved a land element, costs rose dramatically. This was one reason why Rome developed a huge and persistent adverse balance of trade with the East. The East exported luxuries, small in bulk: spices, drugs, incense, perfumes and jewels from India, silks from China. Rome's potential exports were raw materials or bulk cheap manufactures like low-cost pottery. It was economic to ship but not to drag them across the desert by camel. Thus, even in the first century AD, as the Augustan court geographer Strabo noted, Roman ships returned empty to Egypt. In his *Natural History*, Pliny says that India, China and Arabia took an annual sum of one hundred million sesterces from the empire; Tiberius stormed against 'the womanly vanities to pay for which our precious bullion is transferred to foreign or even hostile lands'. Hence Rome's feverish search for gold wherever the legions penetrated: it was her chief viable export.

An effective free-enterprise economy ought to have got round these difficulties, however. But Roman commercial practice was defective. It is true that Graeco-Roman jurisprudence embraced, for the first time in history, the essentials of a commercial code: the idea of private property, underwritten by the rule of law itself; the ability of the individual to enforce his right by law; and, above all, the notion of contracts between two private individuals enforceable in the courts. One might say that the classical world failed to achieve a true economic take-off in so far as these basic concepts were defective or incompletely realized in practice. For instance, there was no concept of independent business capital, distinguishable at law from private wealth, or of limited liability, or of perpetual undertakings which were separate from the lives and fortunes of the existing owners. Associations for business purposes were *ad hoc*. Then too, there was no patent law, and thus no secret and protected processes, at any rate for long, and no incentive to invent. The paper-work and accountancy side of the private-enterprise economy were primitive, and remained so. The notion of the bank was there, but was immature. Greek banks were small – Pasion's, in Athens, was like a pawnshop, and its working capital was tiny – and Roman ones not much better. We know from Cicero's letters how complicated it was to make payments abroad. If banks operating in a vast and secure empire could not get that kind of transaction right, they were clearly crude and inefficient, and it is a fact that the fortunes made by Roman bankers were small compared to the harvests of politicians, generals, mine owners and landlords.

The truth is that Roman prosperity, like that of Athens before it, was due essentially to the spread of empire. Both were built upon the looting, rather than the farming, principle. They had the intellectual elements of a self-perpetuating market economy, and some of its practical features, but they did not travel far along this road because an easier one beckoned – for a time. The Mediterranean provided an excellent means of moving resources from one end to another. Building and looting an empire was a comparatively cheap and effortless process. There was the wealth of great new provinces, especially Egypt and Gaul, to be exploited. The comparative security of the frontiers meant that only a small army had to be paid for. It would be untrue to say that Roman rule was ever exactly popular. As Cicero put it to the Senate (*Pro Lege Manilia*): 'Words cannot express, gentlemen, how bitterly hated we are among foreign nations because of the wanton and outrageous conduct of the men whom in recent years we have sent to govern them.' But Cicero was talking of departures from standards which, in terms of the ancient world, were high ones. What is true is that the republic and early empire never aroused sufficient hostility totally to destroy its liberal spirit, or upset its fundamental budget – that is, the cost of repression did not exceed the profits of colonization.

From the beginning of the second century AD, however, the equilibrium was progressively upset as the growing pressure of the barbarians obliged the authorities to increase their standing forces. At the same time, fresh territories available for conquest and plunder were exhausted, or rather any further advance and occupation had to be purchased at prohibitive military cost. This was the point at which the Roman empire no longer made economic sense; the calculation on which the Romans, quite unconsciously, had created it no longer balanced in the invisible ledgers. But Rome, which never possessed an economic policy as such, and had no administrative means of analysing her total resources and expenditure, simply blundered further into deficit.

To pay for an empire which had ceased to pay for itself, the regime had to raise more money internally. This meant more and higher taxes, and so in turn a bigger bureaucracy, more corruption, tighter central control and a ubiquitous extension of the compulsive principle. One may say that at this stage the cancer eating at the heart of Rome, the all-pervasive acceptance and justification of slavery, of the degradation of man, began rapidly to take over the whole body. With it went the end of liberalism first in a political and then in an economic sense. Under Trajan and Hadrian, when the empire reached its territorial apogee, we get the first evidence of special commissioners, *curatores*, appointed to supervise the internal affairs of the cities and reporting directly to the emperor. It was Trajan who first introduced the system of obligatory state leases and the compulsory recruitment of local officials for the lower grades of the bureaucracy. To this his successor Hadrian added a system of secret police and informers, which he developed from the corps of *frumentarii* or commissariat officials. As the bureaucracy increased in numbers and power, so its interventions in the free-enterprise economy multiplied. The huge and persistent drain of bullion to the East made the empire a victim of a debauched currency and so of chronic inflation. In 301 Diocletian promulgated a universal edict imposing wage and price controls, under the penalty of death. It opened with a notable assertion: 'Uncontrolled economic activity is a religion of the Godless.' For the first time the Roman state acquired a deliberate economic policy, and it was a bad one; indeed, unworkable. The edict illustrated the nemesis of power: though all authority was now centred the emperor's hands, and he might override the law itself, he could not get his controls obeyed, despite the creation of a new bureaucracy to enforce them. Lactantius says the edict was a complete failure, and that in the end there was 'great bloodshed arising from its small and unimportant details'; he adds that there were now more people involved in raising and spending taxes than in paying them.

When an authoritarian and bureaucratic state finds itself ineffective and disobeyed, its frustrated response is invariably to seek more authority and expand its bureaucracy. By the middle of the third century AD the empire was in unmistakable economic decline. The cities were decaying, and with this went a progressive shrinkage of the urban middle class, the very foundation and instrument of classical civilization, which had produced and applauded the Attic drama, the temples and public buildings of Greece – and their sculpture – the histories of Thucydides, Polybius and Herodotus, the science of Archimedes and Euclid, the philosophy of Plato, Aristotle and Epicurus, the poetry of Virgil and Horace, the satire of Juvenal and Tacitus; above all the great infrastructure of Roman law, the ubiquitous artefact and foundation of middle-class morality. Virtually everything of value in the classical world came from the bourgeoisie; hence its political enslavement and its economic destruction – the two went hand in hand and are almost indistinguishable – meant an inevitable return to archaic forms of social and commercial organization, in short a reversal to the oriental tyranny.

We can see the process at work most strikingly in the transformation of a society where movement was free and employment unregulated into an all-embracing corporate state. During the third century, the city trade guilds, or *collegia,* gradually ceased to be honourable and independent associations and were changed into instruments of state domination. By the early fourth century all urban trades and occupations were organized into *collegia,* which were not only compulsory but hereditary. This could be, and indeed was, presented as a form of mixed economy, with the state merely organizing private enterprise. In fact the authoritarian nature of the system increased inexorably. Enrolment in one or another of the *collegia* was enforced as a penalty on any convicted criminal who had hitherto avoided 'incorporation'. Once the system became hereditary, neither a man nor his son or grandson had any prospect of transferring from one trade or occupation to another. Thus the middle and lower orders in the cities were frozen into immobility from generation to generation. An edict of 380, for instance, forbade children of the workers in the mint to marry outside their class and occupation; and, to prevent these workers from escaping, they were branded on the arm.

In what way was their predicament different from that of the slaves themselves? It is hard to say. Indeed, slavery was ceasing to possess institutional importance in the later empire since, as in the archaic despotisms from which free Greece evolved, all men were progressively reduced to the servile level, and then locked into the iron system. As the economy plunged downwards and the towns lost their dynamism, those who flourished put their money into land, and the big estates emerged as centres of power (as well as economic activity). It was, in a number of ways, the beginning of feudalism. The landowners became the most important of the pressure-groups; the countryside became orientated to the manor, and the status-relationships between the owner of the manor and those who lived in the surrounding district more pronounced. Men provided labour-services in return for tenant-land; and so they became tied to the estate. From the beginning of the third century imperial policy supported the landlord in any steps he took to ensure the fields were adequately cultivated, and so able to produce the surpluses to satisfy the government's fiscal demands. As population was falling, from seventy million to about fifty million under the later empire, freedom of movement in the countryside, as well as in the towns, had to be restricted. In 332 Constantine promulgated a basic law binding all *coloni* to the estate. In effect they became serfs, and though they were not actually chattels their status was in some respects worse than slaves because their landlords were forbidden by law either to free them or permit them to leave the district. Their children were *glebae adscripti*, tied to the soil.

By the time of Constantine's death, the Roman empire had become a totalitarian state in both an economic and a political sense. The degree of compulsion was much more marked in the West than in the East, where the nucleus of a free peasantry survived for some centuries (one reason why the Byzantine empire remained viable). But everywhere the state became the biggest, often the only, entrepreneur and manufacturer. In the countryside the landowner acted as the agent of the state, collecting taxes and administering justice. The middle element in society was wholly eliminated in law, and mankind was divided into two classes, the *honestiores* or upper classes (landowners, high officials and clergy), and the *humiliores* – everyone else. Each category had separate functions, rights and punishments. The corporate state was complete.

Needless to say, it was only maintained at all by a steady increase in police terror. Ammianus deals in gruesome detail with the mass-slaughters, tortures and denunciations by which society was regimented. The *Codex Theodosianus* later listed the horrifying punishments which became established: burning alive was the normal penalty for a wide variety of offences against the state. Official savagery, however, was almost wholly ineffective in suppressing corruption, the dominant administrative feature of the late empire – not surprisingly since, by the mid-fourth century, even emperors were accustomed to sell governorships for hard cash. Of course the exactions of those who bought office made Roman rule progressively less tolerable. But in any case, the principle upon which the empire had made itself acceptable – the tolerance of diversity within a unified framework – was inevitably abandoned as the structure became totalitarian.

Here, the change came decisively in the fourth century, when the state ceased to persecute Christians, then embraced Christianity as a state religion, and finally enforced it by terror. The Christians themselves were clear that the survival of their institution was dependent on the degree to which it could remain independent of the state; *they*, at least, saw the dangers of corporatism. As the western fathers declared, in a message to Constantius from the Council of Sardica, 343, any imperial interference in church affairs would be disastrous: 'There is but one way to bring order to what is confused and to bind up what is broken: everyone, freed from all fear of enslavement, has complete liberty of deciding the conduct of his affairs.' The church fought desperately, in part successfully, to maintain a distinction between itself and the state, and for autonomy in its government and doctrine. It was the only group or institution in the empire which kept the regime at bay: hence its survival. But what it claimed for itself it denied to others, and it co-operated enthusiastically with the state in enforcing religious uniformity. From 380 there was a rapid increase in the number and ferocity of statutes against heretics and dissidents of all kinds. Men must believe, Theodosius laid down, what was agreed by the church authorities: 'We judge all others unreasonable madmen, we brand them with the ignominy of heresy . . . and they shall be punished first by divine vengeance and thereafter through the chastisements of the judicial proceedings which we, supported by Heaven's judgement, shall institute.' The Catholic faith was prescribed by law, and heresy ranked as treason. Toleration was withdrawn from pagans, Jews, and other non-Christian groups; and, in areas where Christian heresy was predominant, imperial armies were used to enforce compliance.

Thus one of the most attractive and popular features of Roman rule was destroyed, and the last element of freedom extinguished. The inevitable result was the alienation of many sections of society, which joined themselves to the general undercurrent of protest against the rapacity of the state and its officers, and the terrorism of the police.

From being a liberal artefact, held together by shared freedoms and a respect for reason, the empire degenerated into a coalition of the discontented cemented by the arbitrary use of force. Its characteristics were new dogmas and superstitions, a metaphysic based on allegory, a clerical morality, education by catechism, the rise of an inquisition, and an inexorable drift towards a central control which was both tyrannical and inefficient.

In these circumstances the empire ceased to have either purpose or appeal, and so became vulnerable to internal disruption and external assault. Groups, classes and entire peoples became alienated and moved into opposition as a prelude to revolt. Indeed, peasant revolts became endemic, and they gained new force when they grouped themselves around antinomian religious causes. In North Africa the Donatists became not only heretics but nationalists, anti-imperialists and radicals, campaigning and fighting against absentee landlords who were orthodox Christians. There was the same syndrome farther east, among the persecuted Monophysites of Egypt and the Levant. Such people were prepared to join Rome's enemies whenever they appeared in force.

The claim that the empire was finally destroyed by the barbarians is true, but only in a highly qualified sense. The barbarians had been within the empire for centuries. They had migrated there to find work and fortune, and to enjoy Rome's blessings. They supplied most of Rome's army, and a huge section of her economic work-force. As the blessing of Rome disappeared, and the disadvantages of Roman rule mounted, the barbarians within linked hands with the barbarians without and, indeed, with the whole multitude of the regime's enemies everywhere. Pockets of resistance appeared, spread and defied attempts to reimpose authority. In Gaul, for instance, the *Bagaudae*, or 'those in revolt', occupied large areas and administered their own primitive justice. Paulinus of Pella calls them 'a servile faction . . . raving mad and armed for the special murder of the nobility'.

This violent language was characteristic of the reaction of orthodox, prevailing Roman opinion during the final stages of decay. Writers, reflecting this opinion, portrayed all Rome's enemies as barbarous creatures, no better than beasts; or insane. This was self-deception, which led in turn to racism. What Cicero called Roman *humanitas*, the sense of human decency and humanitarian sentiment, linked to the Stoic belief in the common brotherhood of man, whatever their race or status, largely disappeared. It was another aspect of the collapse of reason, when freedom fled. Typical of the times was the court oration of Synesius of Cyrene, Bishop and Metropolitan of Cyrenaica, given at Constantinople in AD 400: it was essentially an attack on the Goths and other barbarians, and an incitement to riot: 'Let all fair-haired men be banished from the seats of the mighty!' This was followed by an anti-Goth pogrom and massacre. Indeed, Rome's best friends among the 'barbarians', men who had devoted their lives to her service, were often the first victims of the new racism. Thus the Vandal Stilicho, the most successful and reliable of all Rome's later generals, was denounced as a traitor and beheaded. The racism was based on language, culture, religion and, above all, colour, but in a complex manner, since it was directed both against the very fair and the dark. If Synesius attacked blonds, the poet Claudian expressed, almost simultaneously, racial contempt for blacks: there must be no union with African barbarians, he intoned, since 'a coloured bastard besmirches the cradle'. He accompanied this thought by portraying a dream-world of Roman power and pomp, and this only ten years before the actual sack of Rome! Racialism was linked to wishful-thinking, and almost deliberate self-deception. Augustine's pupil, Orosius, a few years after Rome fell, produced his *Historia adversus paganos* (417–18), in which he portrays the future of the empire in absurdly rosy terms since, he says, the barbarians themselves were determined to restore Rome's glory. He invented a speech by Alhaulf, the Gothic king, making him swear that, though his original aim was to extinguish Rome and establish his own Gothic empire, he now realized his people were incapable of such a thing, and he would therefore restore the empire to the Romans.

In fact, the attitude of the barbarian princes was quite the reverse. Once they penetrated the outer fringes of the empire, and saw its condition and strength, and in particular the way in which barbarian minorities were treated, they determined to break it up and establish alternative systems. There is a good deal of evidence that, in certain important respects, the barbarian societies were morally superior, and socially more attractive, than the Rome they superseded. The Christian Salvian of Marseilles, who wrote his *De gubernatione Dei* a little before AD 440, exposes the hollowness of Roman official propaganda in the last phase. Salvian came from the Rhineland, and he writes with detailed knowledge of the Vandals, Goths, Franks, Alamanni and Saxons, and even Huns and Alans. He was better informed about alien cultures than any Roman writer since Tacitus. Rome, he argues, was bound to fall because the greed of the ruling class, which found expression in a ferocious taxation policy, led to the enslavement of the poor. Hence, he says, such outbreaks as the *Bagaudae*. The poor had no freedom to defend, so they did not defend anything. By contrast, the barbarians had a freer and better world. He adds that many educated Romans preferred to live in barbarian territory because there they found freedom and humanity – instead of the restrictions and cruelty of Roman rule.

It is notable that Salvian had linked with the Pelagians, who had for some time been stressing the essential moral equality of barbarians with Roman citizens, and urging that the tribes be Christianized as a prelude to solving the 'barbarian problem'. This anti-racist concept of the essential unity of mankind was a facet of the Pelagian doctrine of free will. But Pelagianism was crushed by Augustinian orthodoxy with the assistance of the dying Roman state; and thus Rome made no deliberately thought-out attempt to come to terms with the aliens.

In the event, Rome and its premises were overturned by grossly inferior forces, a sure indication that, for the mass of the inhabitants of the empire, the way of life the barbarians offered was morally superior and economically and socially more attractive than the Roman totalitarian system. The German fighting forces were far inferior to the regular Roman armies, and even the number of aliens living in the interior as a result of tribal settlement was minute when compared with the non-tribal population. But the fact is that the invaders found friends and allies everywhere, especially on the big estates, which sometimes housed as many as 10,000 unfree workers each. Hence the entire Vandal migration to Africa, which never numbered more than about 80,000, was able to destroy Roman military power in a decade. The Ostrogoths under Theodoric ruled Italy with ease, though outnumbered twenty to one by the Roman population. Most of the invaders were Arian schismatics or pagans, but they brought with them an atmosphere of religious toleration which had long been banished from Roman territories. As Cassiodorus noted, they did not persecute orthodox Catholics, or any other sect; he records that, when asked about his attitude to the Jews, Theodoric replied: 'Religion is not something we can command. No one can be forced into a faith against his will.'

Nor was their attitude to religious freedom the only respect in which the barbarian rule was superior to the one it replaced. Roman official opinion was extraordinarily primitive in that it classified all those who lived outside the empire as barbarians by definition; and, within it, tribes which did not have urban institutions and the classical *polis* were treated as savages. This absurdly crude classification stunted and stifled Roman self-criticism, and prevented them from distinguishing between the tribal federations, which varied enormously in social and political structure, and cultural accomplishment. Above all, the Romans as a whole – there were some Pelagian exceptions – never realized that vital social virtues like freedom, courage and loyalty, virtues they had once possessed themselves, were more secure among peoples whose communal life was founded on blood ties and personal allegiance, than in the *curiae* and *collegiae* of the corporate Roman state, held together by force and police terror. The Roman empire was not, therefore, murdered; it was replaced, in its despotic decrepitude, by what was essentially a superior system. The Graeco-Roman world-civilization disappeared because it had lost the political and economic freedoms, personified in its urban middle class, on which it had been built.

CHAPTER 3

The Western
Time Dynamic

We have spent some time on the Graeco-Roman world because we have there a model of how a civilization works: how it rises, how it falls, and what are the characteristic elements in its composition which cause first the one, then the other. We have seen that its dynamic was the spirit of economic and political liberalism, embodied in an urban middle class; and that the dynamic disappeared once the spirit was extinguished and its carriers enslaved. We now turn to the origins of our own world civilization, and examine to what extent the life-cycle of our model was repeated, and where – and how decisively – it was modified.

Of course, it can be argued that we are looking not at two civilizations, but one: that western society is essentially a part of the great historical *continuum* which began with the Graeco-Roman world and extends to this day. The extent to which this view is valid depends on our estimate of the totality of the Roman breakdown, and the importance of the threads of continuity which undoubtedly link the two epochs and societies. That there was, over a period, a huge regression is undeniable. It is summed up by the Belgian historian Henri Pirenne, in his famous book *Mahomed and Charlemagne*, published just before the Second World War:

If we consider that in the Carolingian epoch the minting of gold had ceased, that lending money at interest was prohibited, that there was no longer a class of professional merchants, that Oriental products (papyrus, spices, silk) were no longer imported, that the circulation of money was reduced to the minimum, that laymen could no longer read or write, that the taxes were no longer organised, and that the towns were mere fortresses, we can say without hesitation that we are confronted with a civilisation that had regressed to the purely agricultural stage; which no longer needed commerce, credit and regular exchange for the maintenance of the social fabric.

One index of the extent of the calamity, judged in purely material terms, is that the wealth of western Europe did not begin to exceed that of the Byzantine empire, the residual legatee of Rome, until the twelfth century, nearly seven hundred years after the western empire collapsed. Those seven centuries of obscure and almost unrecorded labour were the price our forebears paid for the toppling of Roman order.

On the other hand, there is a strong case for saying that the essential matrices of Graeco-Roman civilization were preserved, and passed on to the societies of the Dark Ages. Thanks to industrious compilers, like Cassiodorus and Isidore of Seville, and thanks to the thousands of monks who copied and recopied key texts in monastic scriptoria, the essential knowledge of the ancient world was at all times available to at least a few leaders of opinion in Latin Europe. It is true that in most cases the original Greek texts did not become available in the West until the fifteenth century, and that it was a prime achievement of Renaissance scholarship to transmit ancient culture in its full glory for the first time. Yet there was no essential discovery which was wholly lost, even in the seven dark centuries. The problem was not access to knowledge: it was lack of administrative capacity, finance and, above all, trained man-power to make use of it.

Yet in one respect the societies which emerged north of the Alps, from the debris of the western empire, had an advantage, and a new matrix, which the Graeco-Roman world had never enjoyed: the concept of rural freedom. Freedom, to the Greek, was something indissolubly associated with city life; they could not conceive of it being created, let alone flourishing, in any other context. They thought, in fact, that all good things came from cities, and this belief, endorsed and fortified in Roman times, was the chief reason – as we have seen – why the ancient civilization could not accommodate those they called barbarians because they rejected urbanization.

But it may be that the 'barbarians' themselves regarded Roman society as inferior because, despite all its material advantages, it was, manifestly to them, less free. In his book on German society written at the end of the first century AD, Tacitus noted that domestic chattel slavery was unknown among the tribes. Where slaves were employed in agriculture, they possessed their own homes (they could own property in fact) and were to some extent their own masters. In any case, the number of slaves was small; they were mainly non-German; and they were owned only by the upper classes. In short, slavery was a very marginal feature of German society. It was in fact an importation, since it was found in developed form only in the most advanced political and social areas, that is those nearest to Rome. It is very likely that the communal element in German tribal society proved resistant to the idea of one man owning another, just as, initially, it rejected the idea of freehold land (both were Roman concepts). Thanks to Christianity it came to accept the second, when Christian bishops set down its unwritten law-codes in Latin documents. But it never embraced the first as a basic ingredient of the social structure. That men should be tied to the land and, as it were, indissolubly linked to the place and its lord as a result of some notional bargain, was not abhorrent to the German tribal mind. Thus they came to develop varieties of feudalism wherever they settled. But whereas in the Roman world the infection of slavery had gradually poisoned the whole body, in the Germanic world the reverse process took place: the dynamic element of freedom gradually cleansed the rest. It is evident that from quite an early stage a distinction was made between the mass of peasants, who were unfree in the sense that they could not move, and the true slave. As Marc Bloch, the most perceptive historian of early rural society, was able to demonstrate, by the tenth century this differentiation had reached a technical form, since the word slave or *esclave* had been developed to denote slavery in its true sense, and was a minority condition on its way to extinction; the original word *servus* or serf had ceased to describe chattel-slavery and was now applied to the unfree farmer who formed the base of the feudal pyramid. Within a hundred years, slavery had virtually ceased to exist north of the Alps.

The point needs to be emphasized because it helps to explain the curious fact that western society acquired economic momentum and dynamism throughout the Dark Ages, while the other two great international systems, Byzantium and Islam, became arrested. Let us briefly see how. Byzantium survived the collapse of the western empire because it had a strong currency and urban base, because it had a central administration which gave the state financial resources beyond the capacity of any other organization at the time, and not least because it had a free peasantry who supplied its militia. It had better ports than the West, and Byzantium itself was easily defensible. But it had the essential characteristics of a totalitarian state, indeed of a theocracy. The supernatural was ubiquitous. Public games began with hymns, holidays were religious festivals, trade contracts were stamped with the cross or an invocation to the Trinity, wars were crusades, the emperor called himself the vice-regent of God, political decisions were dominated by omens, the imperial council was the 'sacred consistory', and the finance department was the ministry of 'sacred largesse'. In the West the supernatural impinged too, but at least there was a clear and growing distinction between ecclesiastical and secular power, and profane matters were never so firmly in the grip of magic, superstition, astrology and the miracle-cult as in the eastern empire. Moreover, in Byzantium the notion of freedom was not insurgent but decadent. Since the aristocracy declined to invest their surpluses in anything but land, the free peasants were gradually bought out. The state continued to be the sole manufacturer and the principal trader; the free-enterprise section of the economy remained small, struggling to survive at all in the midst of a suffocating network of monopolies, privileges, protectionist devices and repressive decrees termed 'divine delegations'. As Byzantium stood at the commercial crossroads of the Dark-Age world, and the government charged a flat rate of 10% on all goods passing through the Straits, the system remained financially viable until the twelfth century. But once the western economy had developed to the point where Italian (especially Venetian) merchants penetrated the eastern Mediterranean, they quickly took over the Byzantine private sector, and from there collared all its trade. From this stage Byzantium was a husk, doomed to be smashed by one or other of its neighbours.

Islam, which finally got the prize, was an expanding society from the seventh to the seventeenth century, but never a dynamic one. In some ways this is surprising. It had, from the start, enviable technical and intellectual advantages which the West conspicuously lacked. In their astonishing expansion, the Arabs allowed themselves to be served by able men of all races and faiths. Converted Christians, Persians and Jews were promoted to the highest places in the state; some were not even Moslems. Islam preserved Hellenic culture, or at least its science; and transmitted to it the Hindu principle of numerical position and the zero – thus founding arithmetic and algebra, two of the skills on which all modern civilization is built. There was no religious circumscription of trade since the Prophet himself had been a commercial gentleman and came from an entrepreneurial tribe. Geographically, Islam formed a homogeneous trading block, with its natural centre of mass consumption in Baghdad. Yet Islam never developed a dynamic economy, and once again the missing ingredient was freedom. The desert tribes which were the original carriers of the creed had a social structure not wholly unlike the Germanic confederations. But they were pastoral, not agricultural, and deeply penetrated by slavery; indeed, slavery was ubiquitous in the East and became a constituent part of the Islamic view of life. Thus, when Islam became city-based, the free element in its original tribal matrix atrophied, and the notion of individual rights was submerged by the all-embracing theocratic state. A man and his property were always at risk; state confiscation was liable to afflict a rich man at any time in his life, and certainly at his death. No free-enterprise economy can develop without a real degree of security for private property, and this the Islamic world possessed neither in law nor in fact. Indeed, the Islamic teaching, as a basis for social organization, was defective in various ways. Broadly speaking, men tend to direct and develop their activities in a way their metaphysical beliefs point to. Islam had no sense of urgency, no firm historical structure, and above all no sense of time.

Herein lay the great economic strength of Christianity: it is a time religion. It is progressive in the strict sense since it does not revolve end-lessly around the cyclical span of life, but proceeds relentlessly from one historical point to another. Of course it owes this historical perspective to its Judaic origin, but early Christianity heightened the sense of the millennium and the idea of an approaching apocalypse in which all the books would be balanced and an account rendered. St Augustine pro-vided a firm historical structure for past, present and future, and his notions became part of the basic repertoire of western thinking. Hence the morality of Latin Christianity is obsessed by chronological factors, and dominated by the sense of urgency, the thought that time is 'pre-cious'. 'You know not the day nor the hour' – the time-threat is branded on the Christian conscience. The scarcity of time on earth, which must never be 'wasted', is sharply contrasted with timeless eternity, and the archetypal devout Christian is one who proclaims with Andrew Marvell:

> But at my back I always hear
> Time's wingèd chariot hurrying near

Or, as Francis Bacon was to put it in his *Novum Organum* (1620): 'The human understanding is unquiet, it cannot stop or rest and still presses onward but in vain. . . .' Our spirits, he says, are obsessed 'by the obscurity of nature, the shortness of life, the deceitfulness of the senses, the infirmity of judgement, the difficulty of experiment, and the like'. Christianity had its contemplative orders; but for most of its believers it tended to induce a sense of anxiety about time, which made men dissatisfied by progress but for the same reason determined to pursue it. The image is summed up in the dying words of the great Dark-Age chronologist and historian, the Venerable Bede, addressed to his scribe: 'Write faster . . . there is so little time.'

Against this background of a time-centred religion, there were also solid economic reasons why the fulcrum of progress would shift northwards across the Alps; it may be that this displacement would have taken place even had the western empire survived. For both halves of the empire were chronically short of iron supplies. The artifacts found at Pompeii give us the impression that it was more a Bronze-Age than an Iron-Age city. Mediterranean armies constantly ferreted for iron in their conquests, with a view to using it for re-smelting. Thus, the great monumental buildings of Rome finally collapsed only after they were looted of their iron supports and clamps during the Justinian reoccupation of the sixth century. North of the Alps there was much more iron, and the long process of exploitation began in earnest after Islam closed the Mediterranean to Christian shipping in the late seventh century. The Carolingian armies were based on armoured cavalry, and the empire was based on iron. We get a striking vignette of the impact of northern iron in the *Gesta Karoli*, written by the Monk of St Gall. When the Carolingian army appeared outside the walls of Pavia, capital of the Lombard kingdom, the besieged King Desiderius was deeply depressed by the glitter of its metal. He exclaimed: '*O ferrum! Heu ferrum!*' – 'Look at the iron! Alas, the iron!'

The greater availability of iron enabled western civilization to adopt a number of key devices which in theory had been available for many centuries, but had never been fully exploited. One of the most striking facts about economic history is the slowness with which absolutely crucial innovations have been adopted. As we have seen, one of the reasons why the Romans were so uninterested in non-human power is that they were so effective in mobilizing human power, and had such seemingly inexhaustible supplies of it. They were blind to the potentialities of the horse. The saddle was a first-century barbarian innovation, and a heavier horse was introduced about the same time. But the Romans never adopted the stirrup, which moved slowly west from China through Asia. Only under the Carolingians did the iron stirrup come into standard use in western Europe. Combined with the saddle, it enormously increased the offensive power of the armoured knight. As Lynn White, the historian of medieval technology, puts it, 'The stirrup, by giving lateral support in addition to the front and back support offered by pommel and cantle, effectively welded horse and rider into a single fighting unit capable of a violence without precedent.'

The stirrup was not the only way in which technology increased the efficiency of the horse. The Greeks and Romans, and later the Franks, had only primitive hipposandals for their beasts. Carolingian times saw the introduction of the iron horseshoe, and by the eleventh century they were common. Then, too, carriage-power in the antique world was based essentially on oxen rather than horses, and the yoke-harness, though suitable for oxen, was hopelessly inefficient when placed on a horse, which tended to strangle itself if it pulled with its full strength. In the Dark-Age West, for the first time, the collar-type harness came into general use, and this, combined with the introduction of more powerful horses produced by selective breeding for military use, made possible the four-wheeled heavy wagon. This made a big difference in the land transport of bulk goods, and hastened the change from subsistence to cash-crop agriculture. Scattered hamlets now concentrated into larger villages, as the peasants no longer had to live so close to their fields. And, in these large villages, there was now invariably a smithy, a symbol that iron was at the command of every peasant family.

It was, in fact, at the level of basic agricultural work that these Dark-Age changes in the West brought the greatest returns. Greek and Roman tillage had been based on the light wooden plough, run twice over square fields of thin soil. In his *Natural History* Pliny describes the heavy iron plough, but it was only in northern Europe that it was slowly adopted in the late Roman time, and then more generally under the Franks. The consequences were formidable. The heavy iron plough, with its ability to tackle the most ponderous type of soil, literally changed the pattern of agriculture. The square fields changed to long strips, up, down and over the contours of the landscape, ensuring some crops even in very dry or very wet seasons. These ploughs were pulled originally by teams of eight oxen, and they were adopted as part of a cooperative process, under which the cost of the new technology was shared. In due course, the peasants were able to transfer from oxen-power to horse-power, as the collar-harness was introduced. A horse produces 50% more foot-pounds energy per second than an ox, and moves much more rapidly; it has more endurance and can work about two hours longer each day. Today, it costs 30% more to maintain an ox for the equivalent amount of work a horse can produce; in medieval times the difference was probably about 100%. It was the spread of oat-growing which made the feeding of vast numbers of horses possible. To quote Lynn White again: 'The ox is a grass-burning engine, the horse is a much more efficient oats-burning engine.' With oats, the northern peasants produced surpluses, and could keep more horses. In northern Europe in the twelfth century, we find the horse taking over from oxen over huge areas.

Growing oats to sustain horse-power was only one part of a long, slow but decisive agricultural revolution overtaking northern Europe. The spread of Benedictine monasteries, with their acute sense of time and rigidly kept daily timetables, and their devotion to the discipline of work, set the pace of the new agriculture; and in due course, where their impulse spent itself, the Cistercians arose to pursue large-scale 'modern' farming, especially on the frontiers of the cultivated world. From the fifth to the twelfth centuries, thanks to iron technology, a huge area of western and northern Europe was brought into cultivation for the first time in history, as marshes were drained and forests cleared. Even by the end of the seventh century, the population in central and south-western Germany was perhaps four times as great as in Roman times. The population throughout the West continued to grow until by the end of the eleventh century the pressure on available land, even granted the clearances, led to the eastern migration we call the Crusades, and accelerated a switch to three-field crop rotation, perhaps the greatest agricultural novelty of the entire Middle Ages. It was spring planting, unimportant in Roman times, which made possible the widespread use of oats, and so of horse-power; and the alternation of legumes with cereals brought a 50% production advantage by the twelfth century. Legumes, especially beans, improved the soil and added a large amount of vegetable protein to the human diet. Cooperative farming also produced fundamental social changes, notably the evolution of powerful village councils, which institutionalized the Germanic concept of rural freedom, and slowly but surely transformed the serf into a free peasant or even a yeoman farmer.

The link between town and country was provided by the new use of power-driven mills, another example of the slow exploitation of techno-logy. As long ago as the first century BC, Vitruvius had described a geared water-mill, the first great realization of a continuously powered machine. The Romans never developed the concept, or employed it at all except to grind grain. During the Dark Ages it was applied in iron-forges, for fulling cloth and making hemp, and for the first time many thousands of mills were brought into use. The Domesday Book (1086) lists 5,624 water-mills in the 3,000-odd communities it describes; water-power, in short, was now a universal part of agricultural techno-logy. In the wake of the water-mills followed mills to harness tidal rivers, and catch the wind: by the thirteenth century the windmill was a familiar feature in the landscape of northern Europe. Even more important was the emergence of an attitude of mind which scanned the horizon, looking for more ways in which to apply existing technology.

Almost from the start, the powered technology of the early Middle Ages was linked to the development of textiles for sale and export, and so to the rise of urban trading centres. If the Roman towns were 'hives of drones' and centres of administrative tyranny, the medieval town was first an episcopal fortress-residence, then an adjunct to trading-fairs on the big pilgrimage routes, finally a centre of trade and industry in its own right. We have the beginning of another Greek-style cycle of urban growth. Once more we see an urban middle class emerge, its develop-ment promoted by the growth of economic and political freedoms. But whereas the Greek and Roman *polis* was the heart of the classical politi-cal system, and thus involved in its degeneration, the society of Dark-Age feudalism really made no provision for the urban merchant, since he scarcely existed when its ideas solidified into a mould. He sub-sequently emerged, as it were, through cracks in the carapace of society, without status but also without obligations and social ties. Thus, tenants of urban land could let, pledge or transfer their properties without the intervention or even agreement of the proprietor, and could so raise capital for industrial or commercial schemes. Men liked to invest in urban property because they knew their money was safe and could easily be realized; it also went up in value as towns expanded. Hence capital was available.

The merchant, without status, had a social as well as a financial incentive to use capital effectively, for only by the deployment of wealth could he buy prestige and political power. This was the driving engine of the cloth industry, whose members acquired first influence, then actual power in the running of cities in Italy, the Low Countries and north-west Germany. Town councils, dominated by the most enterprising citizens, made their prime object the promotion of trade. The corporate principle or *collegia* had been carried over from the classical world by the church, but it had lost its repressive function as part of the state apparatus of control. Or, lost it in some ways. Medieval merchant guilds were tightly organized oligarchies, seeking the widest freedom for themselves, but denying it to others where possible. They tried to prevent the formation of craftsmen's guilds – they were, for instance, prohibited in Dinant in 1255, in Tournai in 1280, in Brussels in 1291 – and allowed them later only under the strictest control of the urban patriciate, especially of wages. But if the *bourgeoisie* kept the lower classes down, they also balanced the power of aristocracy and crown. Many wealthy towns in Italy, the Rhineland and Burgundy were virtually independent powers; and even in, say, England, a unitary state, they negotiated with, rather than deferred to, the central authorities, which accorded them political and economic privileges in return for taxes. As Henri Pirenne put it, 'Liberty is a necessary and universal attribute of the townsman.' The social basis of urban liberty was a narrow one in the later Middle Ages, but it was expanding; and, combined with the quite different tradition of rural liberty which had grown up in northern Europe, it expressed itself in a variety of mixed parliaments and assemblies, which added to the political plurality of society and inhibited the growth of a voracious central tyranny, of the type which devoured economic and political liberty in the Roman empire.

Historians have often asked the question: why, given the conjunction of dynamic factors which had come into being by the thirteenth to fourteenth centuries in the West, was there no take-off into self-sustaining industrial and trading growth? Instead there were symptoms of arrested development. 'Everywhere,' wrote Pirenne, 'the world was in labour, but it produced only abortive births.' Of the period from the early fourteenth to the mid-fifteenth century he adds: 'There was a definite feeling abroad that it was waiting for a spiritual renewal.' Population growth seems nearly always to be a pre-condition of rapid economic expansion. In England, between Domesday Book and 1300 the population grew fast, perhaps by as much as 250%. By the early fourteenth century, the territory of Naples, with a total population of 3,300,000, had a population density of 100 per square mile. The territory of Florence had over 200 per square mile, and this was true of parts of France, which had a total population of 16–17 million. Growth at this rate makes a take-off possible, but it also invites a Malthusian corrective if a wide range of other benign factors are not present. These include, among other things, the capacity to expand agricultural production, and hygienic and climatological luck.

In the second decade of the fourteenth century western Europe fell into the Malthusian Trap. A series of excessively wet seasons brought famine. Europe was already up against the limits of exploitable land, given the technology available, and a good deal of marginal land seems to have gone out of production at this time. In the 1340s came the Black Death, which struck at least three times, and was followed by a century of repeated plague-outbreaks. Between 1326 and 1500, for instance, there were seventy-two 'plague years' in Germany. Quite by how much these Malthusian correctives reduced Europe's population cannot be established. One informed guess calculates the figure for all western Europe at 61 million in 1200, rising to 73 million in 1300 – higher than for the entire Roman empire at its zenith. The total fell to 51 million in 1350, and then to 45 million fifty years later, not regaining and then passing the 1300 figure until the mid-sixteenth century. A parallel series of calculations for England puts the figures at 3,757,000 in 1348 (just before the Black Death), falling to 2,100,000 in 1400. These figures are more reliable in indicating trends than aggregates: there can be absolutely no doubt that population everywhere fell heavily in the fourteenth century, and took a long time to recover. There could be no question of a take-off against this demographic background.

There was, however, continuous development in a number of key technical fields. As far back as the twelfth century, bills of exchange emerged at the big trade-fairs and gradually changed from a currency-instrument into a credit-medium; thus moneylenders became bankers, and the European banks quickly outdistanced anything known in the classical age, both in complexity and size. In the fourteenth century the Venetians invented, or adopted, a working method of double-entry book-keeping, and this spread everywhere. Long distance maritime commerce undoubtedly helped to spread plague, but continued to increase despite its ravages, and made possible the development and adoption of a variety of new devices, financial, economic and technical. From 1300 the compass came into regular use, followed by the fairly rapid introduction of complex ocean-going ships with highly sophisticated sailing equipment and procedures; these vessels opened up the prospect of inter-continental trade, and the age of oceanic discovery.

There were restrictions on enterprise, notably the development of the guild system. These corporatist devices, based as they were on the exclusion or limitation of competition, acted against the development of a free enterprise economy. Craft guilds in particular, with ever-increasing minuteness, regulated work-techniques, working hours, wages, prices, types of tools, and raw materials to be employed. They curtailed advertising and limited the numbers of apprentices. Like modern trade unions, they acted as an anti-capitalist force, since they militated against the free movement of labour and the efficient employment of capital. But at the same time there were powerful forces working to enlarge economic freedom. The rapid fall in population in the fourteenth century enormously increased the bargaining strength of the farm-worker, even though governments rushed in to enforce maximum wages. Over large parts of western Europe, the peasants ceased to be serfs or vassals, tied to the land, and became part of a pure wage economy. The medieval manor, with its emphasis on status and stability, ceased to be the microcosm of the economy, and yielded to a cash-nexus society based on wage-contracts between freely negotiating individuals.

We have here a society whose economic complexity already outstrips any conceivable classical parallels, and which is evidently preparing the world for unprecedented patterns and rates of growth. Equally, Europe was entering an entirely new age of technology. In some cases, as with the powered water-mill, there was a classic prototype, or theory. Roger Bacon's 'brazen head', the earliest type of boiler, and the prefiguration of the steam-turbine, made concrete a point noted by Vitruvius. This and other devices are more important as illustrations of the growing curiosity of the European mind than as a contribution to actual growth. More and more clever men were becoming interested in the concept of physical power – the forms it took in nature, and the means to harness them. Since 673, when Kallinihos invented 'Greek fire' for Byzantium, men had begun to look for aggressive combustibles. They made primitive rockets, they experimented with saltpetre, and they devised long tubes for projecting fiery masses. Western metallurgy was, indeed, unable to keep pace with western chemistry, but even by the fifteenth century, the evolution of the cannon-ball and developments in gunpowder had begun to make the cannon an efficient engine of war.

Indeed, by the time the growth of population had resumed, the search for mechanical power, and for the principles of force and movement, was spreading to embrace an ever-widening circle of technology. The use of gravity-power enabled the West to replace the unreliable Roman-style water-clock with the late-thirteenth-century weight-driven mechanical timekeeper. This itself was the product of an advance in machine design. The crank, perhaps the most important mechanical invention since the wheel, because it allows the transformation of rotary into reciprocating motion, and vice versa, had again been known in rudimentary form to the Romans, but remained undeveloped. When mechanical clocks based on this principle became really efficient early in the fourteenth century, they captured the imagination of Europe, and some amazingly complicated examples were built – as, for instance, the Strasbourg 'crowing' clock, built in 1352, and still functioning today.

Hence, by the end of the fifteenth century, with population rising again, the West was beginning a new Malthusian cycle, and a new cycle of growth. But this time it had developed ocean-going ships capable of establishing colonies all over the globe, so ensuring undreamed-of outlets for surplus population. Its technological base, moreover, was much more solid than ever before. It had more diverse sources of power, animal, natural and mechanical, than those known to any previous society, and it had a range of technical devices for grasping, utilizing and guiding non-human energy incomparably more varied and ingenious than had ever been available before, anywhere on earth.

Finally, the large, growing and multitudinous cities of western Europe contained within them huge numbers of skilled mechanics and technicians, on whose practical abilities modern empirical science was to be based. These were, moreover, free citizens, and above them was a powerful, wealthy and politically emancipated bourgeoisie who created the climate of tolerance and security in which intellectual experimentation could proceed.

Once again, then, we see the importance of the 'middle people', those distinct from the near subsistence level peasant and city-dweller, on the one hand, and the ruling landowning aristocracy on the other. As we saw, by the time the Roman civilization broke up, there was nothing between the *humiliores* and the *honestiores*. But over the next ten centuries, an agricultural revolution took place over western Europe, which produced large numbers of free peasants, tenant-farmers or freeholders, who constituted a median element on the land; and, at the same time, an urban middle class, based on trade and small-scale industry, grew up once more, on the pattern of its ancient Greek prototype. The first carried through a vast improvement in agricultural husbandry; the second recreated a world trading pattern, and re-established mechanical technology on a much firmer basis than it had ever possessed in ancient times. Both these classes presupposed a measure of political and economic freedom to exist at all; both, as they grew and flourished, demanded more freedom. By the year 1500, the combination of an economic median element in society, and a degree of political freedom, had produced a new civilization which was already more advanced in many respects than its classical archetype. The moment for the real, irreversible take-off had almost come.

But now we must make a brief detour. We have so far discussed the rise and fall of ancient civilization, and the reconstruction of western society in the Middle Ages, very largely in terms of political, social and economic structures. We have left out the arts. Yet the arts are plainly an essential element in any civilized society. What we must now examine is how closely they are linked to technical progress and economic health. Have the arts an existence independent of economic and political factors? Or do they rise and decay with the social systems of which they are part?

CHAPTER 4

Art, Science and Freedom

Only a superficial view portrays the arts as a kind of non-essential superstructure, erected on an economic and technological base, with the inference that success in constructing the latter must precede the former. In fact men engage in artistic activities as soon as they can assure themselves of a subsistence living: such pursuits seem to be almost as important to them as food and drink. But of course in primitive societies art and technology are almost indistinguishable; that is to say, the distinction is one we make in modern conditions, but which becomes steadily less important the farther back we go in time.

When the Spanish Altamira Caves, with their astonishing wall-paintings, were first discovered, the academic authorities were at first inclined to dismiss them as a hoax. Leading paleo-ethnologists, who had recently found and identified some of the tools of Ice-Age hunters, saw these creatures as *Homo faber*, a brute who made tools, rather than *Homo sapiens*, a reasonable being capable of dealing in artistic images. They thought it impossible that such beings would have had the leisure or the mental inclination to produce art showing powers of observation of a high order. Only slowly have we come to accept that Ice-Age man did not divide hunting weapons and paintings of hunting into wholly separate compartments: both were instruments of his food-collecting technology. One provided information, the other the means to utilize it.

Indeed, virtually all cultural activities are designed to convey information in one form or another, or have their origins in such an objective. Animals react only directly to natural stimuli. Man goes further. By speaking, painting, sculpting, writing, the human learns to create sources of stimulation for his fellows. They are essentially artificial sources: they generate a new kind of perception in man – knowledge, or perception at second hand. Of course speech came first in chronological order: the ability to convey complicated information by means not of noises but of sentences is the real dividing line between *Homo sapiens* and the rest of creation. Ultimately speech was recorded in writing. But long before that, painting, or to be more accurate, scratchings and signs conveyed information of a type in visual form. The non-representational display is much older and more primitive than the image. It is, in a sense, a wholly invented structure, which does not specify anything. As J. J. Gibson, the great optical theoretician, puts it in *The Senses Considered as Perceptual Systems,* an abstract pattern or mark 'contains information, but not information *about,* and it affords perception, but not perception *of'.* Gradually, man acquired the skill to construct a representative display – the Cro-Magnon animals are the earliest that have survived, or which we have discovered. Such images, of mammoths and so forth, have the cultural and technological merit of providing information about something other than what they are. They are no longer mere marks on a cavern wall, but information about supplies of food. 'The structure of a natural optic array,' as Gibson puts it, '. . . specifies its source in the world by the laws of ecological optics.' The earliest such structures, of which we are aware, date from about 30,000 BC, and precede writing, an alternative or additional source of information, by more than twenty millennia.

Not only, then, is painting older than writing; but it is not a means of conveying information, in all its potentiality, which writing can easily replace. Animals, like men, argued William James, can have 'knowledge of acquaintance' (direct knowledge), but only men 'knowledge about', or knowledge at second hand. This is the great advantage of socialized over individual knowledge. But the virtue of images over words is that they permit socialized knowledge to be closer to knowledge by direct acquaintance, to primary perception. The knowledge they convey is more real, immediate, striking and impressive.

The visual image, whether in paint or stone or marble, thus goes close to the sources of a culture, and the way it makes itself understood. It is a remarkably sensitive index. The dynamic of Greek culture was the desire to know about man and explore his potentialities; it was humanist, and because it was humanist it devoted enormous trouble to portraying the human form in its exact likeness, and to placing it by structures of natural optic array in its true setting. The freedom of man in society, as an economic and political being, was paralleled by the freedom with which the artist could accurately depict him in his optical environment. Only when this freedom was secured, by a process of trial, error and improvement, was the information about man complete.

It is not entirely surprising, then, that we find the representational skills of the classical artist rise with the acquisition of human freedom, and fall with its extinction. Antique art survives only in fragmentary form, with many *lacunae*, but we can none the less trace this parabola with some precision. Of course, the real difficulty in portraying mankind truthfully consists not so much in depicting the human body but in relating it to its setting – that is, giving it spatial location. One of the most majestic of all discoveries of the classical world was the conquest of pictorial space. The process can be studied in all its stages thanks to the survival of a large number of high-quality black- and red-figure vases, or kraters, painted in Magna Graecia (that is, the central and eastern Mediterranean) between the seventh and fourth centuries BC. Here the artist was reducing chariots, rows of horses, people in a room sitting at table or on stools, from the solid world of reality to a one-dimensional curved surface. The vases, which can be dated reasonably accurately, show a progressive line of development, based on successive innovations, towards a true sense of perspective, and thus towards the natural and accurate location of the human being in his spatial framework. This step-by-step development of artistic skill is almost wholly akin to the technological changes taking place at the same time in the ancient world (indeed, it was essentially part of them), and to the enlargement of political and economic freedom in the urban societies for which the kraters were made.

At some stage in classical antiquity, the skills acquired by the vase painters were passed on to painters proper, working on the flat surface of boards and walls. Alas, what they achieved has proved much less impervious to destruction and decay than the sturdy kraters. Very little of antique painting survives in any form. What we do possess, however, are three precious written references to the theory of perspective, which underline the close connection between cultural discovery and refinement, and the progress of society as a whole. The first reference, in Euclid, deals with perspective purely in optical terms, and suggests that in the antique world the real innovator here was the mathematician: the painter working on vases was merely applying principles already explored theoretically by the academic technologist. A second passage, from Lucretius' *De Rerum Natura*, and dating from about 50 BC, gives a poetic discussion of a colonnade in terms of perspective. Here again, the writer does not have the painter in mind, and is dwelling on a theoretical and intellectualized concept, part of the (to him) common coinage of recent discovery. Vitruvius has two references, both in *De Architectura*, written about twenty-five years later, and both incidental to his purpose of writing an architectural textbook. He says: 'Sceno-graphy is the sketching of the front, and of the retreating sides, and the correspondence of all the lines to the point of the compasses.' In a second passage, he adds that the development of both theory and prac-tice was the work of Agatharcus, who designed and constructed the scenery for Aeschylus, and used vanishing-point perspective to portray buildings on the stage; apparently he wrote a book describing his methods. What is remarkable and constructive about these fragmen-tary glimpses of the ancient world is how the discovery of perspective brings together a whole range of activities – geometry and optics, stage-scenery and architecture, poetry, ceramics and painting. Nothing could illustrate more clearly the unity of a civilization, and the close connec-tion between knowledge, technology and creative achievement.

Although so little of antique painting survives, we may presume that its use of perspective evolved between the fifth and first centuries BC, and probably not earlier than the third to second. As it happens, some poor quality or mediocre wall-painting has been recovered beneath the ashes of Pompeii, a Samnite city, colonized by Rome under Sulla in 80 BC. About thirty years later, the first of the paintings was carried out on the walls of the three most important sites, the Villa of the Mysteries and the House of the Labyrinth at Pompeii, and the Villa of Publius Fannius Sinistor at Boscoreale (now in the Naples Museum). Examination of these shows that they are not of particularly high quality, and there is no reason to suppose they are original or innovatory. They vary greatly in competence. Clearly, some knowledge of perspective, and the principles by which space is depicted, was common among professional painters, though some, on this evidence, had a much firmer grasp of it than others. The inference is that the leading artistic centres of the republic and empire produced far superior work, masterpieces even. If so, they have vanished for ever. It is thus dangerous to judge the full extent of Roman mastery of pictorial space from these routine productions.

All the same, it is notable that the wall-paintings which exhibit an interest in perspective are among the earliest found at Pompeii. On the evidence available, it looks as though the system reached premature fulfilment and was then discarded. If so, it would fit in with other evidence about the arts in the Roman period. We must remember that, in terms of the artistic parabola of classical civilization, even the first century AD comes very late. The finest productions were already in the past. As we have noted, Graeco-Roman art, at its best, concentrated on the faithful presentation of the human form, in its real and natural setting. The abandonment of perspective would, of course, have been a retreat from this objective, and evidence of a trend in other directions. It may be that the failure of antique painting to develop on lines later followed in the European Renaissance is itself part of the process which produced intellectual and technological atrophy in the antique – some failure of the creative mind and spirit induced by the loss of freedom.

Certainly, in other spheres of creative activity, the loss of a sense of purpose and development is very marked; the cultural horizons narrowed steadily. By the fourth century, it concentrated very largely on what might be termed literature, and literature itself was based on grammar and rhetoric, the arts of the public speaker. The type of training a clever young man like St Augustine received, in Rome and Milan, when he was still intended for a career in public life, was intended to produce an orator. The point is made neatly by Andrew Alfoldi in his famous study of fourth-century intellectuals, *A Conflict of Ideas in the Late Roman Empire:* '. . . the age had no humanistic or scientific horizon, no historical culture, no system of thought based on ethnology or sociology, no clear definition of its attitude to natural science, to say nothing of technology – all it had was literature. The man of letters trained in the classical dialectics, then, was the only type of educated humanity known.'

Moreover, such men, with all their cultural limitations, were evidently rarities by this stage. A letter survives from Symmachus, the leading Roman senator of his day, expressing indignation that a distinguished rhetorician had obtained no higher advancement than the governorship of a small province. This attitude would have been unthinkable in the early empire, for the implication was that the state should cherish such men, since there were so few of them. There is a parallel here with mandarin China, where proficiency in a stagnant literature-culture was the passport to high administrative office. In Symmachus's time, promotion in the civil service depended on the capacity to master the flowery court style of the imperial edicts. But, as has been well said, if literature is used to train bureaucracy, both must suffer. Since the assumption was that only men versed in literature were fit to rule, and since few men possessed literary gifts and training, there was a resort to falsification and flattery. Ammianus says that the emperor Valens had tinselly rhetorical addresses delivered at his headquarters even when he was on campaign; and he adds that Valens' 'woefully crude manner of speech was described as a diction worthy of Cicero'.

Thus literature drifted away from real life, and became a façade. Dislocation, disjunction, an inability or unwillingness to cope with reality seem to be characteristics of civilization in decline. 'A loss of perspective' – the phrase, both in its literal and figurative sense, is apt. And not only was man no longer seen truthfully in his spatial context; he was distorted in his human situation also. We see this particularly in the monumental sculpture of the Late Antique, with its drift away from humanist realism to symbolism and artistic magic. The Arch of Constantine, with its supernaturally huge emperor towering over dwarfish and dumpy soldiers, is a conscious and deliberate departure from the classical style. The men in the ranks of the army and the populace are uniform, identical, mere stereotyped figures in the style of folk-art; not individual human beings. The emperor alone is a recognizable character, but he also is de-humanized by being made gigantic and unreal. He has become an inhuman deity, his subjects subhuman hominids.

The loss of interest and confidence in the human mind and spirit is, to some extent, concealed by the gigantic triumphalism of late imperial architecture – the huge Roman baths of Septimus Severus, completed by his son Caracalla; the Palace of Diocletian at Split; the vast buildings at Leptis Magna and Baalbek, and elsewhere. But in time the buildings themselves were no longer attempted; in the last century of the western empire, there were no new *thermae* or triumphal arches. Farther east, the Constantinian decadence was further developed. In the reliefs on the obelisk set up by Theodosius in the Hippodrome at Constantinople, the size of the various figures and the degree of detail devoted to them is clearly determined by their status. All are uniform dolls, seen from the front, without movement or life, and with a total absence of perspective. The style is hieratic, and the retreat from realism or individuality complete. The figures are units in a totalitarian society, and the relief does not so much record an actual event as express an eternal order. The same process is seen in statuary, where the autonomous personality – the real man as he was in life – which stands at the very centre of classical art, is replaced by the symbolic figure. Portraits represent not actual appearance, but rank. Thus the huge bronze statue of an emperor at

Barletta, often called the last great achievement of Roman sculpture, is in fact a precursor of the medieval world, since it is not a real person but a symbol. The person disappears; the archetype supervenes; the real world fades and is replaced by a metaphysical one.

Throughout the Dark Ages and the early medieval period, the art of humanist realism was lost; or at any rate unpractised. Realist art starts with the space, in which the painter then proceeds to locate figures and objects. Medieval art starts with the figure – itself stereotyped – which is dislocated and floats; it is unattached by observed spatial relationships to its natural surroundings. Thus kings loomed over diminutive noblemen and microscopic serfs, in toy symbolic castles. All are seen from the front. Sometimes the frontal pattern is complicated, or there is a partial attempt to suggest solidity by an intermixture of foreshortened frontal constructions. Medieval artists may well have glimpsed occasional surviving models of true perspective, though they clearly did not grasp its importance.

At any rate, the recovery of pictorial space was a slow business, indicating that the skills, or rather the intellectual and ocular adjustments needed to direct the skills, were difficult to acquire. In a way, the struggles of the painters, beginning in the thirteenth century, were a prototype of the whole economic, social and political struggle in the West to recover a progressive civilization. The progression is not essentially dissimilar to that of the Greek vase painters, though it seems likely that the painters received less assistance from geometers and scientists than in ancient times. So far as we can judge, they tended to work more on their own, as empirical innovators, learning from trial and error. The first notable stage was the wall-painting of Cimabue in the Upper Church of San Francesco at Assisi. There, the attempt at perspective is obvious enough, but unrealized. Around 1305, Giotto painted the Arena Chapel in Padua, a deliberate and schematic adaptation of the viewpoints in the scenes themselves to the vision of a spectator standing in the centre of the chapel. Giotto, an artist of great power and intellectual capacity, seems to have expanded an originally more modest scheme as he proceeded; it is as though he became suddenly conscious of the massive artistic forces he was unleashing by reconquering pictorial space, and raised his ambitions accordingly. Here is one of those rare occasions when we can see civilization taking off in a cultural sense, rather as it takes off in an economic surge of self-sustaining growth. Giotto followed this triumph with the Bardi and Peruzzi

Chapels in Santa Croce, Florence, which marked further refinements and developments. Then, thirty years later, appeared Ambrogio Lorenzetti's 'City of Good Government' in the Siennese Palazzo Publico, another major step forward in that it is the first full perspective vision of landscape, and an indication that the achievement of Giotto was not that of a lone genius, but of an age and culture.

At no stage does the recovery of perspective seem to have been easily accomplished. Curiously enough, as in the history of economic recovery, there was a hiatus in the second half of the fourteenth century, during which the frontiers did not advance. We have absolutely no reason to connect this with the drop in population which clearly accounts for the lack of development in the western economy; it indicates, rather, that neither the social nor the cultural development of a civilization proceeds in smooth acceleration, but instead in periodic and almost unpredictable surges. Until the early fifteenth century, the innovatory painters appear to have been working largely on their own, apart from the main developments of intellectual and scientific thought. But with the beginning of the true Renaissance there is a coming together of the main streams of discovery and innovation. In the first quarter of the fifteenth century, Filippo Brunelleschi painted a pair of panels, of S Giovanni and the Piazza del Duomo, Florence, which formed a kind of pictorial manifesto on perspective. Both have disappeared, but we have a detailed description of them by Antonio Manetti, in his *Life of Brunelleschi:* 'Thus in those days, he himself proposed and practised what painters today call perspective . . . and from him is born the rule, which is the basis of all that has been done of that kind from that day to this.' It is notable that Manetti calls the art of perspective a science – not to be distinguished from the other advancing technologies of the day – and says that the painter accompanied his efforts with an optical experiment. He made a hole in the rear of the panel, at the point of vision, and asked people to look through this and see the actual perspective painting reflected in a mirror: 'It seemed,' says Manetti, 'as if the real thing was seen: and I have had it in my hand, and I can give testimony.' The historian of Renaissance perspective, John White, argues that it is clear that Brunelleschi had developed

a complete, focused system of perspective with mathematically regular diminution towards a fixed vanishing point. . . . It is the final crystallisation of the increasingly close connection between the observer and the pictorial world which had been growing up throughout the previous century. The ever more confident attempts to relate pictorial space to everyday experience of the three-dimensional world . . . are transformed into a logically-precise mathematical system.

Indeed, within a few years the connection between pictorial realism on the one hand, and abstract knowledge and scientific theory on the other, was made explicit when Leon Battista Alberti published his *Della Pittura* in 1435. This is deliberately based on the principles of Euclidean optics, but it is also an attempt at an artistic and cultural theory, which itself was related to the humanism at the core of the Graeco-Roman civilization. Alberti points out that the appearances of all things are purely relative, and that the human figure alone provides the index or measure of whatever it is the artist chooses to portray. Man occupies the central position, as observer of the pictorial world, of which he himself is the guiding unit. Thus perspective is doubly established, by man as the external focus of the painting, and by man as the matriculating arbiter of its content. From either point of view, man re-establishes his centrality in the pictorial universe, which ceases to be hieratic and metaphysical, and now resembles the real one he sees around him.

As with other aspects of civilization-building, the return to visual realism was a collective effort. Very likely Brunelleschi, building on the empirical efforts of his predecessors, was the inventor of the basic geometrical constructions which underlay the new perspective. He was an architect, and he may well have proceeded by first drawing up the plans and elevations of the buildings he proposed to draw in perspective. Alberti then improved on his method by a semi-simultaneous use of a three-dimensional system. Of course different artists utilized the discovery in their own ways. All perception varies to some extent, since optical information is rearranged in the brain in the light of knowledge and intuition. Uccello, described by Vasari as working through the night in his enthusiasm, exclaiming, 'Oh, what a sweet thing this perspective is!', adopted a modified aerial viewpoint which gives his rare and beautiful works great singularity. Leonardo da Vinci worked on, and wrote down, his own theory of synthetic perspective which, in its imaginings of space, was not totally unlike Einstein's vision, since it was based on curves. These, and other, variations sprang from the natural problem of containing the real world of space in the flat, two-dimensional world of the painter's panel or canvas, a problem very similar to that of the mapmaker, who was tackling it with a variety of mathematical and geometrical aids at precisely this time.

The discovery of reliable scientific laws – or what appear to be laws – always brings with it an exhilarating access of freedom. The uncivilized world can best be defined as a familiar prison; civilization is the opening of doors to infinity. Nowhere is the process seen more clearly at work than in the rediscovery of perspective. For the painter it is the true discovery of liberty. Alberti's book reflects the sense of autonomy achieved by the realized idea of space. Earlier, in the thirteenth to fourteenth centuries, the painter had gradually extended space outwards from the mere individual solid object; progressively, space was emancipated from its tyranny. By the mid-fifteenth century the process was effectively complete, for the painter first created space with his canvas square, and then arranged and ordered the objects in it according to its rules. As John White puts it, 'Space now contains the objects by which formerly it was created.'

The completion of this process, analogous to other achievements of high intellectual or scientific importance, raised the popularity and prestige of the Renaissance painter. The *Della Pittura* perspective, as it were, was used as a lever to raise the humble craft of painting into the lordly circle of the liberal arts. Nor was this entirely inappropriate, for it was only at this point that the painter became master of his craft, and became a freeman of the visual world. He was out of his optical prison and could roam at large: nothing was beyond his attempt.

We have been able to establish, then, that there is a connection, and sometimes a very close connection, between the cultural progress (and decline) of a civilization, and its technical achievements and economic health. The experimental painters of the fourteenth to fifteenth centuries, for instance, were part of the same dynamic which produced the technical craftsmen and empirical scientists of the expanding cities during the same period, and indeed of the merchants who employed both. All, in their own way, were seeking forms of freedom; and their accomplishments were roughly correlated to the degree they secured it. Moreover, all were operating in the middle degree of society and in an urban atmosphere, where the cultural, political and economic limitations on freedom were least oppressive.

A picture, therefore, is beginning to emerge of the absolute centrality of freedom, in the widest sense, in the growth of civilization. Now let us return to the main thread of our investigation, and see how the late-medieval society we have described gave birth to the capitalist system.

CHAPTER 5

Lift-off at Last

In an economic sense, the most important single characteristic of our present civilization is the mass production of industrial goods, financed by the system we term capitalism. In order to test the health of our civilization, therefore, we need to discover, as precisely as we can, what were the factors which brought this system into existence. To what does capitalism owe its origins? How did the Industrial Revolution come about?

In Chapter 3 we traced the growth in western Europe, during the Dark and Middle Ages, of an increasingly technical-minded society, with a firm agrarian base and an expanding middle class. In the fourteenth century, this society fell into a 'Malthusian Trap', from which it began to emerge only a hundred years later. Towards the end of the fifteenth century, however, a new population cycle began, and this time the trap was evaded. Humanity moved into an entirely new situation.

What caused this qualitative change has been endlessly debated during the last hundred and fifty years. There are as many rival theories as there are for the causes of the decline of the Roman empire. In the late nineteenth century, following Marx, it was fashionable to provide a purely economic explanation, with a marked flavour of determinism: capitalism *had* to evolve from the decaying economic carcass of feudalism. In the first half of the twentieth century, this approach was modified by the sociologists, who produced an ideological theory, first elaborated by Max Weber: the capitalist class, with its unprecedented propensity to systematic work and saving, was the product of an anxiety neurosis, or 'salvation panic', induced by Calvinism. Neither of these theories can now be maintained. Marx's thesis fails because it tried to

explain capitalism in terms of its own internal elements, and thus constitutes a kind of tautology. The views of Weber and his followers, though
superficially attractive, simply have not stood up to close historical
examination. At best, both schools confused an element of the truth
with the whole. Recently, historians, economists and sociologists (those,
that is, not already committed to Marxism by faith) have tended to
embrace some kind of political explanation.

Here, for instance, are three typical analyses published since 1970.
The French sociologist Jean Baechler, in *The Origins of Capitalism*,
insists that the explanation is wholly political. The theory of feudalism
'left out' the merchant, who thus had the incentive (and by omission the
opportunity) to legitimize himself by creating wealth. We have already
glanced at this theory, and seen that it may have some application in the
medieval context, but chiefly in explaining the abortive take-off of the
twelfth to thirteenth centuries. Another political explanation is put
forward by the American historian Immanuel Wallerstein, in *The
Modern World System: capitalist agriculture and the origins of the
European world-economy in the 16th century*. He argues that throughout
ancient history, when an economy, usually on a city-base, started to
expand, it tended to turn itself into an empire, or disintegrate. But
empires (as in Rome's case) lead to the export of industry, rather than
manufactured products, and thus do not create economies of scale and
advanced industrial processes. In the end they decay and the economy
conflates. What happened in the sixteenth century, he contends, was
unique: the European economy expanded but did not turn into an
empire because the Habsburg effort to create it failed. Instead, strong
states – 'capitalist core-states', as he terms them – emerged within an
international economic system. This made global capitalism possible:
'National homogeneity within international heterogeneity is the formula of a world economy.' Again, there is something to be said for this
view. The multiple city-state economy, rather on the ancient Greek
pattern, which appeared to be developing in the late Middle Ages,
especially in Italy and Flanders, was submerged by the parallel development of the nation state; while, at the same time, the collapse of religious
unity made a continental empire impossible. But Wallerstein's book is
essentially a summary which includes all the facts rather than a causal
diagnosis which explains them.

A third attempt, by the English economists Douglas C. North and
Robert Paul Thomas, is *The Rise of the Western World*. It stresses the

importance of the institutional arrangements which enable economic units to realize economies of scale. Thus: 'Growth will simply not occur unless the existing economic organization is efficient'; and: 'Individuals must be lured by incentives to undertake the socially desirable activities.' Capitalism was the product of a favourable legal situation, itself a product of a certain type of political system.

All other recent explanations of capitalist origins tend to follow one or other of these lines of thought, or a combination of them. Let us now attempt to assemble our own reconstruction of how the 'capitalist miracle' occurred. The first thing we need to do, I believe, is to discard the distinction commonly made between the medieval and the modern (or 'early modern') world. As we have seen, by the end of the fifteenth century, western Europe was already more advanced, from an economic and technological point of view, than the classical world had ever been. It had also developed a far more efficient agriculture, and a habit of searching for technical explanations which the Roman world had never possessed. Above all, it was a society where slavery was virtually non-existent, and where freedom, especially among the urban middle class, was expanding. These characteristics, moreover, had been developing over a very long period. It is hard to see how a society which possessed them *could* become arrested. One is tempted to argue that western Europe would have continued to advance economically and technically even if special factors had not intervened from the sixteenth century onwards.

But of course there were special factors, which operated in addition to the growth-propellants we have already examined. At the end of the fifteenth century, the development of ocean-going ships and navigational aids opened up direct trade-links with Asia. These voyages were immensely profitable, since the European appetite for eastern products was almost insatiable. Vasco da Gama returned to Lisbon in 1499 with a cargo that paid for the cost of his expedition sixty times over. Drake's world voyage, 1577–80, gave a return to its investors of 4,700%. During the 198 years of its existence, the Dutch East India Company paid an average yearly dividend of 18%; and the profits of the English East India Company, at any rate during the seventeenth century, were very much higher. The wealth generated by this trade was itself an immense stimulus to commerce generally, and those seeking to participate in it, as opposed to any other kind of money-making activity (agriculture, war, government) – a complete reverse of the situation in the Roman world. But, since Europe, at this stage, had very little to export to Asia, eastern imports had to be paid for, by and large, in bullion. As under the Roman empire, Europe threatened to acquire an immense balance of payments deficit with the East, which must have led to debased currencies, runaway inflation, political tyranny and so economic collapse.

Happily, oceanic exploration, at the same time, also opened up the route to the gold and silver of the Americas. New silver mines were developed in central Europe; and the Portuguese brought in gold from Africa. These fresh supplies of bullion bridged the trade-gap between West and East until western industry was sufficiently developed to mass-produce textiles for export. Of course, injecting bullion on this scale into the money supply was bound to produce inflationary pressures of its own. The upthrust began slowly about 1475, gathered speed in the next fifty years, and began to die down after about 1620. Its intensity varied. In Spain, commodity prices rose 500% during the sixteenth century, about twice as much as in England and France over a longer period (1475–1663); and in Spain the inflation continued for half a century after it had exhausted itself elsewhere. The great sixteenth to seventeenth century price-rise hit the traditional elements in society – especially monarchs, aristocrats and clergy – but it made commercial profits easy and so encouraged enterprise. As Keynes put it in his *Treatise on Money* (1930), 'Never in the annals of the modern world has there existed so prolonged and rich an opportunity for the businessman, the speculator and the profiteer.' The process undoubtedly assisted the formation of capital, and so the industrial take-off.

The opening up of the Americas brought space as well as bullion. It was one answer to the Malthusian Trap. But here we must be precise. In large areas of Europe, agricultural productivity rose steadily in the sixteenth and seventeenth centuries, and even if the western escape-route had not been open there is no evidence that population would have outstripped food supplies during this period. There was very little European emigration during the sixteenth century, except from Spain (which did not have a surplus, and where the effect was damaging to the economy). Large-scale emigration only began (from Britain) in the late seventeenth century. It was only in the late eighteenth century, when the death-rate began to fall very fast, that the Malthusian Trap appeared about to operate – in the 1780s, many French families had to spend 95% of their income on bread alone during some years. It was then that the American drain proved immensely beneficial, and for the next 120 years it regularly syphoned off the European surplus. This was, of course, the crucial formative period of industrial capitalism. And, by a neat paradox, exporting people from crowded Europe to empty America made rapid industrial growth possible in both.

This, then, is the general international background to the global take-off – a number of special factors operating on a firm base built up over a thousand years. But this broad explanation does not elucidate the key questions. Why did capitalism, and its pendant, industrialization, first begin to operate effectively in one country (Britain) rather than others? And how, precisely, did the process get going?

To answer the first question, we need to look closely at four countries: Spain, France, the Netherlands and Britain itself. Why, to begin with, did Spain, the most powerful European state in the sixteenth century, the prime beneficiary both of the bullion of the West and the trade of the East, fail to become the initial theatre of self-sustaining growth? Why, on the contrary, did it enter a period of profound economic and political decline in the years after 1600? The sheer physical efforts of Spain in the sixteenth century were extraordinary, but they were achieved at great human cost. At the beginning of this century, the key element in Spain was Castile. Not only did it supply the national leadership, to a great extent it supplied the manpower. Unlike the rest of the country, it could almost be described as overpopulated. During the first half of the century, 150,000 Castilians had moved to the Americas. Even so it provided more than three-quarters of the Spanish population. As late as 1590, the central part of Castile alone accounted for nearly 31% of the total population against 16% today; and Castile's density (in 1594) was 22 per square kilometre, against 13·6 in Aragon, the next most populous area. Yet throughout the century Castile was bled – by emigration to the New World, by conscription for Spain's endless wars (Castilian peasants were always preferred for the army's *tercios*), and by an internal migration from the countryside to the Spanish towns, where the peasants were lured by the prospect of New World wealth, but where in fact there was no work. Then came the great Spanish plague of 1599–1600, which marked the end of Castilian demographic dynamism. Rural depopulation seems to have produced an actual decline in agricultural production, though elsewhere in Europe it was generally rising. As a result, Spain imported more and more grain from eastern Europe as the sixteenth century proceeded; most manufactures were already imported. A recent analysis of Spain's decline sums it up thus: 'We have, then, the spectacle of a nation which, at the end of the 16th century, is dependent on foreigners not only for its manufactures but its food supply, while its own population goes idle or is absorbed into economically unproductive occupations! ... The nature of the economic situation was such that one became a student or a monk, a beggar or a bureaucrat. There was nothing else to be.' Above all, there was no middle class. Gonzales de Cellorigo, the ablest of Spain's sixteenth-century *arbitristas*, or economic writers, lamented in 1600: 'Our republic has come to be an extreme contrast between rich and poor ... there are rich who loll at ease or poor who beg, and we lack people of the middle sort, whom neither wealth nor poverty prevents from pursuing the right kind of business enjoined by natural law.'

This anti-growth society did not come about by chance or the workings of blind economic laws. All the causes of Spain's decline can ultimately be traced to political decisions. It was the decision of the Spanish crown and the ruling oligarchy to expel the Moors and the Jews, and so eliminate a huge section of Spain's medieval middle class. It was the decision of the same groups to superimpose religious uniformity on top of this racial uniformity, to kill the Erasmian reformation in Spain, drive its intellectuals and many mercantile reformers into exile, and so replace the inquisitive and entrepreneurial spirit by obscurantism, censorship and thought-control. And, again, it was the crown and the landed aristocracy who jointly decided that the nation's representative body, the Cortes, should hand over control over taxation to the absolutist monarchy, in return for 'stability' and 'order'. Thus one of the most progressive tendencies of the later Middle Ages was reversed. The end of effective parliaments meant not only loss of control over state taxation but loss of security for individual property, whether of the rich or of the poor. One reason why peasants moved to the cities was to escape tax-gatherers and recruiting sergeants. Savings were invested in private or government bonds, which paid high interest rates, but which were spent on war, bureaucracy and conspicuous consumption rather than on trade, industry and agriculture. Such loans in any event were fraught with political risk, since the state, being omnipotent, could treat the individual with contempt. In effect, there was no real law of financial property in Habsburg Spain, since the state seized and confiscated goods at will, altered contracts unilaterally, and if necessary simply went bankrupt, as it did in 1557, 1575, 1576, 1607, 1627 and 1647. The only section of society which could defend itself against the robber-state was the regular army, which enforced payment of its arrears of pay by well-organized mutinies. Peasants, intellectuals and entrepreneurs went on strike, by emigrating. In these circumstances capitalism could not possibly develop.

When we turn from Spain to France, we find many of the same factors at work, though in a less extreme form. Of course France had many advantages which Spain lacked. It was intrinsically much richer; it had a larger population, including an educated middle class; it escaped the worst of the inflation which Spain underwent in the sixteenth to seventeenth centuries; and in some ways it had much more intelligent political leadership – Colbert, for instance, tried hard to create the preconditions for commercial growth by unifying tolls, weights, measures and other standards of value, and by seeking to create a nation currency. But France remained in many ways a feudal assemblage of provinces rather than a unitary economic state until the Revolution. In so far as her unity was insisted upon, the political decisions taken were the wrong ones. In the 1590s, France escaped from the religious wars by the crown opting for Catholicism rather than religious tolerance and diversity; and nearly a hundred years later the retrogressive step was taken of abolishing the legal immunities of the Huguenots, which led to the destruction, by emigration and impoverishment, of a substantial section of France's commercial middle class. As in Spain, the representative tax-authorization body was abolished, since the States General did not meet from early in the seventeenth century until the eve of the Revolution. France was the model of absolutist monarchy, and the rights of private property were only marginally better protected than in Spain. Until the Revolution, a successful trader or manufacturer could always be disposed of, and his fortune seized for the crown, by a *lettre de cachet*.

Turning from France to the Netherlands, we see a very different pattern of development. The cradle of modern economic society was the loose federation of states, counties and free towns which, in the later Middle Ages, acknowledged the sovereignty of the Dukes of Burgundy. All had their economic and political liberties guaranteed by charters, some of great antiquity. It was the policy of successive dukes to enlarge these freedoms in order to expand trade, and so tax-revenue. The rise of Antwerp testified to the effectiveness of liberal policies. There, the exclusiveness of the guilds was reduced; restrictive practices were limited; foreign merchants and capital were welcomed. In the countryside, the production of cloth was freed from municipal regulations, and expanded; and the privilege restricting admission of burghers only to the trade was abolished. Under the first of the Habsburg rulers, Charles v, the Low Countries and Flanders continued to prosper, since Charles had been born in Burgundy and understood how the system worked. His Spanish son and successor, Philip II, sought to impose by force the system of religious and political uniformity already established in Spain, and this involved abrogating all the libertarian charters of the cities. The result was nearly a century of warfare, during which Flanders was crushed and its economy destroyed, and the seven northern provinces, now the Netherlands, liberated themselves and assumed the economic leadership of the world.

It can be argued that the Netherlands were the first country on earth to escape the Malthusian Trap. During the seventeenth century, they generated a substantial and sustained increase in per capita income, while supporting a much larger population. The relative freedom with which trade operated there allowed for the rapid development of paper techniques (bills of exchange, etc) and banking facilities. A genuine European capital market, centred in Amsterdam, developed. As security grew, rates of interest fell. The average had been 20–30% in 1500, and throughout the sixteenth century 12% was regarded as a good rate, especially for a government; during the seventeenth century, Dutch commercial rates were often as low as 3%. The development of commerce was accompanied by (and this is important) a sustained rise in agricultural productivity, as a result of capital investment and specialization, and a free labour force. In many agricultural methods, the Dutch were pioneers, and, though they had to import some food, they increased domestic supplies by land recovery and the more effective use of labour. The Dutch were the first people in history to achieve a measure of self-sustaining economic growth.

Why, then, did the Netherlands fail to pioneer the Industrial Revolution too? Why did economic leadership pass to Britain? The question has only to be asked to demonstrate the frailty of the Weberian thesis that it was the Calvinist 'anxiety neurosis' which generated modern capitalism. Of course Weber himself had Calvinist blood through his maternal grandmother; and, though an agnostic himself, he retained the creed partially in that he accepted the idea of negative predestination – the majority are damned by God from the beginning and their efforts to achieve virtue are wholly futile. Weber's eclectic Calvinism may have distorted his ideas as to how Calvinists actually operated. At all stages, the Netherlands was much closer to a Calvinist country than England, where Calvinism was never more than a minority movement (usually a small minority). If Calvinism was the key to capitalism, then the Industrial Revolution should have taken place in the neighbourhood of Amsterdam, rather than in Lancashire and the English Midlands. England's northern neighbour, Scotland, *was* predominantly Calvinist from the mid-sixteenth century on; but there, the characteristic medieval restrictions on trade, commerce and industry were retained much longer than in Anglican England. In fact, it was not until the theocratic grip of Calvinism was broken, following the union with England, in the mid-eighteenth century, that Scotland entered into a phase of commercial development, marked by religious toleration, intellectual adventurism, and the penetration of liberal modes of thought. The take-off in the Scottish lowlands which followed was post-Calvinist, indeed anti-Calvinist. In the Netherlands, periods of intense Calvinist theocracy were marked by religious persecution, censorship and a loss of individual liberty, and resulted in emigration, usually of the commercial middle class, to England and America. Nor is this surprising, since strict Calvinism, as anyone who actually reads Calvin's *Institutes of Church Government* will find, not only does not promote commerce and the profit motive but militates against them. The entrepreneurial elements whose migrations, in the sixteenth and seventeenth centuries, helped to fix the pattern of future capitalist development, were not primarily Calvinist, and certainly not supporters of theocracy. Some were Lutherans, some Calvinist, some Catholic, some sectarians. What they had in common was their dislike of imposed religious uniformity, whether Roman Catholicism or anything else. Like Erasmus, their spiritual progenitor – who died a Catholic in so far as he was anything – they believed in a minimum creed, toleration and good works. They wanted religion to be private, not public; and, above all, they were profoundly anti-clerical. They settled in north-west Europe, and especially Britain (later in North America) because there the religious background most conducive to their personal well-being and commercial bent was to be found.

The Netherlands, therefore, had no special advantage over nominally Anglican England, as a result of her Calvinism. Moreover, having achieved a very powerful commercial and agricultural base in the seventeenth century, she gradually accumulated self-imposed disadvantages. The Netherlands was engaged in war from the 1560s with virtually no interruption until the Treaty of Utrecht in 1714. These were wars of survival but also of commerce, and during them, for times at least, some sectors of the Dutch economy drew great benefit. It was a mark of the comparative sophistication of the economy that the wars were paid for by high taxation and the funding of public debt. But ultimately the tax-burden became a seriously depressive factor in the economy. Taxes were not only high, but exceedingly complicated, and many of them were imposed on food at various points. English travellers and diplomats in the seventeenth century willingly conceded that the Dutch had superior commercial skills, in the technical sense; but thought these were somewhat offset by ridiculous tax levels. In January 1659, George Downing, English agent at the Hague, noted: 'It's strange to see with what readyness this people doe consent to extraordinary taxes . . . a man cannot eate a dish of meat in an ordinary [inn] but that one way or another he shall pay 19 excises out of it.' Sir William Temple, ambassador under Charles II, calculated that a fish dish paid 30 excises. In 1696, Gregory King, father of English statistics, calculated that Dutch taxes were £3.1.7 per capita, against £1.4.0 in England. The high level of taxation was undoubtedly a political decision; and it was also politics which dictated where the weight fell. The cost of heavily taxed food made urban wages very high, and this meant that industry, especially industries with a high labour-content, were hit much harder than commerce or agriculture. The tyranny of over-taxation was the biggest single avoidable factor which prevented a Dutch industrial take-off in the eighteenth century.

So we come to England, where the take-off actually occurred. To what extent can we isolate the unique elements in this process? Of all the European powers, England, later Britain, took the most decisive advantage of the American escape for surplus population. By 1640 there were fourteen permanent English settlements in the Americas, and at the end of the seventeenth century half a million Englishmen and Scotsmen lived in the Americas, growing chiefly plantation crops for the home economy, and taking back manufactures in return. Britain expanded this initial overseas foothold by the Navigation Acts – the one aspect of restrictive legislation even Adam Smith later justified – which effectively excluded the Dutch from English international commerce, and constituted the beginning of an English-controlled world market. England, Ireland and Wales formed a unitary kingdom, without internal tolls or other regional restrictions on commerce; after the union with Scotland in 1707, the United Kingdom became by far the largest single market in the world, even ignoring overseas dependencies.

This market was also an area where the notion of personal property was most fully developed, and its ownership most stringently guaranteed. In England, unlike France and Spain, the crown, over a very long period, attempted but failed to take over taxation powers, which were decisively secured by parliament in the mid-seventeenth century. The victory of parliament not only ensured that a comparatively low level of taxation (unlike the Netherlands') was a characteristic feature of the economy, but it enshrined property rights in a body of impersonal law, guarded by the courts and safe from crown and government interference. What a capitalist needs most of all is convincing assurance that the law is clear, stable, objective and enforced. As Professor Hayek puts it in *The Constitution of Liberty*, 'There is probably no single factor which has contributed more to the prosperity of the West than the relative certainty of the law which has prevailed here.' Moreover, the law as it stood, and as it was refined, gave a number of distinct advantages to the progressive owners of property. In Elizabethan times, monopolies were deliberately created by the crown to create new manufacturing industries, and attract skilled foreign workmen. More than half a century later, when metal industries had been successfully established, and England was already a net exporter in manufactures, Sir Edward Coke persuaded parliament that monopolies were an unconstitutional impingement by crown prerogative on the private sector, and the Statute of Monopolies (1624) not only proscribed royal monopolies, but embodied a patent system which turned true innovation into a new form of property protected by law. This meant that the private rate of return could justify the substantial cost involved in seeking for and introducing innovatory techniques. The parliamentary law also intervened, at a number of points and over a long period, to promote the triumph of freehold over common land – a process which went back to the thirteenth century and continued until the nineteenth. Initially enclosures were opposed not only by the peasants but by the crown, and to some extent by parliament; the last had accepted enclosure as a progressive movement by the end of the sixteenth century, and the crown by the end of the seventeenth. It was the universal establishment of rights of freehold property which encouraged the cultivator to invest in agriculture, and so brought about the slow but cumulatively astonishing agricultural revolution which marked the seventeenth and eighteenth centuries, and which produced not only Britain's escape from the Malthusian Trap but a sizeable cash surplus to invest in industry.

Finally, it was in this framework of parliamentary law that feudal restrictions both on agriculture and industry were abolished, that the joint-stock company was established, insurance, securities and commodity markets were organized, and that the banking system expanded into a system of deposit and note-issuing banks, presided over by the central Bank of England (1694). By the year 1700, England had not only caught up with the Dutch in terms of financial and commercial techniques, it had established a hospitable legal environment for industrial growth. This was essentially a political process. It assumed that parliament would be dominated by those sympathetic to entrepreneurial interests and property-owners. It is notable that not only Adam Smith but Karl Marx saw the development of efficient property rights to be essential to successful growth. In fact, in a capitalist's ideal world, government is simply an organization that, in return for modest taxes, provides protection and justice, that is the establishment and enforcement of property rights. In the eighteenth century, that is in the world created by John Locke and Blackstone's *Commentaries*, British society came close to proving that ideal. Virtually everything was a freehold, calculable in cash terms, from a clergyman's benefice to government office-jobs and army commissions. And, therefore, most offences against property were punished by penal servitude, transportation or hanging.

The result of this network of English financial institutions and property laws was to increase the efficiency of the market, and in particular to remove obstacles – human, legal and institutional – to the maximization of profits. As the market was very large, by contemporary standards, and, in the eighteenth century, growing rapidly with the development of a protected overseas empire, the only other obstacle to an industrial lift-off was technology. But there is no evidence that this was a serious obstacle at all. Granted the protection of patent laws, the inventor will always emerge when the market really exists. That, certainly, is the lesson of the British Industrial Revolution. Of course there must be a minimum level of technical proficiency, and enough skilled labour. In England, this situation had been in process of creation over several centuries, especially during the so-called 'scientific revolution' of the seventeenth century.

It is not true, however, to see the Industrial Revolution as a product of a scientific explosion. Science is important in the long run not so much because of individual scientific discoveries but because the growth of a vast body of scientific knowledge encourages inventors to see the world differently and to imagine new solutions to old problems – the process is analogous to the development of the realistic artistic vision we examined in the last chapter. Given the practical turn of mind of inventors, the appearance of a new invention is more likely to stimulate them than scientific discoveries. Intellectual stimulation, as such, seems to play little part. Over the past quarter-century, the intensive study of the history of patents and inventions, and their relation to other factors, shows that inventions do not just emerge from an intellectual climate. Jacob Schmorkler in *Invention and Economic Growth* studied four industries (agriculture, railways, paper and petrol refining) over a period of 150 years, and concluded that the chief stimuli to inventions were recognition of a costly problem to be solved, or a potentially profitable opportunity to be seized: 'Many of the important inventions scrutinized used no scientific knowledge at all . . . and many of those that did used science that was old at the time.' The most significant finding of this study was that the market is the most important factor in influencing inventions.

This study is confirmed by others, and indeed by an analysis of the crucial period in Britain during the eighteenth century. Figures of patents taken out testify to the gradual build-up of market forces:

> 1700–1709: 22
> 1730–1739: 56
> 1750–1759: 92
> 1760–1769: 205
> 1770–1779: 294
> 1780–1789: 477

If these figures are further broken down, they show that the number of patents taken out corresponds to cyclical variations in trade: men took out patents in years of prosperity, when demand was high and money cheap – this is particularly true, as a study by T. S. Ashton has shown, of major inventive figures like Arkwright, Watt, Wedgwood, Wilkinson, Cartwright, Curr, Cort, Onions, Bramah, Trevithick, Symington, Horrocks, Brunel, Musher, Maudslay, Roberts and Biddle – most of the great names of the Industrial Revolution. Other studies suggest that this close relationship between invention and market nearly always applies: thus in a survey of patents since 1854, Sir Arnold Plant produced close correlations between the inventive faculty and sudden changes in prices, wages and costs. And, as Schmorkler points out, the fact that invention is largely an economic activity, pursued for gain, to solve economic problems or capitalize on economic opportunities, is a point of great importance for economic theory. It destroys the widespread belief that invention is essentially a non-economic activity and, as a corollary the doctrine that individual inventions are inevitable because of the accumulation of knowledge and the presence of social needs. There was nothing inevitable about the technology of the Industrial Revolution: the inventions appeared because the market asked for and paid for them; and the market was able to function in this way because political decisions had given it the freedom to operate.

Of course, sustained economic growth requires a high level of capital formation to bring the new market-stimulated technology into use. Before the Industrial Revolution, economic growth tended to be slow and small because – as under the Roman empire – it was due to the opening up of new physical resources, and the spread of existing methods, rather than to new technical developments. We might have got stuck, as the Romans did. Without a mass-rise of living standards, and so the creation of huge consumer markets, industrialization was not a possibility. As W. W. Rostow writes, in his famous study of take-off, it 'requires a massive set of pre-conditions going to the heart of a society's economic organizations and its effective scale of values'. In terms of eighteenth-century Britain, that 'scale of values' was determined by the sanctification of property by the political system. Gregory King's estimates of the English experience in the seventeenth century indicate an annual rate of productive capital-formation of a little over 3%, mainly in an increase in the number of farm-animals, buildings, ships and bullion, whose earning power was erratic. People could in fact save, if given the opportunities; as Keynes often remarked, the 'propensity to save has generally been stronger than the inducement to invest'. Before the eighteenth century, there were simply not enough safe investment opportunities to produce take-off. With the creation of the 'property state', capital became far more secure, and interest rates accordingly fell. That brought the entrepreneurs into the market to finance their expansion and inventions; so the opportunities multiplied, and the investors poured in. It was cheap, secure capital, as T. S. Ashton points out, which dug the deep mines, built the solid factories, constructed the ingenious canals and substantial houses of the industrial revolution. The increase in capital formation rose from 3% of the national income in 1700–1750 to 5% in 1780, 7% by 1800 and 10% by 1850. The 1780s marked the lift-off, when the growth-rate rose from 2 to 4%, where it remained until the mid-nineteenth century. The lift-off itself was based on the marriage of coking coal to iron production, marked by the foundation of the Carron works and the building of Roebuck's first blast-furnaces in 1760, and the introduction of factory-made textiles, made possible by Hargreaves's spinning-jenny of 1764. Thus about twenty years separated the technological and the mass-production commercial breakthrough.

The common philosophical thread which runs through all aspects of the Industrial Revolution story is a libertarian one. The more perceptive men realized this at the time, and argued that, once property was effectively guaranteed, the fewer regulations the better. As early as 1702, parliament passed the motion 'That trade ought to be free and not restrained'. The view was growing, even in absolutist France, where it was voiced by Mirabeau, that laws which conformed to nature were unnecessary, and those which contradicted it were impracticable. As Adam Smith showed with great force in his *Wealth of Nations* (first published in 1776), the system of state intervention in trade and industry, which he characterized as 'mercantilism', was designed to bring about an excess of exports over imports, and so increase the country's stock of bullion, under the illusion that 'wealth consists in money, or in gold and silver'. But wealth was in fact the sum of goods produced and services provided. Moreover, once the state drew up rules and regulations, powerful, well-organized and interested men would manipulate them for their sectional purposes. Thus nine-tenths of the inventive ingenuity of the seventeenth century was employed not in exploiting the resources of nature but in 'the endeavour to manipulate the power of the state and the wealth of the community for the benefit of individuals'. As Adam Smith put it, 'The sneaking acts of underling tradesmen are thus erected into political maxims for a great empire.'

Hence, Smith argued, the first principle of the economy should be for the state to stand back. 'On the great chessboard of human society, every single piece has a principle of motion of its own, altogether different from that which the legislature might choose to impress upon it.' All that government interventions produced were distortions, usually to the benefit of the few at the expense of the many. 'The statesman who should attempt to direct private people in what manner they might employ their capital would ... assume an authority which could safely be trusted, not only to no single person, but to no council or senate whatever, and which would nowhere be so dangerous as in the hands of a man who had folly and presumption enough to fancy himself fit to exercise it.'

The second principle was to break up the corporatist elements in the state which sought both to restrain the initiative and protect the interests of groups in economic society. As we have seen, corporatism was a compulsory feature of the late Roman empire; it had grown up again in the Middle Ages, the transmitting agency being the church, and to some extent had received the sanction of government, since all governments have an inherent tendency to favour a tidy society, where individuals are classified in groups, preferably self-regulating ones. To Smith, government support for corporatism was anathema, the compounding of an evil: 'People of the same trade seldom meet together, even for merriment or diversion, but the conversation ends in a conspiracy against the public, or some contrivance to raise prices.' Hence: 'though the law cannot hinder people of the same trade from sometimes assembling together, it ought to do nothing to facilitate such assemblies, much less to render them necessary.'

As Smith grasped with great clarity, a central feature of a free commercial society, as opposed to a restrictive feudal or authoritarian one, was the movement away from corporatism, based on status, towards freely negotiated contracts between individuals. Hitherto, all states throughout history had limited the free market in labour by one device or another. One reason why the Industrial Revolution occurred in England was that there the system of restriction was breaking down. The basic Statute of Artificers, of 1563, only applied in practice to market towns and trades established before 1563; hence new industrial centres like Manchester, Birmingham and Wolverhampton were not restrained. By the early 1700s, in any event, the courts were declining to enforce it (it was not repealed until 1814). Smith felt the whole system of regulation was nonsense anyway: 'Long apprenticeships are altogether unnecessary.' What particularly irked him were the so-called Laws of Settlement of 1698 and 1714, which obliged workmen changing jobs to produce legal certificates, and in effect inhibited the free movement of the worker. 'There is scarce a poor man in England of 40 years of age,' he wrote, 'who has not in some part of his life felt himself most cruelly oppressed by this ill-conceived law of settlements.' For Smith had the foresight to see that the transition from status to contract, which to him was the essence of free-enterprise capitalism, must result in a huge access of liberty to the ordinary working man, who throughout history had been prevented by governments, lords and guilds from seeking work in the best market. The property state was designed to uphold his interests too: 'The property which every man has in his own labour, as it is the original foundation of all other property, so it is the most sacred and inviolable . . . to hinder (a poor man) from employing his strength and dexterity in what manner he thinks proper without injury to his neighbour is a plain violation of this most sacred property.' As Smith realized, political and economic freedom are at bottom inseparable; indeed, the political freedom to vote is pretty meaningless without the economic freedom to work where you please. It is no coincidence that the Industrial Revolution and the creation of the capitalist system were followed by the development of democracy in the West.

It must not be supposed that the ideologists of the free-enterprise economy thought freedom to follow the commercial instinct came before any other consideration. Smith defended the Navigation Acts on the grounds that defence came before prosperity in the last resort; he thought that to expect total freedom of trade to be established in Britain was 'as absurd as to expect that an Oceania or a Utopia should ever be established in it'. Capitalism, it is true, was based on the assumption, first popularized by Leibniz, that the selfish deeds of each combined into social forms for all; or, as Pope put it:

> That Reason, passion, answer one great aim;
> That true self-love and social are the same.

The sub-title of Mandeville's industrial analogy, *The Fable of the Bees* (1714) was 'Private Vice, Public Benefits'; and Smith himself wrote of 'the invisible hand' which amalgamated the selfish individual pursuit of wealth into a collective beneficence. But the motivating agent in Leibniz's theory was a beneficent providence; the 'invisible hand' belonged to the divinity. There was never any doubt in the minds of those fighting for the free economy that it would and must be operated in the spirit of Christian justice, as they understood it. It was not an amoral world; quite the contrary.

Indeed, if we study the actual lives, careers and sentiments of individual entrepreneurs during the last quarter of the eighteenth century in

England, we find that the great majority were not only professing Christians but activists, who deliberately introduced non-commercial criteria into the conduct of their businesses. Thus, to give one of many examples, the Crossley family in Halifax: 'When Mrs Crossley entered her works at 4 a.m. she made a daily vow: "If the Lord does bless this place, the poor shall taste of it." And she left this advice with her sons on the conduct of business in bad times: "If you can go on giving employment in the winter, do so, for it is a bad thing for a working man to go home and hear his children cry for bread when he has none to give them."' The truth is, these earlier entrepreneurs were often conscious and systematic philanthropists; and nearly all had a sense of the moral moment of their work and innovation, and what has been termed 'an almost ferocious enthusiasm in their industrial faith', later enshrined in the historical philosophy of Macaulay. Almost from start to finish, the classic era of capitalism had a religious and moral dimension, which in a sense contradicted its non-interventionist economic theory. Its last great ideologist, Alfred Marshall, probably spoke for the majority of capitalists when he wrote that the privilege of the entrepreneur was not so much his higher income as the greater meaningfulness and creativity of his efforts.

It is vital to bear the moral dimension in mind when we turn to the darker side of the take-off, the cost in human suffering. Achieving lift-off into self-sustaining industrial growth requires a colossal national effort – particularly for the pioneer nation, entirely dependent on its own skills, capital goods and finance. Obviously, it involves heavy voluntary savings on the part of the entrepreneurial class; it also involves a degree of compulsory saving on the part of the work-force. It is the second point which has dominated the imaginations of writers from Engels and Marx onwards. The assumption has generally been made that the Industrial Revolution in Britain led to an impoverishment of the working class, a reduction in its standard of living, and an incalculable amount of cruelty, deprivation and human misery. The picture thus presented has been used not only to condemn capitalism but, much more important, to discredit the principle of freedom in economic (and so in political) arrangements.

The cruder human consequences of the Industrial Revolution, as seen for instance in Manchester (where Engels studied them), struck many people at the time as unacceptable. There were two reasons for this. The first was that the industrial lift-off, beginning in the 1780s, coincided

with a new phase of human sensibility, which expressed itself in evangeli-
calism, the agitation against the slave trade, the campaign against
hanging for theft and the ferocious game-laws, and not least in the
poetry and music of the Romantic movement. A great many middle-
and upper-class men and women suddenly became conscious of phenomena which had always existed but had never seemed important
before – the beauties of natural landscape, the sufferings of deprived
sections of the population. Thus, chimney sweeps in London had employed infant 'climbing boys' since the end of the Middle Ages; not
until the 1780s do we first hear of an agitation on their behalf. The
coming of industry coincided with and helped to generate a new kind of
humanitarianism.

The second, and related, reason was that industrialization made the
more horrific aspects of economic life not only visible but unavoidable.
The world of the eighteenth century was still hideously poor. In the
whole of Germany, even in 1800, there were less than 1,000 persons with
incomes of £500 a year or over. The great majority of human kind, even
in relatively prosperous western Europe, spent most of their incomes on
basic foodstuffs, which did not include fresh meat as a rule. But poverty
and degradation were concealed and scattered in the countryside.
Industrialization, by concentrating the poor in factories and city housing, brought the perennial sufferings of the working class to the attention
of the new humanitarians. In fact, in strict material terms, the poor were
better off in the factories. All the worst abuses of the factory system – the
mass employment of women and children, the twelve-hour day (or
more) – merely continued the essential characteristic of the domestic
system. Indeed, on the whole factory work was characterized by shorter
hours and better conditions, as well as much higher pay – that, of course,
was why the exploited domestic workers flocked in from the countryside.
In the cities they were better housed, too; rural housing in the eighteenth,
even the nineteenth century, was infinitely worse than anything Engels
inspected in Manchester. A study of even the 'model' villages provided
by the better type of landlord reveals an occupation density far higher
than in the slums of Manchester, Sheffield or Leeds. Pre-industrial rural
poverty was something the new urban philanthropists could not comprehend, for they had never seen it. Hence they tended to categorize the
urban poverty they *could* see, and smell, as something new and unprecedented.

Industrialization, in fact, meant higher working-class living standards.

The rise would undoubtedly have been much higher, and more ostensible, and the conjunction between industry and prosperity would have become clearer in men's minds, had it not been for political errors of judgement, and in particular the decision of the British government to oppose the French Revolution. If it was political forces which made the Industrial Revolution possible, it was also political mistakes which made it needlessly costly in human terms. The tragedy is that in the three critical decades in the middle of the take-off, Britain was not only carrying through a massive investment programme but fighting, and paying for, the costliest and one of the longest wars in her history; working-class private consumption was squeezed in consequence. This is reflected in an exhaustive examination of the statistics, which reveal that living standards went up until about 1795; thereafter there was a pause, possibly even a decline, as a result of heavy capital investment and world war; this was followed by slow recovery, with good and bad years; after the mid-1840s, the rise was steady.

Other government errors compounded the original one of fighting France on behalf of royal legitimacy. It was the Corn Laws which were the chief cause of malnutrition and, indeed, unemployment; and it was agricultural protectionism which tended to switch the terms of trade against manufactures. The new government public-relief system aggravated the evils it was designed to cure. One victim of government errors was working-class housing in town and country. The Speenhamland method of poor relief, and the laws of settlement, not only held back house-building in the countryside but actually led to the pulling down of cottages. In the towns, housing was limited by a chronic shortage of timber, produced by the government's vast naval programme and its absurdly high duties on imported timber. At the same time, government was aggravating the demographic effects of a falling death-rate by encouraging a massive Irish immigration to English towns which had no houses to accommodate them; and it failed even in its most elementary duty to provide an adequate supply of coin – thus producing the monstrous abuses of the 'truck' (payment in company money) system.

The capitalist system, and the men who operated it, were not on the whole to blame for these mistakes, for the government represented the landed classes. What can be said is that the sudden and providential growth of industry prevented widespread starvation during a demographic avalanche. Those who criticize the industrialists for exploiting child labour overlook the fact that the central problem of the age was how to feed, clothe and employ generations of children outnumbering by far those of any other time in history. It was not capitalism which produced these children. What it did do was to enable England to avoid an Irish solution of mass starvation and emigration. As Professor Ashton puts it, England 'was delivered not by her rulers but by those who, seeking no doubt their own narrow ends, had the wit and resource to devise new instruments of production and new methods of administering industry'.

If we take a longer perspective, the achievements of the new economic civilization become undeniable. In the end, capitalism brought much greater equality. Gregory King calculated in 1688 that Lords got £3,200 a year and gentlemen on average £280; the mass of the poor got £2. There seems to have been very little change between 1688 and 1800; thereafter the equalizing process began to operate, and the gigantic disparities between rich and poor, so characteristic of all pre-industrial societies, slowly narrowed, a process which continues today. What, in material terms is more important is that, at the same time, the real wealth of all increased. In nineteenth-century Britain, the size of the working population multiplied four-fold; real wages doubled in the half-century 1800–1850, and doubled again, 1850–1900. This meant there was a 1,600% increase in the production and consumption of wage-goods during the century. Nothing like this had happened anywhere before, in the whole of history.

Moreover, as capitalist industrialization spread, to the United States, Germany and Belgium, later to Austria and France, then to Russia and Japan, the positive benefits were acquired more easily and more rapidly, and the incidental miseries gradually eliminated. No other country had to go through Britain's sufferings, in part at least because Britain was able to supply the industrial matrix she had forged for herself – capital, patents, capital goods, skilled labour and management. The United States and Germany were thus able to industrialize on a scale and at a speed which would have dazzled the British pioneers of the 1780s; and feudal empires like Japan and Russia were able to telescope a development process which in Britain had stretched over centuries into a mere generation or two. Yet, curiously enough, the attention of analysts and ideologues remained almost exclusively fixed on the original British experience; and conclusions were drawn from it long after it had ceased to be relevant to the actual world. In particular, the enormously complicated prophetic structure of Marxism was erected on the diminutive basis of what happened in Manchester between 1780 and 1840, and thus itself became the fallacious plinth on which successive monuments of fantasy have been erected from Marx's day to our own.

There were, indeed, aspects of industrial civilization which hardly anyone liked. As Sir Robert Peel, himself the rich son of a cotton pioneer, told the House of Commons: 'If you had to constitute new societies, you might on moral and social grounds prefer cornfields to cotton factories, an agricultural to a manufacturing population. *But our lot is cast and we cannot recede.*' By 'our lot is cast' he meant in effect that there was no other way but through industrial capitalism to feed the teeming new millions. That alone justified the creation of capitalism, for nothing else could have saved us from a demographic catastrophe, and so another recession of civilization and culture. But a further question remained: could the capitalist system continue to justify itself by spreading the enjoyment of the goods it was able to produce to the great mass of mankind? To this we shall now turn, and we shall see how, and why, the answer has varied over the past hundred and fifty years.

CHAPTER 6

The 'Permanent Miracle'

Until the late 1840s, the erratic performance of early industrial capitalism, the violence of its trade cycles, and the visible dislocation and misery which marked its implantation – especially in Britain, its birthplace – made it seem not so much a mixed blessing as an unpredictable dispenser of good and evil, an invisible hand operating at the whim of an unfathomable intelligence, a Frankenstein monster beyond human control. But from about 1845, the accumulating benefits which the system was seen to produce, especially in terms of real wages, became undeniable, and its essential superiority to any other in the whole course of human history became the central proposition in the received economic wisdom. In the three decades 1850–80, world trade expanded by more than 270% and during this period industrial capitalism became a world phenomenon. In the late 1870s there was a serious recession, the first for over thirty years, and a revival of protective tariffs. But expansion of trade was resumed, albeit at a lower rate – 170% between 1880–1913 – and the growth-rates of twelve leading capitalist countries averaged 2·7% in the fifty years up to the First World War. This should be contrasted with the pre-Industrial Age performance, when 1% growth was excellent, and there were many years of nil or minus growth. During this period, the international monetary mechanism based on the gold standard and centred on London functioned smoothly and was largely self-regulating. As a result of legislative changes and the need for larger capital investment, modern capitalism took shape with the emergence of the industrial and commercial corporation – multitudes of small shareholders, boards comparatively remote from day-to-day decisions, professional executives, a divorce of ownership from control.

The connection between industrial capitalism and Christianity, or indeed morality of any kind, was thus severed, and the invisible hand now projected from an agnostic stratosphere; at the same time capitalism acquired a solidity and indestructability which banished many of the nightmares of the past.

This was the world that Adam Smith had, indeed, predicted would come to pass, granted the economic freedom he had enjoined. The warnings of Malthus were now a subject for mirth. Economists were no longer hag-ridden by problems of scarcity, the fear of diminishing returns in agriculture, and the spectre of uncontrolled growth of population. Alfred Marshall, whose standard capitalist bible, *Principles of Economics*, was published in 1890, wrote optimistically: 'Cheap transport by land and sea, combined with the opening up of a large part of the surface of the world during the last 30 years, has caused the purchasing power of wages in terms of goods to rise throughout the western world, and especially in Britain, at a rate which has no parallel in the past, and will probably have none in the future.'

In fact this late note of warning proved well-founded. The year 1914 marked the turning point since war dislocated the international money market and the ordinary patterns of world trade. But a change was coming anyway. The first third of the twentieth century was marked by a sharp decrease in the growth of western populations, the end of territorial expansion and so the opening of entirely new markets, and a change in the quality of technological progress which, though still rapid, required less 'deepening' of capital. All these factors made it more difficult for western economies to recover from the effects of business-cycles; and when governments were called in to help, they did not know how to provide it, even if they were willing to do so. The Great War also saw the end of European predominance, since it forced former markets, especially in the New World, the British Dominions, and the Far East, to become more self-supporting. Capitalist leadership passed to the United States, which had already, in the years 1870–1913, achieved an average annual growth rate of 4·3%, much higher than its nearest European rival, Germany (2·9%).

It was, in fact, primarily the United States' performance which kept the world economy comparatively active in the 1920s. In the seven years up to 1929, industrial production and national income in the US both rose by 40%. By that year, US productive power exceeded that of all continental Europe, and its productivity was already twice that of Britain; with only 7% of the world's population, it produced a third of its coal and iron, 60% of its oil, and a quarter of its manufactured goods (consumer durables). The US economy went into recession on an equally generous scale: in the years 1929–32, its national income fell by 38%, and at one point there were probably as many as 15 million Americans unemployed. The economic devastation caused by the combination of world war followed by US economic collapse was so profound that, for the first time since the early 1840s, there was widespread questioning of the very foundations of industrial capitalism. Was the whole system so inherently unstable as to outweigh its productive merits? Was the invisible hand ultimately malign? Was the pursuit of economic freedom a hideous mistake?

The universality of these doubts sent men scurrying off in pursuit of alternative, non-capitalist solutions. The only complete alternative system available was the one erected by Marx. Now here was a paradox. Both Marx and Engels discounted the impact of ideas. As Engels put it, 'The mode of production in material life determines social, political and spiritual evolution in general. It is not the conscious thought of mankind that determines its modes of existence, but on the contrary, its modes of existence determine its conscious thought.' This formulation immediately raises the (unanswered) question: How, then, did the conscious thought of Marx come into existence? In any case, the most cursory historical inquiry shows it to be false. Much nearer the truth is Keynes's observation:

... the ideas of economists and political philosophers, both when they are right and when they are wrong, are more powerful than is commonly understood. Indeed, the world is ruled by little else. Practical men, who believe themselves to be quite exempt from any intellectual influences, are usually the slaves of some defunct economist. Madmen in authority, who hear voices in the air, are distilling their frenzy from some academic scribbler of a few years back.

The most convincing proof of this observation, and therein lies the paradox, is the acceptance of Marxism itself.

For by the 1930s, Marxism had not only, to all appearances, established itself in Russia, but it seemed to provide the theoretical explanation of what was happening in the rest of the world. Marx himself had prophesied it all! He had said that competition would lead to the concentration of capital into fewer and fewer hands. Then:

Along with the constantly diminishing number of the magnates of capital, who usurp and monopolise all advantages of this process of transformation, grows the mass of misery, oppression, slavery, degradation, exploitation; but with this too grows the revolt of the working-class, a class always increasing in numbers, and disciplined, united, organised by the very mechanism of the process of capitalist production itself. The monopoly of capital becomes a fetter upon the mode of production, which has sprung up and flourished along with it, and under it. The centralisation of the means of production and the socialisation of labour at last reach a point where they become incompatible with their capitalist integument. This integument is burst asunder. The knell of capitalist private property sounds. The expropriators are expropriated.

Thus *Capital*, Chapter 24. In fact, looked at closely, this prediction, like most prophecies, has very little relation to what actually happened in the Great Depression. But it had the right apocalyptic ring. And it made the point, which to many then seemed evident, that capitalism would collapse of its very nature.

Of course, Marxism itself did not provide an alternative to capitalism. The only alternative to economic liberalism is some form of state management. But Marx did not believe in the state. He identified it with capitalism. As Engels said: 'The modern state, whatever its form, is essentially a capitalist machine.' The retreat of the state, after the expropriators are expropriated, is the very core and essence of the Marxist solution. What was being applied in Russia was not Marxism at all. Lenin had made this clear even before he seized the opportunity to apply it, in *Will the Bolsheviks Retain State Power?* (1917):

The state is an organ or apparatus of force to be used by one class against another. So long as it remains an apparatus for the bourgeoisie to use force against the proletariat, so long can the slogan of the proletariat be only: the destruction of the state. But when the state has become an apparatus of force to be used by the proletariat against the bourgeoisie, then we shall be fully and unreservedly for a strong state power and centralism.

Nothing could be plainer. In fact the Communist alternative was merely one form of state totalitarianism. It had much more in common with the Nazi or Fascist solution to capitalist crisis, than any of them had with free-enterprise capitalism. Indeed, all these state-power theories sprang from the same root: Hegel. He taught that the state represents the principle of absolute reason and spiritual power, which bestows upon man whatever value he has. Far from losing his liberty in the collective whole, the individual is lifted to a higher sphere in which his real will is realized. As the state is the embodiment of absolute power, its actual policies must not be judged in terms of 'subjective morality'. Power is the basic fact of political life, and the political order must be judged and justified within its own terms – this is the central argument of Hegel's *Philosophy of Right* (1821).

But, as we have already noted, the elevation of the state is a very common feature in primitive storage cultures, in stagnant civilizations, as in imperial China, and in civilizations in process of decay. It was the salient principle of the later Roman empire, with its total abolition of economic and political freedom, and its compulsory corporations. Italian Fascism, in fact, consciously based itself on the Roman model. Nazi Germany was equally frank in imposing control of labour and eliminating all foci of political and economic power other than the party-state. Stalinist Russia was in all essentials a similar creation, though the compulsory workers' corporations were nominally labelled trade unions on the western model. All these totalitarian societies tended towards the total elimination of the middle class from economic or political decision-making, leaving the population, for all practical purposes, divided into an official elite, and the rest – the old *honestiores* and *humiliores* of Rome's decay. The distinction was most clearly developed in Russia, where party membership, grudgingly awarded and speedily withdrawn, was introduced as the badge of 'honest' status. In addition, both the Nazi and the Russian systems quickly began to employ slave-labour, thus conforming to the late Roman pattern, with the supposedly free being very little better off, in terms of movement and choice of occupation.

The problem confronting capitalism in the 1930s was whether it could modify itself sufficiently to avoid this gruesome alternative. The prevailing wisdom was that, tempting as it might be to seek a little state interference with the economic process, the result would be ineffective at best, at worst disastrous. Winston Churchill voiced this sentiment in 1929 when introducing his budget: '. . . whatever might be the political or social advantages, very little additional employment can, in fact and as a general rule, be created by state borrowing and expenditure.' A plan for state intervention on these lines, put forward by Sir Oswald Mosley in 1930, was rejected by all three British political parties. But cracks were beginning to appear in orthodox theory. Marshall himself had chipped away at the principle of absolute competition; so had

Pigou. Both found technical economic arguments, derived from pure liberal theory, to justify state intervention in certain circumstances designed to produce 'more efficient allocation of resources'. Marshall, towards the end of his life, described 'a cautious movement towards enriching the poor at the expense of the rich' as 'beneficial' – even though 'socialists say it is a step in their direction'.

The process was carried further by Marshall's pupil, Keynes, one of those providential men who, like Adam Smith, encapsulate a coming mood. A government as well as an academic (and commercial) economist, Keynes became increasingly critical of the orthodox monetary arrangements during the 1920s. The international rules were 'unstable, complicated, unreliable and temporary'. Capitalist economies were forced to steer between deflation and inflation; the first was 'inexpedient', the second 'unjust'. Except in the case of hyperinflation, deflation was the worse of the choices 'because it is worse, in an impoverished world, to provoke unemployment than to disappoint the rentier' (*Tract on Monetary Reform*, 1923). An agnostic in religion, he was an agnostic in economics, too; no 'invisible hand' for him:

> It is *not* true that individuals possess a prescriptive 'natural liberty' in their economic activities. There is *no* 'compact' conferring perpetual rights on those who Have or those who Acquire. The world is *not* so governed from above that private and social interests always coincide. It is *not* so managed here below that in practice they coincide. It is *not* a correct deduction from the Principles of Economics that enlightened self-interest always operates in the public interest. Nor is it true that self-interest generally is enlightened; more often individuals acting separately to promote their own ends are too ignorant or too weak to attain even these. Experience does *not* show that individuals, when they make up a social unit, are always less clear-sighted than when they act separately (*Essays in Persuasion*, 1926).

This iconoclastic assault on classical theory was all very well. But what should replace the discredited self-regulating market? How, and when, and to what extent, and on what theoretical basis should the state move into the market? It is important to get clear that Keynes was never a socialist. One of the reasons why his theories penetrated the orthodox world so rapidly is that he was an academic figure of great standing, had a mastery of orthodox doctrine, and argued within many of its assumptions. At heart he believed in liberal capitalism not only because he thought it more likely to produce the goods than any other imaginable system, but for moral reasons: he thought the destruction of economic freedom must, in practice, lead to a progressive diminution of political freedom. As he once told Sir Roy Harrod (1938): 'Economics is essentially a moral science and not a natural science; that is to say, it employs introspection and judgements of value.' He shared Dr Johnson's view that, in a society under the rule of law, making money is a comparatively innocent canalization of dark human motives:

There are valuable human activities which require the motive of money-making and the environment of private wealth-ownership for their full fruition. Moreover, dangerous human proclivities can be canalised into comparatively harmless channels by the existence of opportunities for money-making and private wealth, which, if they cannot be satisfied in this way, may find their outlet in cruelty, the reckless pursuit of personal power and authority, and other forms of self-aggrandisement. It is better that a man should tyrannise over his bank-balance than over his fellow citizens . . . (*General Theory of Employment, Interest and Money*, 1936).

As he later put it in *Democracy and Efficiency* (1939), he wanted a middle way, '. . . a system where we can act as an organised community for common purposes, and to promote social and economic justice, while respecting and protecting the individual – his freedom of choice, his faith, his mind and its expression, his enterprise and his property'. This is a formula not for socialism, nor even for a mixed economy, but for occasional state regulation of the economy as a whole.

It took Keynes some years of thought to produce his prognosis; perhaps he might never have done so had he not lived through the collapse of the early 1930s. For he needed, in effect, to invent a new economic science. Classical economics had dealt with scarcity, value, choice, resource-allocation and efficiency; it took the stock of economic resources as given, and their level of utilization, and it dealt with their allocation – whether by market, planning or a mixture of the two. Keynes classified this form of investigation as micro-economics; on top of it he erected macro-economics, using aggregate variables such as 'national income' and aggregate demand, to analyse and explain the general level of economic activity at any one time. Viewed in this context, he felt he had detected an inherent downward instability of the economy as a whole, that is a deficiency in aggregate demand requiring some kind of offsetting action by the government. Why was there this downward instability? Because of a defect in the system of savings. Saving was not an invariable virtue; it could become a social vice if investment failed to use savings effectively. Thrift is an aid to economic growth only if the propensity to invest is strong; if it is weak, thrift will tend to make it all the weaker. The harmony between public and private interests was thus a myth, and could not be relied on to produce full employment. This had to become an object of state policy, the government balancing uninvested private saving by its own spending policies.

The theory was neat; it fitted all the known facts. Even before publication, Keynes confidently predicted his *General Theory* would 'revolutionise the way in which the world thinks about economic problems'. In fact Keynes claimed that the more enlightened democracies were already moving in the direction he wished. In December 1933, in an *Open Letter to Roosevelt* he praised the 'reasoned experiment' of the New Deal: 'If you fail, rational change will be gravely prejudiced throughout the world, leaving orthodoxy and revolution to fight it out. But if you succeed, new and bolder methods will be tried everywhere, and we may date the first chapter of a new economic era from your accession to office.' His view, as he made clear in a private letter to Roosevelt in February 1938, was that the New Deal did not go far enough in using public expenditure for pump-priming. His criticism was adopted, and the United States began to run budget deficits, as Keynes had urged, though there is no evidence that Roosevelt himself understood the Keynesian argument.

It was the Second World War which really marked the introduction of Keynesian macro-economics. Indeed, it is impossible to fight a total war efficiently without interfering with aggregate demand. Keynes's real triumph was to persuade the British government, and by example other governments, to use macro-economics to tackle post-war problems. It is more difficult to run a peace-time economy, especially in the immediate transitional period, than a wartime one, and Keynes feared the breakdowns that had followed the defeat of Napoleonic France and the Kaiser's Germany. In 1944, Sir William Beveridge published *Full Employment in a Free Society*, written by five Keynesians, Joan Robinson, Barbara Wootton, Nicholas Kaldor, E. F. Schumacher and Frank Pakenham; and this was followed the same year by the official *White Paper on Employment Policy*, which for the first time embodied the central Keynesian doctrine that the maintenance of high demand (and so of high employment) should be a primary object of government policy. A parallel development took place in the United States, where the American Employment Act, 1946, accepted federal management of the economy. As passed by Congress, the Act was considerably watered down, since it embodied a commitment not to full but to 'maximum' employment, which must be consistent with 'and in a manner calculated to foster and promote free competitive enterprise'. But the rapid adoption by European economies of Keynesian management strategy, and its empirical success in the US led to a gradual acceptance of Keynes's doctrines in Washington. The triumph of the theory in the world's largest economy was saluted by President Kennedy's Yale Commencement Speech in June 1962, described by a leading US economist, Walter H. Heller, as 'the most literate and sophisticated dissertation on economics ever delivered by a president'. Arthur Schlesinger Jr called Kennedy 'unquestionably the first Keynesian president'.

Keynes, in fact, became the new capitalist orthodoxy. As his pupil and biographer, Sir Roy Harrod, put it during the first Keynes Seminar at Canterbury University (1974):

... to the best of my knowledge the majority of people now are Keynesians and have been for some time. I am not only talking about economists or professors lecturing in universities; the practical people have become Keynesians, have accepted this idea that you can regulate the economy, regulate aggregate demand, by your monetary and fiscal policies ... you will find that these ideas are taken for granted: they are almost universally accepted.

The chief reason for this, as with Adam Smith's establishment as the repository of truth in the early nineteenth century, is that Keynes's theory appeared to be matched by actual economic performance. From 1945, and for nearly thirty years, nearly all the major capitalist economies sustained high growth rates. In the 1950s, for instance, the twelve leading economies cited before had an average annual growth of 4·2%. France, traditionally a slow-growth country, averaged 4·4%, Switzerland over 5, Italy over 6 and Germany 7·6. In all the western European economies the rate of investment in the 1950s was half as high again as it had ever been on a sustained basis. In Germany and the Netherlands, investment averaged 25% of the Gross National Product, in Norway it was even higher, and in several other European countries it was over 20%. Moreover, this high capital formation took place not at the cost of private consumption but during a rapid and sustained rise in living-standards, particularly of industrial workers. These tendencies were prolonged throughout the 1960s and into the 1970s. So far as the 'mature' economies were concerned, the 'second Industrial Revolution', 1945–70, was entirely painless, and largely so even in Japan, where even higher investment and growth-rates were sought, and obtained, to catch up with Europe.

What was the cause of this phenomenon, which for the first time brought affluence within the reach of entire nations, and which seemed to justify capitalism not only as a source of plenty for all but as a system which could be manipulated and improved to produce steady growth within a framework of stability? There were those, all along, who denied the credit to Keynesian methods. They argued that the long boom would have happened anyway. Had not the United States set the pattern, leaving out the Depression years, between 1870 and the 1950s, when the advantages of vast natural resources, fast population growth, relative security from the effects of war, and relative invulnerability to export markets – together with the absolute size of the economy – produced continuous high growth over a very long period? As with the Industrial Revolution itself, once one nation has shown that a new kind of economic activity is possible, others will find ways to imitate it. Moreover, experience of growth generates its own momentum, especially among managers and entrepreneurs, and the men who finance them, just as it strengthens confidence by diminishing the fear of failure. Thus it could be argued that objective factors which have made for high and sustained post-war growth, especially in Europe and Japan, were recovery from war, elimination of disguised unemployment, the reduction of tariff barriers (a once-and-for-all gain), and the drive to reach US productivity levels and standard of living. The post-war international payments mechanism worked reasonably well during this period, so there were no trade and tariffs wars; clearly, the system of convertibility, with fixed exchange-rates, liberal trading policies and a non-retaliatory code of behaviour, was favourable to steady growth.

But of course this payments system was itself part of the Keynesian formula, itself made workable by the fact that all governments concerned pursued, by and large, policies which promoted high demand. And it was undoubtedly the enormous level of investment, stimulated by extremely high demand (and high profits) which led to the sustained rise in productivity, output and living-standards. What gave a variety of governments the courage and self-confidence to go on stimulating demand was undoubtedly their knowledge that they were operating within a convincing theory which now had the support of all orthodox economic opinion. If Keynes cannot claim posthumous credit for assisting the post-war boom, no thinker in history can claim credit for influencing anything.

Yet, at the very moment when capitalism, as the West had learnt to manage it, had been set upon its feet again, more firmly than ever, was steadily fulfilling all the promises of even its most ambitious partisans, and was displaying the most protean capacity to adapt itself to situations and regimes all over the globe, the entire system suddenly, for no apparent reason, staggered and lost confidence in itself. How did this come about? Why was it necessary to fight the battle for capitalism all over again, and this time against a cultural background almost wholly hostile to it? We now, at last, turn to the problems of the 1970s.

CHAPTER 7

Ecological Panic

The essence of civilization is the orderly quest for truth, the rational perception of reality and all its facets, and the adaptation of man's behaviour to its laws. So long as we follow the path of reason we shall not move far from the lighted circle of civilization. Its enemies invariably lie among those who, for whatever motive, deny, distort, minimize, exaggerate or poison the truth, and who falsify the processes of reason. At all times civilization has its enemies, though they are constantly changing their guise and their weapons. The great defensive art is to detect and unmask them before the damage they inflict becomes fatal. 'Hell,' wrote Thomas Hobbes, 'is truth seen too late.' Survival is falsehood detected in time.

The acceptance of Keynesian theory, and the use of economic management techniques based on it, had by 1972 raised the national income per head of the advanced industrial countries of North America and western Europe to more than twice its pre-war average. This huge increase in goods and services, greater than hitherto achieved at any time in history over a comparable period, had come about without human suffering and, indeed, had been accompanied by the rapid development of welfare services and a slow but persistent tendency towards an equalization of incomes. Capitalism was not only the physical mainstay of western civilization; it was also, it appeared, in the process of becoming civilized itself.

Then, in 1972 and for the next three years, the international economy, and many of the larger national economies which composed it, began to behave in ways for which the Keynesian model provided no guidance; in ways which, indeed, seemed to contradict its assumptions. The international exchange system, based on fixed parities, broke down, and there was a reversion to more primitive methods of floating rates. More important, the slow but steady inflation which had been a characteristic of the managed Keynesian economies – and was seen as an acceptable concomitant of growth – began to accelerate very rapidly. Not only this, but the new inflation was accompanied by conjunctive trends which, in the Keynesian analysis, seemed impossible – a fall in growth and a rise in unemployment. The art of Keynesian management had been to steer the ship of state between too much growth and high inflation on the one hand, and too little growth and deflation on the other. Now, for no discernible reason, all the associated causes and effects had become confused, and the world found itself confronted with a new combination of evils: hyperinflation, high unemployment, and low, nil or negative growth. Theoretically, the conjunction was impossible. But the figures proved otherwise. Therefore the theory must be wrong, and Keynesianism was discredited.

So the argument ran. But to attack Keynes was absurd. Keynes was an empiricist and an original who had no attachment to theory – hated theory in fact. His method was to look at new facts squarely, and then seek to explain them, and devise methods to cope with them. The only trouble with Keynesianism in the later 1970s was that Keynes was dead, and so unable to bring his uniquely creative mind to bear on its problems. Of course he reflected his age. He did not study, because the materials did not exist, the effects of highly organized and aggressive trade unions on wage-inflation. As one of his leading followers, John Kenneth Galbraith, has noted, Keynes detected an inherent downward instability of the economy as a whole, and his prognosis provided for this; what he did not foresee – because there was then no evidence – was the possible development of instability in an upward direction. But Keynes had no illusions about the cruel ravages of inflation. As long ago as 1920 he had written in *Economic Consequences of the Peace*: 'There is no subtler, nor surer, means of overturning the existing basis of society than to debauch the currency. The process engages all the hidden forces of economic law on the side of destruction, and does it in a manner which no one man in a million is able to diagnose.'

Rationally considered, then, the great recession of the 1970s is not the proof that demand management is useless and dangerous, and the occasion to revert to the primitive controls of the market, or the in-humanity of totalitarianism. On the contrary, it is an invitation to enlarge our understanding, and refine our armoury of weapons. We are already beginning to explain some of the new paradoxes. Thus, to cite one characteristic but important example of the way in which the crisis can be turned to our profit, there is the Cambridge study which has revealed the dangers of raising taxation to reduce demand (Dudley Jackson, H. A. Turner, Frank Wilkinson, *Do Trades Unions Cause Inflation?*). The authors demonstrated that the 'impossible' double conjunction of high inflation *plus* high unemployment, and high unemployment *plus* intensified labour militancy, also coincided, for the first time in history, with the entry of the mass of the manual wage-earners into the net of direct taxation, deducted from wage-packets at source. Hence, to obtain modest net increases in income, they had to ask for much higher gross wages. As firms had to pay the gross, profits fell and thus unemployment rose. Prices rose too, and so inflation increased, and a new cycle of wage demands. The gainer was the profligate state, which added to inflation in two distinct ways. Thus, the Keynesian management policies most specifically directed in the 1960s towards restraining inflation – high direct taxes – may in fact have done most to increase it in the 1970s.

Yet, at a deeper level, the great depression of the 1970s, which must be the starting point for any investigation of the ills of our civilization, was not brought about merely by defects in management technique. These alone cannot account for the manner in which the recession has been exploited to cast doubts on the entire purpose and workings of the free economy, and the democratic social systems built around it, and the concerted endeavour to push off course the western pursuit of rational progress. It is important to realize that all civilizations contain the elements of their destruction. Each casts its shadow: a sinister doppelgänger which denies its aims, belittles its achievements, and predicts and plots its demise. All societies contain not only creators and builders but apocalyptics. Our Christian-based society, with its acute sense of time, necessarily possesses its own eschatology. For most of its history, most of its inhabitants have believed, with greater or less conviction and with varying degrees of immediacy, that the world was coming to an end. For a thousand years, St Augustine's chronology, teaching that the sixth and final epoch had begun, was standard doctrine. Hence Donne's line: 'I was born in the last age of the world.' In the eighteenth century, Archbishop Ussher's detailed chronology of creation not only dated its beginnings, but worked out that 5,500 of the allotted 6,000 years were over.

There was, however, disagreement about when, precisely, the Second Coming would take place. This being so, the creators and builders pushed the prospect to the back of their minds, rather on Hamlet's reasoning: 'If it be now, 'tis not to come; if it be not to come, it will be now; if it be not now, yet it will come – the readiness is all.' The apocalyptics and millenarians, on the other hand, constantly predicted the event and the precise form it would take; and, this strain of human nature being what it is, the repeated failures of such precise prophecies in no way deterred men from framing and believing in new ones. What is even more remarkable is that apocalyptic prophecy survived the coming of the secular age, and took on a more materialist form. Marx, with his highly detailed and imaginative presentation of the eschatology of capitalism, can be described as the last of the Judaeo-Christian prophets, or the first of the secular ones. Nor, as one would expect, has the discrediting of Marx's vision by the actual unrolling of events prevented fresh generations of the millenarian-minded from modifying and updating it, or indeed from devising new secular eschatologies. Any unexpected, brutal or ominous conjunction of events is enough to conjure up new visions of the end, as Yeats noted:

> Things fall apart; the centre cannot hold;
> Mere anarchy is loosed upon the world,
> The blood-dimmed tide is loosed, and everywhere
> The ceremony of innocence is drowned;
> The best lack all conviction, while the worst
> Are full of passionate intensity.
>
> Surely some revelation is at hand;
> Surely the Second Coming is at hand?

This syndrome of symptoms is at work at many levels of our society, as we shall see. But in relation to the future of the international free economy, it takes the particular form of ecological eschatology. The Four Last Things are to be the poisoning of the air, the exhaustion of the soil, the final consumption of the earth's natural resources, and mass-starvation of an over-populated planet.

This apocalyptic scenario is presented at just the time, as Sir Peter Medawar has put it, when science has made it 'the ordinary received opinion that the world has a future extending far beyond the most distant frontiers of what can be rationally imagined'. Ecological alarmism is characterized by a marked distrust of the free-enterprise economy, and indeed incorporates many aspects of Marxist mythology, especially the idea that capitalist society creates, then satisfies, artificial and wasteful appetites, and is ultimately self-destructive. But it is even more characterized by an irrational fear of science. Its visions are infested by Gothic devils in the shape of mad scientists and their lunatic benefactors, engaged in horrific experiments which must end in the destruction of the human race. At one time this form of millenarianism saw the H-bomb as the death-agent; the popular nightmare of the 1950s and early 1960s was of an incinerated planet made uninhabitable by radiation; and the level of argument – and the misunderstanding of how science and sciences actually work – was illustrated by an Anglican bishop, who wrote to *The Times* asking all nations to agree to destroy 'the formula for the thermonuclear bomb'. The level of argument has not improved but, the thermonuclear war having failed to materialize, there has been a change of location. The dangers of radiation remain as a carry-over from the thermonuclear eschatology, but they are now seen as part of a permanent peace-time threat posed by the demands of capitalist economies and the pursuit of unlimited growth.

This new death-vision itself draws on an earlier secular tradition, perhaps best illustrated by Freud's melancholy posthumous book, *Civilization and its Discontents* (1930). Like other melancholic irrationalists, Freud wrote in terms of a collective nervous breakdown – itself a relic of social Darwinism, which compares societies to individuals. Of course, to speak of civilization having a nervous breakdown has no meaning; one might just as well say it has a hernia, or piles. But this misuse of figures of speech is characteristic of secular eschatology, and helps to explain the horror its faithful feel towards scientists, forever portrayed in cataclysmic or violent activities, such as the 'conquest' of space, age, etc. – expressions, needless to say, coined by journalists, not by men of science.

What makes ecological eschatology important and dangerous – and, as we shall see, even destructive – is that it is part of a very widely based movement in the West. The ecological lobby should be seen as the 'respectable' end of a spectrum of middle-class cranks which embraces such sects as the Christian Scientists, the anti-vivisectionists and those who campaign fanatically against the fluoridation of water-supplies. But the lobby itself includes a large number of presentable intellectuals, and even a few distinguished scientists; it has political appeal and even electoral impact. Some of its assertions have virtually passed into the stock of the prevailing wisdom. It is important to understand just how, and why, it can be misleading.

The first point to grasp is that there is an internal contradiction in the anti-growth philosophy. Those who hold it are divided between those who say growth is intrinsically bad, whether or not it is impossible; and those who say it is impossible, whatever its moral merits, because we are up against the limits of our resources. However, the second group are not necessarily exorcised of their fears if it is demonstrated that our resources are, in fact, ample for any foreseeable growth. They then fall back on arguments centring around pollution, thus indicating that they are closer to the first group than they care to admit. Indeed, it is characteristic of the ecolobby, as of most irrationalist systems, that when faced with reasoned opposition they constantly discard old arguments and replace them with new ones. Osmosis, of course, is the normal state of invalid theory.

First, then, we must deal with those, the minority, who are opposed to growth itself, on the grounds that it consists chiefly in the creation of new and wholly unnecessary needs by what is termed 'the consumer society', and that any desirable elements in it are greatly exceeded by undesirable ones. The answer, at the level of first principles, is that man seems to fulfil himself by imagining and acquiring new needs. The ultimate value of the new artifacts he creates can only be determined by testing and experience. Some are discarded as meretricious; others, retained, permanently enhance his condition. If we look closely at the detailed analysis of recent growth, we can see that the beneficial elements greatly outweigh the others. The increase in leisure, to use a clumsy term for a complex thing, has been enormous. One American study by A. W. Sametz (1968) shows that, whereas the Gross National Product in the United States rose from 9·4 billion dollars in 1869–78 (average) to 315 billion in 1966, welfare and leisure-spending rose much faster, from 1·2 billion to 240 billion. Similar studies reach the same conclusion by different routes. Nor is this surprising, since with increasing growth the proportion of income required for essentials must fall, and therefore the area of choice for man must rise. Of course, there is no arguing with those who believe that any increase in human felicity is itself undesirable; but they are never likely to be more than an insignificant minority.

More substantial is the argument that such growth, however desirable, is bought at too high a cost in terms of pollution and similar evils

attendant on industrial use. Here, we must first deal with those members
of the ecology lobby who distinguish between capitalist and other
economies. Evidence of pollution in the free-enterprise world is much
more extensive, simply because awareness of the problem came sooner,
as did calculations of its magnitude and efforts to deal with it. But from
what we know of the collectivist economies, the pursuit of production
goals can be as destructive of the environment as the pursuit of profits.
We now have a good idea of the extensive damage done in the areas of
Lake Baikal, the Volga, the Caspian and the Aral seas, and other
Soviet areas of industrial waste-disposal. There is serious air-pollution
over a number of East German, Czech, Soviet, Polish and Hungarian
cities, and acute river-pollution throughout the eastern block. Only since
1972 have environmental factors been included in planning criteria
during the drawing-up of Soviet and satellite industrial programmes.
Action against pollution has not only come later than in the West but
has been less stringent, since there is no role in collectivist states for
private agitation, and therefore no ecological lobby. This emerges
strongly when direct comparisons can be made: thus the attempt to deal
with 'noise pollution' in the creation of the Anglo-French supersonic
transport has no parallel in the Soviet SST, which in consequence has a
much higher decibel rating.

The distinction, then, between capitalist and communist pollution is
false. The argument follows the same lines on either side of the ideological frontier. Let us turn, then, to the heart of the problem, which is
a question of scale. Most Domesday predictions, such as (to cite two
very characteristic examples) E. J. Mishan's *The Costs of Economic
Growth* and the study sponsored by the Club of Rome, *The Limits of
Growth* by Dennis and Donella Meadows, J. Randers and W. W.
Behrens, leave out of account the magnitude of natural forces. Nature
makes man's efforts seem puny. Thus, the Israeli scientists at the Desert
Agriculture Station at Beersheba scoff at the theory that destructive
Arab methods of cultivation were responsible for the spread of desert in
North Africa and the Middle East: dessication on this scale would be
beyond even modern technology, let alone the powers of the medieval
Arabs. Deserts are usually created by relatively small change in climate.
The fact is that nature itself is both a pollutant and a self-cleansing
mechanism on a gigantic scale. An average-size hurricane releases the
energy of 100,000 H-bombs. Dr Mishan's estimate that there were (1967)
10 million tons of man-made pollutants in the atmosphere should be

set against the 1,600 million tons of methane gas emitted by natural swamps every year. Even cattle produce several million tons of methane gas annually; forests and other vegetation discharge 170 million tons annually of various hydrocarbons. Where artificial pollutants do raise problems, there is a tendency in the ecolobby to confuse questions of local industrial hygiene, which can easily be answered, with the world environment, which is unaffected. Carbon-monoxide emitted by car-exhausts amounts to 200 to 300 million tons a year. This affects local atmospheres, like Los Angeles, and has to be dealt with by the authorities. But it has produced no rise in the average concentrations of carbon-monoxide in the atmosphere, since carbon-monoxide (like sulphur-dioxide) is produced by nature in infinitely greater quantities than by man. In some respects, the car – often identified by the ecolobby as the chief villain of growth – has led to less pollution, since a 1972 United States study shows that the average-size car emits 6 grammes of pollutants per mile, while a horse emits 600 grammes of solid and 300 grammes of liquid pollutants per mile.

If the ecolobbyists exaggerate man's capacity to pollute, they equally underestimate nature's ability to clear up. Those notorious pollutants, volcanoes, sometimes spew out many hundreds of cubic kilometres of ash; but it is a notable rarity if the atmospheric debris is not eliminated within a few years. But the ecolobbyists, for people whose whole propaganda consists in the presentation of massive series of detailed figures, are notoriously inept in handling them. For them, indeed, the use of figures is more a form of emotional rhetoric than an exact science. This is particularly true in relation to noise-levels, classified as a noxious 'pollutant'. In Britain, for instance, the Noise Advisory Council decided in 1971 that 70 decibels was the highest level of noise which can be borne by householders adjacent to motorways, apparently unaware that all-day 90-decibel noise is common in factories and workshops and is designated as the maximum in the code of practice laid down by the Department of Employment. The whole campaign against the Concorde SST was based upon a misunderstanding of the nature of noise-levels and of the decibel system of computation, and ignorance of the fact that measurement and permission of levels vary enormously not only from country to country but within each.

Ecolobbyists are particularly suspect when they get hold of computers and produce horrific forecasts based on exponential calculations of future growth. Technological forecasting, sometimes called futurology, is a good example of a pseudo-science, lacking a background of craft knowledge based on long and successful research experience, and exhibiting faulty techniques in producing data, and misjudgements of what constitutes an adequate argument. A computer is no better than the quality of the material submitted to it; however complex, it does not in itself convey scientific authenticity. If the basic proposition is misconceived, the computer compounds the error. As one critic of futurology, Martin Shubi, has put it, 'vacuous computing' is a case of GIGO – 'garbage in, garbage out'. He adds: 'Tons of computer output are in general a sign of a badly understood job.'

At its worst, the assault on growth, and the misleading stress on pollution, can cause positive harm because it denies the vital part growth plays in improving the human physique and environment and in removing the grosser forms of pollution. If there had been a powerful ecological lobby in eighteenth-century England, it is hard to see how the Industrial Revolution could have taken place – and the Western world would still be condemned to pre-industrial living standards. Ecologists do, indeed, reflect nostalgia for a mythical past. Thus Dr Mishan hails 'the Britain of 1951' as a kind of golden age, 'before the car and the developer had made hideous our cities and suburbs, before TV held people in a semi-bovine state up to six hours a day. . . . The skies in those days were not rent by shrieking aircraft, nor was the air thick with car fumes. People could stroll along the street and converse without screaming at each other.' As it happens, 1951 saw the last and greatest of the London smogs, which killed 5,000 people, and was a typical instance of nineteenth-century-type pollution now eliminated by growth-science. The truth is that if natural conditions are allowed to prevail infantile death-rates tend to be high and life-expectancy low. Improvements in the human condition are largely due to the pursuit of growth. To give some examples, in England and Wales, deaths from respiratory TB were about 25,000 per annum in the 1930s, and are now about 1,000 (Ministry of Health Annual Reports); in the United States, the rate has fallen from over 50 per 100,000 pre-war to about 3 (United States government statistical abstracts). Before the war, there were about 50,000–60,000 cases of diphtheria in England and Wales, mainly among children, and leading to about 3,000 deaths per annum. It has now been virtually eliminated. In both Britain and the US, infantile mortality has been cut from 60 to 20 per thousand over the same period. Other diseases now successfully treated, or rare, include polio, whooping cough and scarlet fever. Fatal industrial accidents, 4,800 per annum in the United Kingdom in 1900, fell to 1,600 in 1950 and are now less than 800.

The ecolobby also embraces those campaigning against the use of animals in medical research and what is termed 'surgical adventurism' (transplants). This hostility denies or ignores the fact that, for instance, experiments with rats and monkeys are essential to elucidate the mechanism of the cyclical recurrence of malaria. Malaria is still, in terms of sheer numbers, the world's most serious disease, since it kills 2·5 million a year and debilitates at any one time over 250 million. Leprosy, thanks to work on mice, is now at last in process of elimination. Transplantation, which of course requires animal experiments, involves the whole science of immunology, one of the great keys in clinical medicine. And animals are needed for basic research into protein synthesis and its mechanisms, one of the main lines of advance to enlarging food-supplies.

One instance where the ecolobby undoubtedly inflicted demonstrable harm was in its ill-informed but successful campaign against DDT. It is now known that the biological ill-effects of DDT have been much exaggerated, and are greatly outweighed by its benefits. Yet the ecolobby got DDT banned in the United States and a large number of other countries. In Ceylon, the ban has led to a rapid rise in the malarial death-rate. In Sweden, a country peculiarly victimized by the ecolobby, the renewed ravages of insects led to a lifting of the ban; other countries have been less slow to respond to the invalidation of ecolobby claims. The technique of the lobby is to put out a scare-story, and then move on quickly to a fresh one when scientific investigation proves the first one unfounded. In fact the kind of public hysteria engendered by these scares is a major obstacle to the systematic control of real pollution because once the public realizes it has been conned, it ceases to take the subject seriously or to authorize the precautions which undoubtedly are needed.

The most vulnerable victims of the lobby's propaganda are the people of the underdeveloped countries, who still suffer from the far more serious aspects of pollution which have been eliminated or greatly reduced in the advanced West. These are: poor water, inadequate or non-existent sanitation, poor housing and slums, endemic diseases – together with all the other evils of malnutrition and chronic poverty. These are the consequences not of high growth but of low or static growth; and if growth were to stop, hundreds of millions of people would be frozen into their present posture. Reasonably high rates of growth in the advanced countries are essential to the growth of the developing countries. The ecolobby also ignores the fact that even in advanced countries the poor remain in huge numbers: here again, steady growth is their only hope – in the United States, for instance, those below an absolute poverty line fell in the decade 1959–69 from 39 to 24 million almost entirely because the economy achieved productivity increases averaging 3% per annum.

As it happens, despite rather than because of the ecolobby, very considerable progress has been made in coping with and reducing pollution in recent years. In the United Kingdom, the total of smoke produced fell from 2·3 million tons in 1953 to 0·9 million in 1968, and is still falling. Over the decade 1961–70 average smoke-concentrations in British urban areas fell by 60% and sulphur-dioxide concentrations by 30%, despite a big increase in output; cities which have taken advantage of powers conferred by the Clean Air Act, such as London, have achieved cleansing rates of 85% – average hours of winter sunshine in London doubled over the 1960s and visibility lengthened four-fold. London is expected to eliminate all smoke by 1980. The official *River Pollution Survey of England and Wales* (as updated to 1972) shows that the percentage of 'grossly polluted' rivers fell from 6·4 in 1958 to 3·7 in 1972, while completely unpolluted rivers rose from 72·9 to 77·4% over the same period. The recent story of the Thames indicates that it now has more varieties of fish than for hundreds of years, and perhaps ever. Following the British lead, the United States passed the Clean Air Act (1963), the Air Quality Act (1967) and the Clean Air Act Amendments (1970) which collectively will bring about a dramatic fall in US air pollution by the end of this decade. River cleansing in the US is now following a similar pattern to Britain's, though it is some years behind. Germany, Sweden and Japan have embarked on equally ambitious programmes. The progress so far achieved has completely falsified the Domesday predictions of *The Limits to Growth* survey which claimed, on the basis of computer forecasts, that existing pollution could be reduced only by 25% over a hundred years. In fact 90% of US air pollution will be eliminated over seven to eight years. Over this whole sector, in fact, the more extreme claims of the ecolobby have now been dropped, and attention switched elsewhere.

Pollution still poses some very expensive problems. Thus, in the OECD area, the amounts involved in reducing sulphur oxides, nitrogen oxides and other major industrial air pollutants to acceptable levels, are in absolute money terms large; in relative terms, however, they are only

between 0·2 and 0·34% of the GNP and the capital costs of the programme are less than 1% of investment in the area. It is all a matter
of scale and perspective. Happily, after the initial loss of balance, there
are signs that governments are beginning to adopt a more rational
approach and are bringing the whole discussion out of the realms of
emotion and subjecting it to the normal criteria of science. A new
technique of environmental economics is coming into existence. Thus,
some 'pollutants' are now classified as beneficial: warm water discharged
from nuclear power stations has actually improved fishing in some areas;
ammonium sulphate particles, characteristic of heavily industrialized
areas, as (in some cases) atmospheric dioxide, can improve agricultural
land. Some pollutants are harmful at some levels, beneficial at others.
Pollution diagnostics are enormously complex. In any case, pollution is
not a function of economic growth but a case of misallocated resources.
It arises chiefly because of defects in standard property laws, which do
not define rights in the environment, and therefore enable infringements
of them to be costed. Once this principle is fully accepted, and applied
over the whole range of practicable possibilities, the avoidance of
harmful pollution can be built into industrial estimates like any other
costs. This is undoubtedly the best long-run solution because it enables
pollution control to be to a large extent self-policing. Of course, absolute
safeguards or prohibitions will be retained in some cases, and for the
moment, until the economics of control become effective, these government limitations will have to be very extensive. But what is already
perfectly clear is that pollution control is not incompatible with high
growth; on the contrary, by bringing about a more efficient use of
resources, lower pollution levels will be a symptom of accelerated growth.

The pollution scar served to generate, at least for a time, widespread
fears that the pace of growth was altogether too fast; the parallel scare
about resources was even more serious, since it presupposed that the
process of industrial production, on the scale to which the world had
become accustomed, would have to be reduced as supplies of vital raw
materials ran out. The factual basis for this second fallacy is even more
slender than the first. Like other aspects of Domesday eschatology, there
is nothing new about it. A century ago, Stanley Jevons, a leading
economist, prophesied an inevitable and imminent shortage of coal.
Today, despite an increase in production far, far greater than Jevons
foresaw, known reserves are now estimated at six hundred years'
supply. Estimates of mineral reserves are always, and necessarily, under-

estimates. Wartime estimates compiled in 1944 would, uncorrected, have predicated that by 1973 the US would run out of tin, nickel, zinc, lead and manganese; in fact in all five cases, more deposits were found in the 1950s than in the previous quarter-century. In 1925, it was predicted tin would run out within ten years; forty years later, *The Limits to Growth* gave it fifteen years! These gloomy prophecies, like the larger eschatologies of which they form part, tend to go unnoticed at the moment they are falsified by events, as they invariably are.

For those whose concern is genuine, as opposed to an emotional need, it should be emphasized that the technical term 'known reserves' means nothing more than reserves considered worth exploiting commercially given existing prices, demand and costs of exploration. It is not worth prospecting for more than a limited time-span of production. One calculation is that metals concealed in the top mile alone of the earth's crust are about a million times as great as present 'known reserves'. This super-abundance is constantly reflected in upward revisions of quantity: iron-ore reserves rose five-fold 1960–73, bauxite reserves seven-fold 1950–72; copper consumption multiplied forty times during the nineteenth century but reserves were bigger at the end than the beginning. In 1945 they had risen to 100 million metric tons, and in 1970, 93 million tons having been extracted in the meantime, to 300 million. The same indefinite extension can be applied to most other minerals. Perhaps the term 'reserves' should not be used at all, since it implies something finite; the word simply applies to specific quantities which are, as it were, in the productive pipeline, somewhere between the process of exploration and extraction. Ecologists who worry about raw material shortages on the basis of reserve figures are rather like the nervous Daughters of the American Revolution, who insist, from time to time, the gold in Fort Knox be publicly counted, to make sure it is still there. The world does not count its real reserves of metal because counting is costly and it does not need to know the answer. Indeed, by an obvious paradox, stress on scarcity tends to shrink actual reserves since it depresses production and so exploration. This, of course, is precisely why the more fanatical anti-growth men labour the point.

Where there seems genuine ground for some anxiety is in future supplies of food and oil. But here again there has been a good deal of mystification by the ecolobby, some of it ludicrous. Men have always worried about population growth pushing up against food supplies; or rather, if they are not worrying about there being too many people, they are worrying about there being not enough of them. Many of these studies (e.g. William Ramsay and Claude Anderson, *Managing the Environment*) are impressed and depressed by the accelerating speed of human growth. Man has been in existence over two million years; but agriculture did not replace hunting until about 7,000 BC, and the next revolution, the industrial, occurred only two hundred years ago. Again, at the beginning of the Christian era, world population stood at about 250 million. It took 1,650 years to double the first time, 100 the second, 70 the third, and is currently increasing annually by 70 million. One UN study projects a figure of 6,800 million by AD 2000, and 25,000 million fifty years later. But these figures based on *extraponential* growth are ridiculous. If, for instance, the same statistical trick were applied to the rise in rice-yields in the Indian subcontinent since 1965 – in itself a very encouraging sign – within a century the world would be covered in rice to a depth of three feet! No one in his right mind supposes this will actually happen, any more than it is really envisaged that people will be standing on each others' shoulders all over the world in the twenty-first century. The science of demography is still disappointingly primitive, but all recorded experience so far suggests that a fall in death-rate is sooner or later followed by a fall in the birth-rate, as incomes rise. This is the universal western pattern, and indicates that the cure is continuing economic growth – not the reverse! In the developing countries, the chances are that the gap between falling death-rates and the fall in the birth-rate – which of course is the danger period – will be much narrower than in the corresponding phase of growth of the advanced countries, because contraceptives are now more generally available. We may see population growth-rates reach a plateau at the end of this decade, and begin to decline, slowly at first, in the 1980s.

In any event, growing enough food is not the real problem. The ecolobby makes great play with the notion, first popularized by Garrett Hardin in *Biology: its Human Implications* that, because of the Second Law of thermodynamics, man is an 'insufficient energy converter', requiring, for example, a ton of fish per year to sustain a mere 150 pounds of human protoplasm. This invocation of thermodynamics is typical of the way scientific concepts are glibly introduced to alarm the public. If the Second Law of Thermodynamics is true (an assumption), all creation is a colossal waste of natural resources, since all its activities result in a continuous dissipation of energy. Producing meat is an expensive way of providing protein – it always has been. Men tend to eat meat if they can afford it, and get it; and societies with a high meat content in their diet tend to produce high growth-rates, by way of compensation. If meat production proves profligate of natural resources, the cost will rise fast, and bring down demand to meet supply. So far as cereals and other foods are concerned, ecolobby arguments about soil exhaustion, dwindling supplies of fertilizers, crop diseases, and so forth, rarely bear expert examination. There are very few unsolved technical problems about increasing food supplies; the difficulties lie in social habit, distribution, and politics. If, *mirabile dictu*, all the land under cultivation were brought up to the standards of, say, the Netherlands, we could feed a world population of 60 billion. The real problem is not so much economic but social – food is not the commodity in shortest supply, but space. Assuming the population stabilizes itself as incomes rise, we shall have to cope with permanent high densities in large parts of the world, and analogies with the animal kingdom hint that these are a fertile source of tension and social breakdown.

Of course, as with meat-proteins, the law of supply and demand will operate whenever a real or possible shortage of raw materials is foreseen: to some extent the market will impose rationing by price, and this in turn will finance additional exploration and so uncover added reserves. This mechanism, simple enough in all conscience, is one the ecolobby does not seem to understand. Some hypothetic calculations have been made by the International Bank for Reconstruction and Development in its *Report on the Limits to Growth:* if the price of iron-ore rose 30–40%, reserves would double; if the price of copper tripled, reserves would rise by 800%. The principle applies, most significantly, to energy resources, and above all to oil, the one important area where talk of a possible shortage has some foundation in the known facts. Here, it is true, reserves may be unable to meet increases in demand at present prices. But the last qualification is all-important. Demand has been increasing by an average of about 8% per annum; the effect of price-rises may slow this to 4%. A study carried out by A. J. Surrey and A. J. Bromley, of the Sussex University Science Policy Research Unit, indicates that, granted the difference is made up from other conventional energy sources, we may have about 300 years' supply of oil, allowing the 4% increment to accumulate to a total eight times the 1973 production rate; and, in any case, within a generous estimate of thirty years, less conventional sources will be in production.

Hence, as the World Bank pointed out at the time, the so-called

'Energy Crisis' was a crisis of policy, not of nature. To handle it, all that was required was a progressive, and non-disruptive change in pricing policy. Instead, the panic generated by the ecolobby, which needless to say has more influence with less sophisticated governments, led the oil-exporting states abruptly to triple the prices of oil. The occasion was the Arab–Israeli war of 1973, but that this was merely a pretext is shown by the fact that the Iranians, who have no quarrel with Israel or the West, took the lead in insisting on massive increases. They were impressed by the argument that the greedy requirements of western growth for low-price oil were robbing them of their greatest, almost their only, national asset, and they jumped at the chance afforded by the war to get the Arab states into line.

The oil panic – the unplanned switch from low to high-cost energy – was a disaster of the first magnitude for our civilization. Almost over-night, it turned a routine slow-down of the world economy into a major depression, by far the worst since the 1930s. It brought to a bitter end the thirty-year Keynesian boom, resurrected the spectre, indeed the reality, of mass-unemployment in the advanced states, cut growth-rates to nil, or even to reverse growth, and induced a new and highly destructive crisis of confidence in the free economy and in free societies everywhere. What made the Middle East price-revolution even more effective in bringing western growth to an end was the fact that another campaign by the ecolobby had succeeded in delaying the introduction of the vast new oil fields on the North Slope of Alaska. The fanatics, as it were, brought down the West with both barrels.

But if the so-called rich were the ostensible target of the lobby, it was the poor who suffered most. In the advanced states, reduced, nil or reverse growth brought hyperinflation, and huge cuts in public spending, which fell inevitably on education, welfare, pensions, hospitals, public housing and anti-poverty projects. The ecolobby, essentially and almost by definition a middle-class movement, usually living in pleasant rural suburbia, thus brought down vengeance for the sin of growth on the innocent heads of the urban poor of the West's great cities. But the vengeance inflicted was even more painful for the poor countries of the world. Most of them have no indigenous sources of energy, except water-power, and are heavily dependent on imported oil for their develop-ment programmes. Tripling the price made nonsense of their planning forecasts, and everywhere brought wholesale cuts in targets. The effects were particularly serious in agriculture, where oil-fueled tractors and irrigation-plants were just becoming familiar features of the African and Asian scene. The drain on precious resources was compounded by the inevitable decisions in the West to cut overseas aid schemes – especially since western electorates and taxpayers tended to confuse the Arab oil states with the poor recipients who were their most pitiful victims. The precise economic effects, in terms of human misery and death, of the ecolobby's *coup* will never be known. But in spring 1976, the United Kingdom House of Commons sub-committee on Overseas Aid published a document which calculated that more than 500 million people were then near the starvation level in the Third World. There were also political consequences. In Africa, the economic climate strengthened the forces pushing the new states away from parliamentary democracy and towards authoritarian rule, and police and army terror. In Asia, it brought down the world's largest democracy, India, which in 1975 abandoned liberty, at least for a time, and so confirmed the views of the pessimists who claimed that western freedom was not for export. In the end, the price-revolution even brought distress to the oil-exporting states themselves, for the drop in world demand curtailed their national revenues in real terms – the inflation in the prices of western capital goods and consumer durables had already largely negated the effects of higher oil export prices. Hence they too were forced to cut their development programmes. One of the worst sufferers was Iran, which by early 1977 was forced to raise loans. The only gainer was the archetypal totalitarian state, the Soviet Union, which saw its own prestige rise, and its effective military and political power enhanced, as the wealth of the West fell and its self-confidence evaporated.

It was this episode, more than any other development since the Second World War, which damaged the faith of our civilization in its own future, and led it to jittery self-questioning. We have examined it at length because it is instructive in indicating how vulnerable even the most solidly based societies are to the forces of unreason, and how powerful are the emotions and instincts which lead educated western man to pre-fer falsehood to truth. Unfortunately, this is not the only example of the enemies of civilization at work. It serves, however, as an appropriate introduction to the irrational modes of thought which fester beneath the surface of our supposedly logical and scientific culture. Let us now examine them in some more detail.

CHAPTER 8

Uncertain Trumpets

One principal way in which our civilization is rendered vulnerable to the assaults of its enemies (and false friends) is by the undermining of linguistic truth. Language is a curious thing. It is the bloodstream of our culture, the real infrastructure of civilization; as I. A. Richards has put it, language is 'a completion and does what the intuitions of sensation by themselves cannot do'. With words, he adds, we can combine regions of sensation which could never naturally come together. Hence words 'are the occasion and means of that growth which is the mind's endless endeavour to order itself. That is why we have language. It is no mere signalling system. It is the instrument of all our distinctively human development, of everything in which we go beyond the other animals.' Thus language has the strength or resilience of humanity itself; but it also reflects the multifarious weaknesses of human nature. Words can be prostituted and debauched, damaged by use, misuse or intent, rendered untruthful or treacherous, devalued or aggrandized, stood, as it were, on their heads, or turned inside out.

There is, indeed, a very close analogy between words and coins, both quintessentially human creations. A word, when fresh-minted, has the objectivity and innocence of a legal penny. Handled by men, it is soon subjected to the processes of inflation or deflation, and acquires moral or immoral characteristics. As Hobbes noted, words are quickly invested with qualities they do not intrinsically possess: 'Words are wise men's counters, they do but reckon with them; but they are the money of fools.' Every word takes on a mask, and hence, as Ruskin argued in *Of King's Treasuries*, we are surrounded by masked words 'which nobody understands, but which everyone uses, and most people will also fight for, live for or even die for, fancying they mean this, or that, or the other, of things dear to them'.

Maintaining the pristine truthfulness of words is thus a constant and endless struggle, like the preservation of the money supply; but it is even more necessary for the defence of civilization. Indeed, it is the first line of defence, for if we can prevent the subversion of words we shall make it extraordinarily difficult for the enemies of civilization to operate in more concrete ways. Let us now examine some of the ways in which language is under attack. We take English as our theme not because it is the only language subject to abuse but because it is the chief one, and one where fresh aggressions tend first to manifest themselves. It has, too, an international aspect because it is the language of world commerce and diplomacy, and increasingly of international communication, since 88% of all scientific and technical literature is published first in English, or translated into it immediately. It is also the nearest we are likely to get to a world language in the foreseeable future. Then, too, English has some special strengths and weaknesses, which make it the chosen battlefield for the warfare we deal with in this chapter. It is huge, with over 700,000 words, and growing fast; it is also grievously under-used by its habituates. The average English-speaker's customary vocabulary is only 600 words, and monitoring experiments carried out by the Bell Telephone Laboratory show that a group of 100 common words constitute over 75% of all conversations. English, then, well reflects the thinness and vulnerability of our civilization, as well as its reserves of power.

The first principle to grasp, however, is that attacks on English are not always or even usually inspired by malice. Would that they were! The enemies of civilization are always easier to deal with when they are bold and open, huge and hideous. Language is a particular victim of the well-meaning since, from an early stage in its use and development, men became aware of the wounding power of words and society thus developed the euphemism. We need not trace its origins, which are very ancient; what is modern is its gross and ceaseless proliferation. In the 1790s Benjamin Franklin listed 228 euphemisms current in his day; now there are many thousands, often stamped with the proto-legality of officialdom or even the full legality of compulsory ideologies. The object is to ease pain by masking or changing the word. We are dealing, in fact, with a linguistics of happiness – an illusory happiness to be sure – or what might perhaps be more accurately termed somo-semantics, a process by which a sleepy numbness of feeling is induced by tampering with the truth of a term. 'Semantics', of course, comes from the Greek *simantikos*, 'significant', and it is notable that, in a somo-semantic world, the desire to deprive an expression of its significance is accounted a virtue, and insistence on it ascribed to pedantry: hence the expressions which use 'semantics' in a derogatory sense – 'simply a question of semantics' (i.e. it does not matter) or 'let's not argue about semantics'.

It is true that a euphemism may serve a positive purpose; may, in fact – though only very rarely – be inspired. President Kennedy's decision to call the 1962 blockade of Cuba a 'quarantine' helped to avert a world war, though it can be argued that this was a case not of euphemism but of accuracy. Equally, and more commonly, euphemism springs from instincts of misplaced generosity. Thus Winston Churchill, often a defender of linguistic truth, who rightly, in 1940, changed the title 'Local Defence Volunteers' to 'Home Guard', wrote a 1943 minute (printed in the Appendix of *The Grand Alliance*): 'I hope the term "Communal Feeding Centres" is not going to be adopted. It is an odious expression, suggestive of Communism and the workhouse. I suggest you call them "British Restaurants". Everybody associates the word "restaurant" with a good meal, and they may as well have the name if they cannot have anything else.' Here, however, the intention was admitted to be dishonest, and in fact proved self-defeating. 'Communal Feeding Centre', though indeed odious, was an accurate expression for an odious thing, and the only result of Churchill's suggestion, which was adopted, was to make the term 'British Restaurant' a by-word for repulsive food served in revolting circumstances. 'British Restaurant' in fact became a kind of contradiction in terms, synonymous with 'anti-Restaurant', thus unfairly adding to Britain's already unenviable reputation for disgusting cooking.

Modern euphemism, which Churchill rightly termed as giving people the name if they cannot have anything else, rarely if ever works, even for a time. The language suffers, but the pains of the deprived are not thereby lessened. Yet the practice is on the increase, and no list could now hope to be exhaustive. A backward child is a late-developer; a cripple is handicapped; the poor are lower-income groups or under-privileged; the deaf are hard of hearing; slums are sub-standard houses; the insane are mentally ill, and drunkards alcoholics; a subject becomes a citizen or a national, and old people are senior citizens, or, worse, geriatrics. Eggs are not big or small but large, medium or standard; cheap becomes budget, thrifty or economy; a second-hand or used car is owner-tested; dustmen (or binmen in the North of England) become refuse-collectors, night-watchmen security officers, and charwomen, having for a short time become charladies, are now daily helps (if employed in private houses) or cleaners (in offices). In fact, the capacity of ordinary persons to accustom themselves to, and so discount, euphemism is almost infinite. Men and women now fear a coronary as much as ever they feared a heart attack, rheumatoid arthritis is no less odious than gout, and sore throats and eyes cause just as keen distress now they are called laryngitis and conjunctivitis.

The euphemist, in truth, has an unrewarding task. 'Criminal boy' or 'criminal girl' was changed to 'juvenile delinquent', but this in turn soon became pejorative and was again changed to 'young offender'; but the last phrase equally fails to conceal the ugly fact, with the additional thought that a young offender will soon become an old one, as usually happens. There is, too, almost invariably some loss or distortion of meaning. A deaf man is not necessarily hard of hearing; handicapped is not necessarily the same as crippled. The result is a degree of confusion. The Waifs and Strays Society conveyed a very clear meaning; its somosemantic reincarnation, the Children's Aid Society, is less precise: aid for what, and for which children? Nebraska's Hospital for the Crippled and Deformed is now Nebraska's Orthopaedic Hospital. The meaning is not the same, it is less.

The ineffectiveness of happiness linguistics (except in the damage it inflicts on language) is seen in the fact that one euphemism must soon be replaced by another. There is no final euphemism that satisfies. In the United States, the poor were officially reclassified as needy, then deprived, then underprivileged. The last term is open to the real objection that a privilege ceases to have any meaning if everyone is given it, the supposed object of the welfare operation. As one philologist has pointed out, a true definition of an underprivileged person is one, for example, who is not allowed to join the Communist Party in a Soviet-type state, or a trade union in a western one. In any case, underprivileged soon became pejorative in turn, and was followed by disadvantaged – open to the same objection in terms of strict meaning.

The same difficulties arose when dealing with poor people in a collective or national sense. The poor nations, it was thought, would object to being called poor, though that was what they were, and what they were complaining about. They were termed 'backward'; but this raised the objection (not a very solid one) that 'backward' implied their condition was their own fault. The term, for United Nations purposes, was changed to underdeveloped, defined by the 1961 *Webster* as 'failing to realize a potential economic level and standard of living because of lack of capital, shortage of trained technicians, medical assistance or culture traits resistant to change'. But this, in turn, was soon discredited, and was replaced by 'developing', a clear misuse of language since it implies that the 'advanced' or 'other' countries are stagnant or becoming back-ward. And when is a country not developing in one sense or another? As it happens, developing itself has now fallen into disfavour, and 'emerg-ing' or 'emergent' is preferred, as being virtually meaningless but vaguely complimentary; such nations are also, following the current rules of international lying, usually described as 'uncommitted' or 'unaligned', though their one common characteristic is that they hunt in packs at the UN.

Behind the difficulties over the poor nations is the spectre of race, a great dissolvant of verbal truth. Almost all expressions now connected with race and colour can be described as 'escape words' – that is attempts, usually unsuccessful, to avoid giving offence or to deflect in advance accusations of prejudice. But of course there is no escape in the end, for truth, like the poor, is always with us. Nigger was once an escape word, intended to avoid hurt feelings. It soon acquired odium and then was used with the deliberate aim of causing offence; it is now frequently employed by the more race-conscious blacks, but only among them-selves. Negro, whether capitalized or not (use of capitals was introduced as an emollient) is now offensive; black, once highly offensive, is for the moment not only acceptable but orthodox and standard in inter-racial use. The erratic and illogical path of racial linguistics is littered with the graves of well-meaning expressions, designed in varying degrees to avoid or conceal primitive truth: 'a West Indian born in London', 'an African born in Britain', 'East Indian', 'West Asian', 'coloured', 'non-white', 'racial minority' and so forth. One miserable newcomer is 'ethnic', a nonsense-word in this context. It originally meant gentile, 'heathen pagan' and, by derivation, national. It has nothing to do with colour or race. In the United States, it was first misused as an escape-word as part of a weird distinction which classified 'racial minority' as implying black or coloured, while 'ethnic minority' implied groups of (white) European origin. Now it has been further devalued by implying 'black' in a cultural sense; thus, 'ethnic dancing' is black ballet, and an Ethnic Studies Centre is a university faculty exclusively reserved for blacks, where forms of 'Black Power' are 'studied'.

Sometimes the difference between escape-words and their opposite, confrontation-words or fighting-words, is miniscule and inexplicable, and reflects nothing more than archaeological layers of usage in inflamed situations. Thus, Asian was first used in 1563, Asiatic in 1631; both come from the Greek, *Asianos, Asiatikos*; the '-*atic*' suffix is Greek, *atikos*, meaning 'of the kind of'; hence automatic, chromatic, Adriatic, Hanseatic, etc. Asian was once dismissed as archaic in dictionaries, Asiatic being preferred; the latter passed into official colonial usage and acquired opprobrium; so now 'Asian' is orthodox and 'Asiatic' taboo, and the title of a famous journal appears as *The Asian Review incorporating The Asiatic Review*.

The currently correct use of escape-words is a matter of some concern for governments. Words or expressions like dole, relief, unemployment benefit, National Assistance, many already obsolete or obsolescent, are gravestones on ancient political battlefields. Much official thinking went into attempts to avoid the word 'slump'; thus we had depression, recession, business-cycle; and a good deal of dishonest juggling took place with unemployment, high employment, underemployment, full employment and overemployment, leaving a state of genuine confusion over the exact meaning of official 'unemployment figures', with the risk of popular misinterpretation and thus of dangerous consequences for economic policy.

The nearer one gets to the heart of politics, and its ultimate expression war, the more the escape-words multiply. Words can kill; 'He is dying of a long word' says Carla of the Marquess in *Brideshead Revisited*. When is a war not a war? When, for instance, it is 'separating the combatants' (Sir Anthony Eden, Suez, 1956), 'a police action' (President Truman on Korea, 1950), 'a struggle' (Robert Kennedy on Vietnam, 1960). In the Korean case, the episode was subsequently redefined as a war by an Appeals Court, which allowed certain insurance companies to escape their obligations, and such financial factors sometimes determined escape-terminology in the case of civil killing and destruction (it was variously argued that the Newark and Watts events were riots, insurrections, rebellions or disturbances). As a rule, however, the function of escape words or somo-semantics in politics is to deceive electorates, opponents or neutrals. As one philologist has noted, whereas in the spheres of advertising, education and economics the use of weasel words tends to be towards gross overstatement, in the field of killing and mass destruction, the tendency is to understate and minimize. Thus the ability to make war is defence; an attack force of bombers and missiles is a deterrent force or deterrent; to fight a preventative war is to launch a pre-emptive strike; weapons are hardwear and bodies softwear; forms of grotesque violence are interdiction and attrition, and the most murderous weapons are described as sophisticated or anti-personnel. In this night-mare world, the infliction of enormous casualties is covered by terms like pacification or peace-keeping, the deaths of millions are described as acceptable or unacceptable, credibility gap is a circumlocution for lying, and statesmen give countenance to such verbal cripples as defoliate, overkill, failsafe, escalate, all words designed to conceal the fact of destruction on an unprecedented scale. And so, too, the simple murder of the innocent is carried out on raids or commando raids, by freedom-fighters or guerrillas. In politics, as in war, truth is always the first casualty.

These words and expressions used as above are still escape-words or somo-semantic words in the sense that they serve to anaesthetize or deaden responses to horrific realities. But there is also a large and grow-ing group of truly 'political' words in which the meaning has been deli-berately changed, or removed, or inverted for base purposes. These are often absolutely key words in the political process, once pregnant and thrilling with meaning. Now they are dead or empty carapaces, com-pletely de-gutted, or mere terms of abuse. In the last category, for instance, there is racist, properly racialist; this springs from racism, defined as the assumption that psycho-cultural traits and capacities are determined by biological race, and that races differ decisively among themselves. The definition of 'race' which applies to these terms is 'stock characterized by more or less distinct combinations of physical traits transmitted in descent'. This would seem to give racism some scientific standing or intellectual justification. What in fact has happened is that racism has been hammered by politics into a blunt portmanteau word embracing more precise terms such as bigotry, intolerance, prejudice and discrimination. Of course, 'discrimination' itself has been devalued since it once meant 'to distinguish between', and had a definite value. Now it implies condemnation by the user of the person who discrimi-nates, unless it is 'positive discrimination', which means discrimination in favour of a group previously discriminated against: this form of racism, by a paradox beloved of the linguistics of happiness, is healthy and commendable.

Another word which has been hammered by politics into meaninglessness or confusion is democracy; as George Orwell noted, 'In the case of a word like democracy, not only is there no agreed definition, but the attempt to make one is resisted from all sides.' Persistent misuse of democracy has dragged down other useful words with it: thus, social democrat means a Right-wing anti-Communist politician of the centre; a People's Democracy or a People's Democratic Republic is a form of Communist totalitarian state. Freedom or free can be used pejoratively or approvingly. The phrase 'free world' is used aggressively by opponents of Communism; Radio Free Europe has acquired overtones of militarism and other 'cold war' attitudes. Free enterprise is attacked by trade unionists who nevertheless regard free collective bargaining as their sacred birthright. The word free, in fact, has become so poisoned or devalued that one seeks to avoid it – not easy, since it has so many uses. As Orwell put it in his appendix to *1984*: 'The word *free* still existed in Newspeak, but it could only be used in such statements as "This dog is free from lice" or "This field is free from weeds".'

While the Communist world has sought to appropriate 'free' and 'freedom', as well as 'democratic' and 'republic', and so de-gut them, it has steered away from 'liberal', which it uses as a term of abuse, in the same way as 'cosmopolitan'. As a matter of fact, a whole book could be written on the different and successive uses of the words liberty and liberal, or on the group of expressions which centre round the terms human rights, civil rights and civil liberties. Here, political hammering has reduced all to confusion. Right, Anglo-Saxon *riht*, goes back to the Indo-European *reg*, which is 'straight' or 'king'. Words which come from the same root are rajah, regal, royal, rule, rich. The *Oxford English Dictionary* defines 'right' as: 'that which is consonant with equity or the light of nature; that which is morally just or due; justifiable claim, on legal or moral grounds, to have or obtain something, or to act in a certain way'. In the light of this, and similar definitions of right, it is very difficult indeed to be clear about the meaning of such expressions, very commonly used, as civil rights or human rights. The dictionaries contradict each other, and even themselves. Some contrast civil with political rights, which makes nonsense of the phrase 'civil rights' as it is used today. The 1961 *Webster*, for instance, calls civil rights 'those rights the enjoyment of which does not involve participation in the establishment, support or management of government'. But these are precisely the rights which civil-rights campaigners are working for. Even more striking is the fact that civil rights, as interpreted to include such efforts to correct racial imbalance as busing, 'positive discrimination' and multi-racial housing regulations, directly contradict civil liberty as defined by *Webster:* 'freedom from arbitrary government interference, specially by denial of government power, and in the US especially as guaranteed by the Constitution.'

In the wake of these central linguistic confusions tramp the massed battalion of 'political' words, used without reference to their true meaning, but in accordance with a professional or hieratic code: progressive, unity, peace, aggression, peace-loving, provocation, mercenary (and volunteer, expert, technician, its non-pejorative equivalents), cultural revolution and social imperialism, chauvinist, military-industrial complex, non-interference, solidarity, monopolist, hooligan, myrmidon, sectarian, wrecker, national egoism and power chauvinism, diversionist, revisionist, deviationist, dogmatist, capitulationist, conglomerate, multinational, and so on. The process of devaluation continues remorselessly, and though the Communists and the international Left generally are by far the worst offenders, they are by no means the only ones. Recent casualties include moderate, now misused to describe supporters of a central coalition, and legitimate, to distinguish between the 'legitimate Left', working within the democratic tradition, and the far Left. It is extraordinary how rapidly valuable and accurate words disintegrate under misuse, or become contaminated. As T. S. Eliot put it:

> Words strain,
> Crack and sometimes break, under the burden,
> Under the tension, slip, slide, perish,
> Decay with imprecision, will not stay in place,
> Will not stay still.

This constant and growing assault on a vulnerable artifact might be less dangerous if enough well-disposed people were equipped to defend English from within. But not enough of even educated people in the English-speaking world have a professional grip on language-structure, or are sufficiently careful and accurate in their use of words to constitute an effective force of *vigilantes*. Indeed, many of the educated persistently misuse words. Among words often so abused today are: arguable (instead of uncertain), dilemma (instead of choice), mentality (disposition), authentic (true), vulnerable (weak), differential (difference), entitlement (right), phenomenon (fact), hopefully (meaning 'I hope' or 'it is hoped'), alibi (excuse), viable (workable), chronic (severe), ambience (surroundings), idiosyncratic (odd), ambivalence (ambiguity), nostalgia (regret), redundant (out of work) and dichotomy (partition).

The cause of such misuse is the overweening desire to scare or impress the less educated. Language is one of those fields where social or professional groups tend to set up electrified wire-fences of verbosity or special usage to denote their private territory and to discourage intruders. Here, for instance, is a characteristic civil service minefield carefully laid down to warn politicians to keep out (to say nothing of the general public). It is an order-in-council (British) dating from the late 1940s: 'In the Nuts (Unground) (Other than Groundnuts) Order, the expression Nuts shall have reference to such nuts, other than Groundnuts, as would, but for this amending Order, not qualify as Nuts (Unground) (Other than Groundnuts) by reason of their being Nuts (Unground).' Similarly, professional lawyers deter non-lawyers, as in the British National Insurance Act 1964 (1st Schedule, Part II): 'For the purpose of this Part of the Schedule a person over pensionable age, not being an insured person, shall be treated as an employed person if he would be an insured person were he under pensionable age and would be an employed person were he an insured person.'

Both these passages act as guard-dogs: they say 'Bow wow' – keep off, to intruders. There is now a huge list of 'bow wow' words used by politicians, bureaucrats, educationalists, economists and many other groups in positions of real or quasi-authority, without much regard to their real meaning but for purposes of creating a general impression of knowledge, competence and power. Thus: programming, divisive, cost-effective, counter-productive, pluralist, bilateral, adumbrate, encapsulate, purposive, meaningful, charisma, catalyst, pragmatic, pervasive, context, participation, resources, implement, integrate, macro- and micro-, optimum, abrasive, utilize, ongoing, parameters, orientation, structured, permissive, confrontation, complex (noun), integrate, marginal, unilateral, growth-point, amenities, potential, significant (meaning, more or big), continuing dialogue, environment. Ten or twelve times this number of bow-wow words could be compiled from a cursory examination of official papers published by the us and British governments in recent years. Such words and expressions gain currency in the first place in the academic world, being drawn mostly from technical expressions in economics, sociology and the physical sciences. Then, as a result of civil servants meeting 'experts' on committees, borrowing terms from them and passing them on to ministers, they are thrown into the general political pool, and so reach the public through the press.

Of course, academics resent the vulgarization of 'their' words, and are constantly strengthening their own electric fences to protect their perimeters. This means invoking new words from the darker lexicological recesses and bringing them into academic use by using them in their books. Current academic vogue words as used by leading dons (not necessarily incorrectly) include the following I have noted: gnosis (knowledge) topology (place, location), hermeneutics (interpretation), exegesis (explanation), epistemology (science of knowledge and method), entropy (transformation), sclerotic (hardening), doxology (praise), taxonomy (classification), ontological (study of being), helix (spiral), paradigm (pattern or example), polysemy (capacity to mean different things), synapse (junction), morphology (dealing with formation), neologism (new word), monad (unit); and a tramping, sneering elite-corps of others – numinous, osmosis, synoptic, construct, typology, hieratic, animist, eschatology, strophe and androgynous. These words are all, in short, already being processed by dons for eventual public use as bow-wow words. And of course in the meantime, they protect donnish private estates. Here, for instance, is George Steiner, in a recent book, *After Babel*, emitting noises to discourage trespassers: 'Homonyms, paronomasia, acoustic and semantic cognates, synecdochic sets, analogies, associative strings proliferate, undulating at extreme speed, sometimes with incongruous but pointed logic, across the surface of consciousness.'

Such pretensions are best dismissed by Jane Austen's pert comment in *Northanger Abbey:* 'I cannot speak well enough to be unintelligible.' The creation of obscurity, if deliberate, is an offence against reason, and therefore against civilization; and if accidental, is a sign of incapacity. The unfortunate thing, as Sir Peter Medawar points out, is that many accept the false syllogism: 'Profound reasoning is difficult to understand: this work is difficult to understand: therefore this work is profound.' In fact all great philosophers have been at enormous pains to make themselves as clear as their skill allowed. Descartes, for instance, in a letter to the French translator of his *Principles of Philosophy* (1644), said that ordinary readers ought to be able to grasp his meaning, since there was nothing in his writings 'which they are not capable of completely understanding, if they take the trouble to examine them'. The decline in clarity began with Kant, an extraordinarily difficult philosopher to understand, who made obscurity seem respectable. But this was in no way his purpose: he hated to write obscurely. In his introduction to the Second Edition of the *Critique of Pure Reason* (1776) he complained to readers that he was unable to do any better, and said he hoped that others would make his meaning plain.

Civilization, then, is best defended when all those in authority and influence combine to use words in their true and accurate meaning, and unite to denounce their misusage and falsification. But at the same time we have to guard and enhance the imaginative use of words. While avoiding mystification and obscurity, we must recognize that there are two kinds of verbal clarity, the practical and the illuminative, comparable to different kinds of light. As Dr Johnson said of Dryden, 'He delighted to tread upon the brink of meaning, where light and darkness begin to mingle.' The verbal operation, so common in poetry, where the initial challenge enhances the depth of understanding eventually secured, is like the painter's art of *chiaroscuro*, where the density of shadows makes the highlights more brilliant.

This use of language is not merely legitimate, it is part of the very core of civilization in its metaphysical aspects. Words are magic in the sense that they can be creative. All words have undertones and overtones, and in key combinations they acquire extraordinary resonance. They have histories and pedigrees, and particular contexts in our lives. For a community, says Sir Thomas Browne, its language is 'a hieroglyphical and shadowed lesson of the whole world'. The rational and civilized man knows that at certain dramatic and emotional moments metaphysics must be invoked, and that the special use of words is one way of doing it. Hence at marriages and deaths, for instance, the words must be bigger than their meanings. This is where the heritage of language becomes so important, and hence attacks on it become assaults on civilization itself. In a brilliant essay, Dr Ian Richardson has castigated the new biblical translations, by committees of both Protestant and Roman Catholic divines, which, as he says, conjure up a world of ordinary common-sense, of newspaper reports and radio bulletins, of sensible sex-instructions, and of down-to-earth government explanations about how to fill in your income-tax form or claim a pension. He gives, as a characteristic example, the new rendering of *Matthew* 28:5–7: 'After meeting with the elders and conferring together, the chief priests offered the soldiers a substantial bribe and told them to say: "His disciples came by night and stole the body while we were asleep." They added: "If this should reach the Governor's ears, we will put matters right with him and see you do not suffer."' Here, the quest for a mundane and practical clarity merely succeeds in inducing in the reader a mood where the events seem trivial and the characters unimportant. Far from there being, as Coleridge put it, 'a willing suspension of disbelief' there is, on the contrary, an urge to examine episodes thus baldly described more closely, and to find them empty. In great literature, and especially in great ceremonial and metaphysical literature, a passage is more than the sum of its words; its sense far, far more than the aggregate of their individual meanings. The mistake of the new biblical translators is to treat language as mere verbal equipment to be assembled according to the instructions on the packet. Hence the words they use 'become only themselves, and are as dead stones in our mouths'.

The use of language at this level involves an act of faith, just as the very act of constructing civilization itself involves a constant act of faith. The translators of the 1611 King James Bible, who believed unhesitatingly that they were dealing with the inspired words of an all-powerful God, felt that they themselves, in all humility, shared this infusion of spirit, as they say in their Preface: 'And in what sort did these assemble? In the trust of their own knowledge, or their sharpness of wit, or deepness of judgement, as it were in an arm of flesh? At no hand. They trusted in him that hath the key of *David*, opening, and no man shutting; they prayed to the Lord.' The new translators, by contrast, lacked faith in the divinity of their mission; and it shows. Thus the exercise fails, and civilization is thereby diminished. For, as St Paul says, 'If the trumpet give an uncertain sound, who shall prepare himself to the battle?'

Needless to say, it is mistaken to argue that language, least of all any particular language, should be closely guarded from intrusion and change. The theories of Johann Gottfried Von Herder, who saw a national language as analogous to race, which must be protected lest it be weakened by 'impurities', now seem to us as ridiculous as the 'social Darwinism' to which they are related; and we laugh, along with most sensible Frenchmen, at the absurd efforts of modern French governments to prevent the accretion of Anglo-Saxon loan words by fines and threats. The point is not that any particular language is sacred, but that words, and the way we use them, are infinitely more important than a mere system of communication.

Since 1957, when Noam Chomsky first published *Syntactic Structures*, we have come to see that language is more closely related to our existence as human beings than we had hitherto grasped. The debate Chomsky opened is still raging, and some of his later assertions can be discounted, for the moment, as unproved and improbable. Nevertheless, we now have a better understanding of how language is related to human capacity. The curious thing about languages is that though they differ enormously on the surface, that is in the actual noises we make to convey meanings, the way in which these noises are arranged in sequence and conjunction appears to follow certain basic patterns common to all mankind. This is related to another observation, that whereas non-human creatures can make communication with each other by noises, they cannot construct sentences – they lack the capacity to observe rules of syntax and grammar; only humans have this. It looks, then, as though the deep structures common to all languages are directly related to our human condition.

In a sense, this relationship can be illustrated by the way in which a child learns to speak. It is obvious that children are not born with a predisposition to learn one language rather than another. What is less obvious is how the child, by hearing parents talk, learns not so much to imitate them as to acquire the ability to construct sentences, so that in an astonishingly short time he can utter entirely original verbal constructions, long before, indeed, he has learnt to think clearly and logically. The data supplied to him by his parents is limited, often faulty. The thing, when we come to think of it, is a miracle, unless there is another explanation. Chomsky suggests, and more and more people now agree with him, that the deep structures of language are based on principles so specific and articulated that they must be regarded as being biologically determined – that is, 'human nature', genetically transmitted from parents to children. Part of the genetic coding of all children is knowledge of the highly restrictivist principles of universal grammar; hence the child's ability to construct for himself, on the basis of scanty parental data, and in a relatively short time, the grammatic rules of the language he hears around him.

Now there follows from this something of profound importance for the human condition. The prevailing wisdom, over recent centuries, has tended to suggest that human knowledge rests fundamentally on experience. Empirical philosophers like Locke, Berkeley and Hume argued that we simply register impressions of the world around us and formulate them into rules, which then become the stock of human knowledge. Hence it is possible to argue from this, as most psychologists do, that the nature and limits of human knowledge, and the way in which we actually behave, are wholly determined by our surroundings, and that there is no essential difference between us and other animals. The argument is used even more strongly, of course, by materialists, especially dialectical materialists like Marxists, who see man and his behaviour as very largely conditioned by economic forces springing from his situation. We are, then, to a large extent, prisoners of our environment. Our actions are determined.

It is a different matter, however, if we accept that our genetic coding includes ideas and concepts. In that case, Descartes was right to say that our human understanding – what we make of the world and our position in it – rests partly at least on a number of ideas which are innate, that is inborn, native and natural to our species. We have, in short, a number of specific faculties which play a key role in the acquisition of knowledge. These innate faculties are what we collectively call 'mind', and it is our minds which allow us to act, undetermined by external stimuli in our surroundings, as free persons. This line of thought, therefore, allows us to reconstruct the optimistic doctrine of free human will, and to re-establish mankind, not as a victim of his predicament, but as a civilizing agent. It demonstrates, in fact, the underlying reason why freedom, in all its senses and uses, plays so central a part in the civilizing process.

Now we see why language is so important. It is both a consequence, and a guarantee, of the innate freedom conferred on man by mind. So long as we have language, we cannot be wholly enslaved, or wholly uncivilized. Equally, one of the factors which nourishes our freedom and our civilization is the degree to which we cherish our linguistic skills, and relate them to truth and imagination. For language is the framework of reason; unless it is ordered and related to truth, reason cannot express itself. Now let us turn from the framework of language to the core of reason, from how we express our thoughts to what those thoughts actually are. There, too, we find the enemies of civilization busily at work.

CHAPTER 9

From Priests to Witchdoctors

In the last resort, our civilization is what we think and believe. The externals matter, but they cannot stand if the inner convictions which originally produced them have vanished. The western empire collapsed in the fifth century AD because the notions which underlay the creative capacity of Graeco-Roman society – the desire for freedom and the search for truth – had long since been discarded and trampled upon. The walls of the Colosseum, the columns of Leptis Magna and Baalbek, still stood; but their animating spirit had departed, and in time walls and columns fell too.

What are our animating thoughts and beliefs? And to what extent do we still possess them? Certainly, we seem to have more dilemmas than convictions. Our civilization is unique in that it is the first to exist on a secular underpinning. All previous cultures have revolved around a series of propositions about life and death, the real and the invisible world, magic and spirits; all have had gods or God – that is, an external arbiter. We alone now attempt to carry on our civilization on the assumption that it is finite and autonomous, and that we are entirely dependent on our own resources – an audacious venture. Is it a feasible one? The attempt dates back less than a hundred years. Only in that short period have we tried to grapple with the idea of a wholly secular existence. Moreover, we are seeking to erect a secular superstructure on a plinth constructed not merely of religious assumptions but of specifically Christian ones, and Christian ones of the western Latin tradition. We have seen that Christianity was one of the principal dynamic forces in the agricultural revolution on which the prosperity of western Europe ultimately rested, and that it was the Christian ethic,

with its haunting sense of time and its anxiety to accomplish, its ineradicable urge to move and arrive, which gave men in the West the will to
industrialize and to create our modern material structure. And Christianity provided the moral code, the drill and the discipline – as well as
the destination – which enabled the unwieldy army of progress to
lumber into the future. If the marching army is now autonomous, can it
also be self-disciplined?

It can be argued that Christianity itself was the penultimate stage in
the movement of mankind towards a secular existence. Man in his original
innocence, naïvety and fear saw gods in every stream and wood and
mountain, as particular and local explanations of phenomena inexplicable to him. As his knowledge accumulated and his methodology
improved, the range of necessary explanations narrowed, and the local
gods and goddesses coalesced into groups of archetypes. The drift
towards monotheism was itself a sign of progress (and secularization)
since it indicated man's intellectual readiness to accept a single, all-
embracing explanation of mysterious things, as radiating from a solitary
divine agent. Judaism supplied a working hypothesis of monotheism
which, in its Christian interpretation, was accepted by the Graeco-
Roman world. The reason why the Christian version was needed was not
merely its willingness to Hellenize itself but the fact that it had a much
clearer explanation than Judaism of what happened after death, a much
more positive and striking theodicy. Each human society is a society in
the face of death; it knows that sentence has been passed and wishes to
know why – the final necessary explanation. Theodicy is an attempt to
make a pact with death. Christian theodicy was a momentous improvement on any conceived before; hence its triumph. But Christianity,
unlike Judaism, was imperfectly monotheistic. It had not only the
Father but the Son, and the Holy Ghost, and in time a thronging celestial court of saints, martyrs and angels. In time the drive towards monotheism was resumed. The Moslem faith was a deliberate attempt to purge
Christianity of its polytheism, and successfully carried off the bulk of its
African and Asian congregations. The Christian self-purging took place
at the Reformation, when the Protestants returned to the Old Testament, scattered the celestial court, banished the Virgin and reaffirmed
the monotheistic spirit. So the progress towards secularization continued,
indeed accelerated.

On the basis of this line of argument, true secularization achieved a
kind of false dawn in the eighteenth century, with the emergence of forms

of deism which effectively discarded the Christian carapace. Such progress as had been achieved indicated, as Leibniz put it, that all was for the best in 'the best of all possible worlds'. Many of the explanations Christianity had provided were now seen as needless, and therefore absurd. The vessel of deism dropped the Christian ballast, and sailed on faster; but if it seemed to have the wind of history in its sails, it was a more fragile ship in two respects. It had no theodicy; it had nothing convincing to say on death – as Voltaire spitefully pointed out when the great Lisbon earthquake of 1743 intruded on the best of all possible worlds. Nor, in the second place, did the Voltairean alternative (analogous to Locke's empiricism and to some extent shared by Rousseau) of improvements by bits and pieces, cultivating a garden under a vague, distant and non-interfering deity, measure up to the harsh challenge of the French Revolution, when Satanic spirits surged out of the ground again. Thus the deistic false dawn yielded to a religious revival which was clerical as well as romantic, which dominated the opening decades of the nineteenth century and put the varieties of Christianity back on their feet.

Secularization, however, resumed its progress in the mid-nineteenth century, and the advance towards a wholly rational explanation of the world has been uninterrupted, though it has taken many different forms. Let us look at some of them in turn. And in the first place there is the attempt to rationalize, or modernize, Christianity within its own terms. This too has made a somewhat spasmodic progress, most of the spasms originating in Germany (like the Reformation itself). It was in Germany, from the earliest years of the nineteenth century, that biblical scholarship began to strip Christianity of its false historical accretions, and thus opened the way to its reconciliation with scientific development by the abandonment of marginal doctrines. Now it is an understandable but nonetheless important fact that the whole process of secularization advances much faster during periods of worldly optimism, as we have already noted in the eighteenth century. During the triumphant Victorian decades, Christianity steadily 'modernized' and 'liberalized' itself, within the Protestant communions particularly, but even to some extent in Catholicism also, though there it met more tenacious opponents. The horrors of the First World War, like the French Revolution and Terror, brought a check to the secularizing process within the faith – indeed inspired the neo-orthodoxy initiated by Karl Barth, whose famous commentary on St Paul's *Epistle to the Romans* first appeared in 1919. But this return to a more rigorously doctrinal (and historical) Christianity also spent itself in time; and it is significant that the resumption of the secularizing process within Christianity dates from the late-1940s, when Germany began to emerge from three decades of warfare, barbarism and humiliation (the currency reform of 1948 marked the beginning of the post-war German 'miracle'). The dominant theologians of modern Christianity, Rudolf Bultmann and Paul Tillich (and the posthumously published Dietrich Bonhoeffer), as popularized by such best-sellers as Bishop Robinson's *Honest to God* (1963) and Harvey Cox's *The Secular City* (1965), together with the more recent 'Death of God' movement, openly accept, welcome and indeed wish to hasten the secularizing process. A phrase, adapted from Bonhoeffer, has become current: religionless Christianity.

Here we have, in fact, the first of the modern pseudo-religions. What we may call, for want of a better term, Christianity without Christ, tends to leave out the obligatory element in either conduct or belief. The idea of inflexible commandments, or the categories of specific sins, are rearranged and re-presented as modes of approach to moral problems, and the difference between right and wrong ceases to be objective, imposed from without, and becomes wholly subjective, and a matter for personal decision. Hence the readiness with which this type of moral theology accepts sexual promiscuity (and aberration) and individual acts of terrorism, just as once St Augustine accepted 'the just war'. Equally, on the doctrinal plane, the Resurrection, the very core of Christian belief is not presented as an external event but is 'translated' in terms of phenomena existing in the mind of the believer. Thus religion, both in its moral and in its doctrinal aspects, exists entirely within the individual and nowhere else. Christianity ceases to be a community of believers, animated by an external impulse, and becomes a multitude of separate personal universes, each revolving on its own doctrinal and moral axis. There is, then, no *ecclesia*. But there is no factual truth either, since realities are downgraded to mere symbols, and the historical record becomes simply personal biography, or rather autobiographical interpretation. This is fatal to Christianity, which is a historical religion, teaching that certain events actually did happen, or it is nothing. The process termed 'de-mythologizing' in reality merely creates a new series of myths; as some of the early Hellenic Christians attempted to do in the first century AD, it turns Christianity into a form of gnosticism, without an anchor in historical fact, and with every conceivable variety of moral discipline or licence. Had the earlier gnosticism triumphed, Christianity must have disintegrated into a myriad ephemeral sects. The modern gnosticism of Christianity without Christ will similarly disperse its followers into enclaves.

It is precisely the fear of such dispersal which prompts the parallel, in some ways complementary, movement of ecumenicalism. This is animated by the belief that there is an eirenic solution to everything. But of course it necessarily follows from the idea of civilization as the pursuit of truth in freedom that men, so long as they are free, will tend to disagree about everything, including essentials. Agreed truth is something that emerges slowly, from painful delivery: one reason why it is so precious. There *is* a solution to everything, but not necessarily an eirenic one. Ecumenicalism is a true expression of Christianity if it is an attempt to move towards a fuller conception and understanding of Christian truth, and if it springs from a positive fellow-feeling and a genuine repentance for the blind cruelty which opened and perpetuated the divisions of the past. But in practice it tends to be impelled by the thought which struck Chateaubriand in his *Génie du Christianisme* (1802): 'It is natural that schism should lead to incredulity', and to the bitter realization that, when two Christian theologians quarrel, there is a *tertius gaudens* (the 'laughing third'). To join hands against a common enemy, the laughing third, is not a religious impulse and, far from producing a fuller Christianity, produces an ever-emptier deism. Here we have the second of the pseudo-creeds: lowest-common-denominator religion.

Of course one could argue that this form of debased ecumenicalism is in reality merely one example of a third category, what can be termed 'market research religions'. The growth of such, religious sociologists maintain, is almost inevitable when secularization advances to the point where it breaks the religious monopoly completely. A market phase then opens up, and religious systems, to survive at all, must sell themselves like commodities. As a matter of historical fact, this sociological analysis is mistaken if it implies the process is a once-and-for-all event in human history, rather than cyclical. The Roman republic and early empire was a market arena for a multitude of rival private religions, and it was the triumph of Christianity that it scooped the pool. The process could occur again; will in all probability recur, unless someone discovers a satisfactory secular theodicy (which very likely is a contradiction in terms). On the other hand, though the process may be cyclical, it does undoubtedly happen, and the sociologists have a good deal of evidence that we are now in a market phase.

The religious sects, and even to some extent the major groupings, have responded accordingly. Some years ago, Louis Schneider and Sanford M. Dornbusch analysed forty-six best-selling books of religious 'inspiration', such as Norman Vincent Peale's *Power of Positive Thinking*. They discovered that all these works had in common the attempt to turn God, or religion, or both, into a utilitarian human instrument. Religion was to be put to the uses of man so that he might lead a better life on earth. And 'better' was given the widest possible interpretation. The authors quote, as characteristic, Glenn Clark's book *The Soul's Sincere Desire*: 'A man who practises the laws of prayer correctly should be able to play golf better, do business better, work better, love better, serve better.' The aim is thus altruistic as well as utilitarian (not, indeed, unlike Locke's approach to religion and morals: 'Virtue is now much the best purchase and by far the better bargain') but the test of truth is the public response, based on the success of the teaching in their own lives; and the teaching of the sect is adjusted in the light of the market findings.

Schneider and Dornbusch identified four common characteristics in the religion idealized in these uplift books: activism, optimism, individualism and pragmatism. That is the kind of religion western, semi-secularized man appeared to want, if he wants any at all. It is not surprising, therefore, to find that the modernizers of mainstream Christianity also respond to these market-indicators. Pragmatism is reflected in the discounting of dogmatic theology and morals, individualism in the subjective approach to faith and conduct we have already discussed, activism in the concentration on material 'problems', optimism in the conviction they can be 'solved'. In a brash survey of Protestantism in the United States, *Protestant Power and the Coming Revolution*, Will Oursler lists the leading preoccupations of militants among Protestant clerics and laity as 'racism, hunger, drugs, pollution, war, wage-scales, peace-marches, riots, ghettoes, protests and nudity'. Belatedly, but with increasing enthusiasm, Roman Catholic activists on both sides of the Atlantic are concentrating on the same topics; and in Catholic circles, in addition, the note of optimism so stridently sounded by American market-research religions, is now reflected in wholesale changes in the liturgy, such as, for example, the replacement of black vestments by white in the requiem for the dead, and the omission of that daunting but magnificent poem, the *Dies Irae*.

Such efforts to keep up the numbers of Christian communities by exploiting marketing techniques have not, on the whole, been very successful even in their own terms; and the persistence of the churches in using them indicates that they despair of any other approach providing even this degree of success. Yet the three religious types we have so far discussed – Christianity without Christ, lowest-common-denominator Christianity, and market-research Christianity – have all been based on the assumption that secularization is inevitable and irresistible. All hack away at the credal content, all in varying ways de-mythologize, all concentrate on materialist activism. Yet, oddly enough, myths expelled from one human window tend to pop into another. Within many human beings, at least, there is an obstinate and irrational resistance to the secularizing process. Chesterton's paradox is well known. 'When a man ceases to believe in God, he does not believe in nothing. He believes in anything.' Educated people in the West often happily juxtapose in their minds scientific rationalism with crude superstition (e.g. astrology).

No one has yet provided a convincing explanation of why this conjunction arises. In 1959, C. G. Jung published an essay attempting to explain why so many young people believed in Flying Saucers. He argued that modern life does not provide enough to still the craving of the unconscious and the emotionalism it harbours. Hence, 'Undeterred by rationalistic criticism, it thrusts itself to the forefront in the form of a symbolic rumour, accompanied and reinforced by the appropriate visions . . . thus giving rise to unexpected and apparently inexplicable opinions, beliefs, illusions.' Such beliefs are 'a gesture on the part of the unconscious' which is made 'when feelings of . . . the senselessness of a merely functional existence threaten to stifle the personality'. We are all born to believe, argued Jung. The eyes may be wrong – no Saucer really exists – but the psyche is right. The reaction is not unhealthy, because we are looking for the perfect archetype of ourselves, such as Jesus Christ. He added: 'It is characteristic of our time that, in contrast to its previous expressions, the archetype should now take the form of an object, a technological construction, in order to avoid the odiousness of a mythological personification.'

The explanation is not wholly convincing, for modern sophisticates see all kinds of visions, sometimes delving back into the mythological past, as in the cult of the Loch Ness monster, now, in the late-1970s, stronger than ever. On the other hand, it is true that the religious impulse tends to take over striking contemporary phenomena and activities. Some of the forms of deism which flourished in France during the

Revolution had rituals (substituting for the abolished Catholic Mass) conducted by doctors, scientists and members of other then-fashionable professions. It is not surprising that the closing decades of the twentieth century should see the birth of science-fiction religions. One such is the curious cult which centres around the Jesuit priest Father Pierre Teilhard de Chardin. Teilhard is a classic case not merely of a pseudo-intellectual, but of a French pseudo-intellectual. That is, he has no understanding of what makes a logical argument, or constitutes proof, but an impressive fluency of exposition which begins to disintegrate on second reading or when it is translated into English. His most important work, *The Phenomenon of Man*, has been described by one of his fiercest critics, Sir Peter Medawar, as 'philosophy-fiction' appealing to the 'half-educated' or to people 'educated far beyond their capacity to undertake analytical thought'. On its first appearance it was hailed, however, by a number of leading French intellectuals as a remarkable synthesis of religious and scientific thought, and it arrived in Britain and the United States in English translation (1959) with distinguished credentials, including a fulsome introduction by Professor Julian Huxley. Yet Medawar's harsh judgement is just, for Teilhard tends to attract disciples with the same mental habits as the Flying Saucer worshippers, but from a significantly higher social background: he is the idol of upper-middle-class sub-intellectuals (especially ladies), among whom he has replaced such cults as Madame Blavatsky's Scientology.

Teilhard was a botanist, a member of the broad-based scientific tradition which has always been the pride of the Society of Jesus. Indeed, possibly with the Roman Holy Office in mind, he did not seek to present himself as a religious innovator, but as a scientist. He wrote of the *Phenomenon*: 'If this book is to be properly understood, it must be read not as a work of metaphysics, still less as a sort of theological essay, but purely and simply as a scientific treatise.' In fact this approach did not deceive the Holy Office, which put Teilhard's works on its Index, as dangerous and liable to corrupt the faithful. The scientist might add that, despite its claims, it is thoroughly unscientific and liable to deceive the unrigorous. It freely employs narrowly defined scientific words, like tension, force, impetus, energy, dimension, consciousness, but without any attempt to give them their exact meaning. The theme is the relationship of man to nature, and to a redefined, scientific concept of God. Teilhard argues that in addition to ordinary energy, as defined by the scientists, there is also radial or psychic energy. This overrides the

Second Law of Thermodynamics, and evolution is its continual growth from the lowest forms, an 'ascent towards consciousness'. Evolution is not haphazard, either, since it has 'a precise *orientation* and a *privileged axis*'. (Teilhard is fond of italics, and also of new words.) At the head of this evolution is Man, 'a direct lineal descendant from a total effort of life'. The idea is actually a direct lineal descendant of Bergson's life-force, which also defied the Second Law of Thermodynamics, and impressed such intellectuals of the day as George Bernard Shaw. But Teilhard carries it further into the birth of a higher consciousness he calls noogenesis, and the noosphere, where such consciousness is deployed. The supreme consciousness is Omega, 'already in existence and operative at the very core of the thinking mass' – God, redefined in science-fiction terms.

The thesis is not, of course, so baldly stated. But it is not actually argued either. It is merely asserted, in a complicated manner, with a variety of linguistic conjuring tricks. Here is how he explains the noosphere:

> The recognition of a new era in evolution, the era of noogenesis, obliges us to distinguish correlatively a support proportionate to the operation – that is to say, yet another membrane in the majestic assembly of telluric layers. A glow ripples outward from the first spark of conscious reflection. The point of ignition grows larger. The fire spreads in ever-widening circles till finally the whole planet is covered with incandescence. Only one interpretation, only one name can be found worthy of this grand phenomenon. Much more coherent and just as extensive as any preceding layer, it is really a new layer, the 'thinking layer', which, since its germination at the end of the Tertiary period, has spread over and above the world of planets and animals. In other words, outside and above the biosphere there is the noosphere.

Of course Teilhard stands in the long mystic tradition of Christian literature which goes back to *Revelation*, and the Jewish apocalyptics. (He is not as far from Marx as he liked to think!) Hence of course his appeal. His attitude to scientists is condescending: in the last resort they are shallow, their knowledge puerile. The book's unintelligible style is taken as a measure of its profundity, and its message that man is in a sorry state, sick of 'a malady of space-time' appears plausible when presented in a fog of pretentious verbiage. As Sir Peter Medawar noted sharply, the predicament of man is an attractive subject, 'now that people have sufficient leisure and are sufficiently well fed to contemplate it'. Teilhardian phenomenology is a system which enables the more leisured class to accommodate scientific knowledge in a religious setting but which makes no intolerable demands on either flesh or intellect.

All such systems are an impediment to civilization in that they confuse and deflect men from the pursuit of truth. But other religion-substitutes are actively destructive, particularly when, while nominally jettisoning the idea of gods, or God, they in fact deify secular concepts. These are the power-religions, which now infest and terrify our planet. Of course the ruler-God, or the divine-viceroy under God, is almost as old as man; but these crowned icons have always been mortal, necessarily. Much more frightening, because indestructible and perpetual, is the idea of deity incarnated in the state. The concept springs, together with much else, from Hobbes, whose Leviathan was 'a mortal God, to which we owe, under the immortal God, our peace and defence'. He was an agnostic, possibly an atheist, who presented the deification of the Commonwealth as a convenient substitute for conventional faith. The idea was broadened by Rousseau, whose concept of the General Will made it possible, eventually, to deify the Common Man, collectivized as the proletariat and endowed with dictatorial powers.

Power-religions thus encompass a variety of ideas, old and new, which have been forged into ferocious instruments of state tyranny. They ascribe to Nature, Biology, History or other abstractions many of the attributes which Christian theology ascribes to God. These abstractions are then presented as irresistible forces which the new state incarnates. Hence the Nazis deified the blood-force of the German race, which had an irresistible historical role to play for the next thousand years. They retained the old ruler-God worship of Hitler, and huge, pseudo-religious public ceremonies. For the Nazi baptism service, a room was decorated with Nazi flags, the Tree of Life, branches of birch-trees and candles and a centre-altar contained a photograph of Hitler and a copy of *Mein Kampf*. For Nazi weddings, there were runic figures, a yellow sun-disc of flowers and a fire-bowl; the married couple received bread and salt under a picture of Hitler and the Nazi flag, swore oaths and listened to appropriate Nazi music and readings. Communist marriage ceremonies in Moscow's 'Palace of Weddings' are basically the same, though they vary in ostentation and price; Lenin gazes serenely on the couple from the walls, while an official administers oaths of loyalty to the Workers' State. Unlike Nazism, which rested on Nature-Biology, Communism claims its legitimacy from History, which replaces the salvation process, has God-like attributes and is presented as essentially beneficent. The theology of the God-state is expanded or modified as required, to explain away new phenomena or incorporate new political objectives. Of course there are schisms, heresies, excommunications, an inquisition, and the employment of torture to extract confessions and reaffirmations of the true faith. Marxism-Communism in all its myriad varieties loves the splendour and language of ritual: the Red Square parades; the Peking displays of ritual gymnastics and its miracle- and mystery-plays; its hymns, like 'The East is Red', its catechism, the 'Little Red Book', its ritual praises and abuse, so similar to the litanies and anathemas developed in the fourth-century Byzantine church. It even has its own ecumenical movement now, as can be seen from a photograph (1973) of students demonstrating for 'proletarian unity', and carrying embroidered banners to Marx, Engels, Lenin, Stalin and Mao Tse-tung, for all the world like young clerics in a Holy Week procession of expiation for sin, schism and heresy.

But if these power-religions are caricatures of Christianity, they are infinitely more cruel and destructive in their operations, for they operate on naïve theories of world-transformation, and when the theories prove illusory wreak savage vengeance on the men and women whose non-compliance the ruler-priests judge responsible. Religious formulae which evolve slowly over long periods, combine different traditions, and span the needs of varied societies, as Christianity does, are less likely to be destructive, and more likely to advance the purposes of civilization than maniac force-systems which spring from the solitary minds of inspired secular prophets. As Edmund Burke put it, 'We are afraid to put men to live and trade each on his own private stock of reason; because we suspect that the stock in each man is small, and that the individuals would do better to avail themselves of the general bank and capital of nations and of ages.' It is characteristic of the accretive subtlety of Christianity that it ascribes evil in the world to a multiplicity of causes. Marx, by contrast, has a single-cause theory: all the evils of society arise from private property; abolish that, and they will disappear. But the result is not happiness. It is the Gulag Archipelago.

The wise defender of civilization thus accepts the secularizing forces which, to some extent, it encourages; but he does not suppose that civilization will ever dispense with the religious impulse. The idea of religion disappearing is as illusory as that Marxist vision of the withering state. There will always be policemen, judges, gaolers – and clergymen of a kind. Better, therefore, priests than witchdoctors. The Christian might express it by saying that man will always be a prey to evil forces, or in the grip, if you like, of original sin. Jung would go further: 'The evil that comes to light in man and that undoubtedly dwells within him is of gigantic proportions, so that for the church to talk of original sin, and to trace it back to Adam's innocent slip with Eve is almost a euphemism' (*The Undiscovered Self*). If the religious impulse must be accommodated, and the evil contained, the Christian approach seems that most compatible with the aims of civilization, fulfilling, as it does, Burke's requirement, and being, as it is, part of the historical background of civilization itself. Certainly, the pseudo-religions which seek to replace it are, by comparison, grotesquely irrational or monstrously destructive. They are among the major, as well as the minor, enemies of civilization. Now let us turn from the religious to the purely secular side of our intellectual apparatus, and in the first place test the strength and weakness of philosophy.

CHAPTER 10

Dancing Angels and Bottled Flies

It is not true, as is commonly asserted, that medieval scholastic philosophers passionately debated the problem of how many angels could dance upon the point of a pin. It appears this was a fancy cooked up by Disraeli's father, the antiquarian Isaac Disraeli. But they certainly discussed matters which seem to us – and to many at the time – equally absurd. In 1493, for instance, the dons of Louvain University, to the disgust of Erasmus, spent eight weeks debating the topic: do four five-minute prayers on consecutive days stand a better chance of being answered than one twenty-minute prayer, and is a prayer of ten minutes, said on behalf of ten people, as efficacious as ten one-minute prayers? The professional philosophers of the day, absorbed in such topics, had nothing to say about the Renaissance and the recovery of learning, the discovery of America, the passing of the closed world of the Middle Ages, the menace of the Ottomans, the growth of the national state and the power of the crown, or any other of the transcendental topics of their times. They would not move outside the narrow sphere of their technical 'problems'.

Are our own professional philosophers any better today? If we look back to the early fifth century, to the fall of Rome and the progressive disintegration of the western empire, we find that leading philosophers were concerned with the external world, and the devastating forces which were transforming it. Most of Pelagius's writings were lost, but we know that he advocated a reconciliation between the civilized world and its 'barbarian' opponents. St Jerome had no doubt about the momentousness of the forces overtaking the empire; and, above all, St Augustine extracted from the darkening scene around him the germ of his masterpiece, *The City of God*, a gigantic and brilliant commentary on the collapse of a civilization, which unquestionably provided carefully worked-out answers – I do not say they were the right ones – to the great questions intelligent people were asking. We find no such response among philosophers today. That our civilization is crumbling is a matter for debate; that it is under great stress is almost beyond dispute. But mankind's predicament, its causes and possible consequences (or remedies) is not regarded as fit material for philosophical attention. We may be sure no twentieth-century equivalent of *The City of God* is under preparation. No: the philosophical climate in our leading centres of learning is very much Louvain, 1493.

Indeed, we are the heirs to a century-long tradition of philosophical frivolity, eccentricity and obscurantism. Let us look at the record, over that period, of the University of Cambridge, perhaps the most productive, philosophically, of all the major western academies, and certainly, while Russell, Moore, Whitehead and Wittgenstein worked there in conjunction, a repository of philosophical talents unique in modern times. Because of the strength of the Cambridge philosophy school over the last century, we can fairly say that, if philosophy has failed to be effective and relevant there, it has failed everywhere. What, then, do we find?

What we find, in the words of the historian of Cambridge philosophy, C. D. Broad, is that its study there has been 'almost completely out of touch with general history, with political theory and sociology, and with jurisprudence'. Being himself a Cambridge philosopher, he is consoled by the reflection – which will strike non-academic philosophers as a paradox – that such isolation has at least 'saved it . . . from the danger of philosophizing with one eye on contemporary politics'. Cambridge philosophy is not only isolated from other disciplines, it is truncated in itself, by an arbitrary device characteristic of ancient university curricula. At Cambridge, Greek philosophy is treated exclusively as a branch of classical studies. For the student who wants to learn philosophy, which is actually called 'moral sciences', the subject starts with Descartes: hence the philosophic emphasis has tended to be on mathematics and mathematical physics. Between the study of, say, Plato and the study of Kant, says Broad, 'There is practically no overlapping either of teachers or of students.'

In any case, the giants of Cambridge philosophy have not appeared anxious to take a broad and comprehensive view of intellectual problems. The chief contribution of John Neville Keynes (1852–1950), who lived to be ninety-eight and survived his more famous son, was to distinguish between 'conventional', 'subjective' and 'objective'. William Ernest Johnson (1858–1931) spent most of his life thinking about 'probability', on which topic, however, he proved unable, claims Broad, 'to compose a sustained and coherent presentation of his work'. Oddly enough, the economist J. M. Keynes also wrote a Cambridge *Treatise on Probability*, which he actually published; but then went on to more useful work. James Ward (1843–1925), a Unitarian minister who lost his faith and became a deist, or theist, spent his Cambridge career writing a tome called *Psychological Principles*; but, says Broad, 'Ward's book is unread and his arguments completely ignored by most contemporary writers on the philosophy of mind.' George Frederick Stout (1860–1944), for many years editor of the philosophical journal *Mind*, was also a psychologist-philosopher, and developed a weird system of his own, which few understood then, or trouble to assess now.

So the roll-call goes on. John McTaggart (1866–1925) was a metaphysician-mystic, noted for his strong prejudices: 'When he defended in public an opinion which he happened to share with others, he was liable to do so by arguments which acutely embarrassed them.' He wrote a book appearing to accept the transmigration of the soul, or at least the view that we are all eternal, our existence being split up into successive lives; and he produced an immensely complicated and obscure argument proving that we all completely misconceive not only everything we conceive by our senses, but ourselves and our mental processes to boot; 'I do not suppose,' notes Broad, 'that McTaggart made a single disciple.' Henry Sidgwick (1838–1900), who lost his faith and so became Professor of Moral Philosophy, spent many years writing about ethics and eventually reached the conclusion that the notion of moral obligation was impossible to analyse, but anyway ought to be self-evident to any intelligent adult. G. E. Moore (1873–1958) achieved a world-wide reputation as the specialist of 'common-sense' philosophy, but to the non-academic his claim to the title is not immediately apparent. In 1926, he contrived to draw a distinction between 'meaning' and 'analysis', which led to a fierce debate, on both sides of the Atlantic, about 'the meaning of analysis', 'the analysis of meaning', the 'meaning of meaning' and the 'analysis of analysis': a debate still going on.

If we turn to Bertrand Russell, often, indeed usually, regarded as the greatest philosopher of the twentieth century, the record is not much more impressive, for although Russell pronounced on many public topics and even from time to time took part in public life, he did so consciously as a non-philosopher. In his professional field he fought long and hard to retain and strengthen a special or hieratic language for philosophical speculation. He flatly disagreed with those, like Moore, who wanted to debate problems in a commonsense manner and language – indeed, he said 'common sense embodies the metaphysics of savages'. Much of his work was carried out in a highly technical manner, on the limits of comprehension (rather like passages in Aquinas or Occam). His first major work, the *Principles of Mathematics* (never finished), seeks to show that pure mathematics has no concept which cannot be defined in terms of those of logic, and no special methods of reasoning foreign to formal logic. His *Principia Mathematica*, written in conjunction with A. N. Whitehead, is accounted a *tour de force*, but dwells on such problems as 'the class of all classes which are not members of themselves', the distinction between 'knowledge by acquaintance' and 'knowledge by description', and the proposition that, in order to understand a description, one must be acquainted with all the terms in the analysis of it. Russell often later said that his mind had never been so powerful after the strain he imposed on it by writing this work. Afterwards, he became involved in free love, pacifism, and experimental education, and campaigned for many other views and causes, often contradictory; he advocated a preventive atomic war against the Soviet Union but later urged the unilateral nuclear disarmament of the West.

However, the most characteristic Cambridge philosopher, one may say the most characteristic philosopher of our time, as he is the most influential among academics, was Ludwig Wittgenstein (1889–1951), an Austrian engineer and artillery officer, who spent most of his adult life as a Cambridge philosophy tutor. As a prisoner-of-war of the Italians, he had written a philosophical work called the *Tractatus Logico-philosophicus*, which was published in 1922 in both English and German. Apart from this he never published anything in his lifetime, but bits of his writings and notes circulated among his reverential pupils, who edited them after his death. Wittgenstein, though a foreigner, was a characteristic Cambridge phenomenon; that is, he conducted his teaching as though he was head of a secret society, a *capo di mafia*, gathered favoured pupils around him, basked in their adoration, shared their mutual worship, and surrounded himself with quasi-religious mystery. He seems to have changed his philosophical views more or less completely in middle life, and evolved through a turn of 180 degrees. (The same was true of Russell.) There is nothing necessarily wrong in this; on the contrary, change of mind is a reflection of growth and activity. Locke, for instance, changed his views almost completely on the central question (of his day) of religious toleration. But we know exactly why he did so: it was a result of his experience in exile in the Netherlands, and of his practical work in dealing with the American colonies. But in Wittgenstein's case, his reasons for disagreeing with his earlier views are even more obscure than the process of reasoning by which he reached them in the first place.

Wittgenstein shared, enormously deepened, and in his lifework epitomized the preoccupation of modern philosophy with language – that is, not with thought as such, still less with belief, but with the words in which thoughts are conveyed; and, as such, philosophy has left civilization undefended and confused. Moore had said that ordinary everyday language, it would seem, was 'expressly designed to mislead philosophers'. Wittengenstein's *Tractatus* was essentially a critique of this language. But it was not so much a continuous argument, leading to a comprehensive conclusion, or any conclusion at all, as a series of *aperçus*, or 'insights', to use the Cambridge term. Virtually all Wittgenstein's insights relate to the use of language. Thus: 'All philosophy is a "critique of language".' 'Philosophy is not a body of doctrine but an activity. A philosophical work consists essentially of elucidations. Philosophy does not result in "philosophical propositions" but rather in the clarification of propositions.' 'Philosophy is a battle against the bewitchment of our intelligence by means of language.' 'A philosophical problem has the form "I don't know my way about".' 'A main source of our failure to understand is that we do not *command a clear view* of our use of words – our grammar is lacking in this sort of perspicuity.'

As we have noted in Chapter 8, it is vital to use words accurately. But the pursuit of meaning in language, though valuable up to a point, is subject to the linguistic law of diminishing returns; it can be made endless, to little profit (like a child continually saying 'Why?'), and a philosopher lured into this particular maze is unlikely ever to come out of it. Hence, in part, the modern contempt with which the word 'semantics' is invested. Wittgenstein called a philosophical problem one which arises 'when language goes on holiday' or 'when language is like an engine idling'. But this is not what ordinary intelligent people understand by philosophy at all; hence the split between academic philosophy and true philosophy, just as with the scholastics of the Middle Ages. One feels that Wittgenstein would have shone in that 1493 debate at Louvain. Sometimes, indeed, he appears (like Picasso) to be playing a joke on the intelligentsia. Thus: 'My propositions serve as elucidations in the following way: anyone who understands me eventually recognizes them as nonsensical, when he has to use them – as steps – to climb up beyond them. (He must, so to speak, throw away the ladder after he has climbed up it.)' There are times when Wittgenstein seems to oscillate between the desire to be another Delphic oracle and the urge to play logic-games like Lewis Carroll (another mathematico-philosophy don). Certainly, he knew well that the way to the hearts of the educated upper-middle class, at any rate in England and America, is to give them a new writing game for wet afternoons. But in terms of philosophic humanism his work is, to use a phrase of Kingsley Amis's, the search for pseudo-solutions to non-problems.

Wittgenstein damaged himself even among some academic philosophers by his switch in mid-career from a critique of language to a mere study of its usage, which led him to appeal to common speech as a kind of authority. Hence he led his followers away from philosophy, even of an academic kind, into the wilderness of linguistics. What, he said, will help 'the fly escape from the fly-bottle' is analysis of usage, getting straight about how we actually use words. He returned again and again to this idea of the fly in the bottle, using an image which, however dear to pre-1914 Vienna, is unfamiliar to the Anglo-Saxon world, debating whether the fly could get out, whether it was possible to get out, whether it wanted to get out, whether the fly existed, or the bottle for that matter. Even Russell, who saw the lordly academic philosopher, with his professional vernacular, as a long way above the needs of the common herd, exploded with rage at the writing of the later Wittgenstein. He declared it 'completely unintelligible. Its positive doctrines seem to me trivial and its negative doctrines unfounded. I have not found in Wittgenstein's *Philosophical Investigations* anything that seems to me interesting and I do not understand why a whole school finds important wisdom in its pages.' For Russell, despite his professional preoccupation with abstruse problems of logic, held that the general aim of philosophy must be to achieve understanding of the world; and he thought philosophers, to do this, should put forward theories of some kind. Wittgenstein did not do this, and therefore, argued Russell, he was not worth taking seriously; he and his followers were examples of people whose interest in the world was exhausted.

Yet Russell's denunciation did nothing to diminish the influence and practice of parlour-game philosophy; on the contrary, it and its derivatives are more prominent in academic life now than when Wittgenstein was alive. One of his last obsessions was with the question: can there be such a thing as a private language? Private means that it is used by only one person, and is intelligible to him alone, describing his inner mental events. Wittgenstein, in his posthumous *Philosophical Investigations*, demonstrated that such a language was neither a logical nor a practical possibility. His proof hinged on the belief that language is a social phenomenon, which cannot function unless there is at least one other person there to correct mistakes. In a purely notional language there can be no objective check on mistakes of memory. Language is a system of rules, which must be consistent if its propositions are to have meaning; if we check the rules privately, without another person to monitor our checks, we cannot be sure we have actually kept the rules – we may just have *thought* we have done so. So, given the fallibility of memory, a man living as a hermit and using his own private language cannot be sure that today's rules are the same as yesterday's. A community of speakers is required to provide a standard of correct usage; a language must be public because it must be publicly verified. This demonstration has led to an international controversy which has now occupied the best part of two decades and shows no sign of being resolved, or dying down. One is reminded of Parmenides: 'Heed not the blind eye, the echoing ear, nor yet the tongue, but bring to this great debate the test of reason.' Where, we ask, is the 'great debate' of twentieth-century philosophy, against the background of a threatened civilization? There is none in the layman's sense. To be sure, there are these academic 'great debates' – the fly buzzing in the bottle, the hermit and his private language – but philosophy, of all sciences, is the one where the demands of the layman should be paramount; and these are not being met.

The fault does not lie with Cambridge or with any academic centre in particular. As a matter of fact, university or national parochialism in philosophy is dying. Modern philosophers speed by jet from one international congress to another; their preoccupations are, to a growing extent, globally shared. The failures of Cambridge merely epitomize the failures of the profession. We have now had several generations of destructive, and negative, philosophizing. Logical positivism, effectively popularized by A. J. Ayer's *Language, Truth and Logic* (1936), dismissed philosophy as a mere adjunct of the empirical sciences and mathematics. It argued that any proposition which could not be verified empirically either meant nothing, or turned out to be tautology. Most statements in whole areas of traditional philosophy were thus exposed as useless. In effect, all philosophizing on morals, politics, social theory, aesthetics and religion was impossible, and might be dangerous. As a result, large numbers of academic philosophers were reluctant to say anything – a reversion to the Middle Ages, when voices were still for fear of ecclesiastical censure. On top of this came the linguistic analysts, following Wittgenstein, who argued that so-called philosophical problems were just pits into which we blundered, having dug them ourselves by misuse of language. For two whole generations, then, little or no useful work was done in large traditional areas of philosophy. The implication of Wittgenstein is that there is no such thing as a science of human behaviour, psychology or sociology, and that philosophy has nothing useful to say on these topics. The implication of contemporary presentations of logical philosophy is that philosophy can be nothing more than a commentary on other disciplines.

Indeed, academic philosophers today appear to be exceedingly gloomy about the ability of their trade to do anything. Idealist philosophy, which is essentially constructive, as opposed to critical or analytic, is presented as an absurd form of elitism, arrogantly raising philosophy to a higher intellectual status than other types of thinking. The right posture, it is argued, is scepticism, stress on the limitations of the subject. As A. J. Ayer now puts it: 'There is a certain kind of sceptical argument that runs through the whole of philosophy, right back to the ancients, which tends to show that we can't really know lots of things that we think we know.' Or again, Bernard Williams, pressed to define the relationship between moral philosophy and actual moral conceptions among ordinary people, ducks hastily: 'Philosophy must avoid the path of being an armchair sociology or armchair anthropology.' The fact is that, while avoiding arrogance by their own definition, academic philosophers are very keen to keep the people at arm's length; hence their continuing use of hieratic concepts and language. Like the medieval cleric, they want clear distinctions between themselves and the rest of society; since such distinctions can no longer be legal they take the form of intellectual usage and habit (most philosophy dons would, of course, have become clergymen under an earlier dispensation).

It is true that some academic philosophers, particularly in the United States, have constantly urged a wider and more generous view of philosophic concern. Whitehead, who left Cambridge to spend the last twenty years of his life in Harvard, completely lost sympathy with narrow British and European preoccupations, and returned to meta-physics; he experimented with a 'world-system' of his own. Brand Blanchard, another leading American philosopher, also urges the possi-bility of system: 'The notion that the world is a gigantic rag-bag of loose ends, in which nothing is connected intelligibly with anything else, will not stand even a cursory examination. The world as we know it is shot through and through with lines of necessity, and there is every reason to believe that, if we knew it better, we should see those lines to be more numerous and far-ramified than at present they seem' (*Reason and Analysis*). Here, then, is the optimistic assertion that sense can be made of the world, and the implication that it is the philosopher's job to try and make that sense. Some would admit this duty openly, notably Karl Popper in the preface to the 1959 edition of his *The Logic of Scientific Discovery*: '. . . there is at least one philosophic problem in which all thinking men are interested. It is the problem of cosmology: *The problem of understanding the world – including ourselves, and our knowledge, as part of the world.* All science is cosmology, I believe, and for me the interest of philosophy, no less than of science, lies solely in the contributions which it has made to it.'

But such declarations of intellectual courage and ambition are rare among professional philosophers. Even Whitehead would go no further than to say: 'Philosophy is the wielding of imagination and common sense into a restraint upon specialists, and also into an enlarge-ment of their imaginations' (*Process and Reality*) – another way of say-ing it is a mere comment on other men's work. Rudolf Carnap put it more bluntly: 'Philosophy is to be replaced by the logic of science – that is to say, by the logical analysis of the concepts and sentences of the sciences, for the logic of science is nothing other than the logical syntax of the language of science' (*The Logical Syntax of Language*). It was an axiom of the logical positivists that, non-empirical propositions being illusory (or tautology), the task of extending true knowledge had to be handed over to the scientists and mathematicians. After experienc-ing Wittgenstein's parlour-game philosophy as the dominant mode, the majority of young philosophers active today again assert that the complex of science-mathematics is the ideal form of human thinking. Where Popper sees the quest for a true cosmology as one explored by philosophers and scientists working in tandem, the academic consensus is that only scientists can be entrusted with the job.

Among the radical Left, or those among them willing and able to interest themselves in academic philosophy, this abdication is seen as a betrayal of humanity by those traditionally and pre-eminently entrusted with its protection. While the radicals dismiss the linguistics philosophers as complacent, or 'decadent' (one of their favourite words), viewing the task of the philosopher as marginal, a process of tidying up at best, they are even more hotly opposed to logical positivism, or analytical philosophy or, as they call it, scientism. They regard it as propaganda for technology. Anthony Quinton sums up their position:

The hatred of a technologically dominated civilisation extends to what looks like its philosophical justification. Indeed it is frequently alleged by people on the far critical left that analytic philosophy as a whole is a handmaiden for science, that science is a destructive monster, and that the blame for its monstrosities which attaches to science also attaches to the philosophy which plays the part of its support, or rhinocerus-bird, or jackal.

Certainly, there has been an abdication. But to describe an abdication as a betrayal implies that the recipient of the role thus handed over by philosophy is as malevolent in its intentions as the radicals claim. What, in fact, *are* the intentions of the scientists? Have they any?

CHAPTER 11

The Scientist
and his Doppelgänger

The Victorian scientist T. H. Huxley, hero of the fight to establish Darwin's theory in the teeth of clerical resistance, relates that when he went to Osborne, to receive the accolade of a Privy Councillorship from the hands of Queen Victoria herself, he took the opportunity, while he knelt at her feet, to steal an upward glance, and look at the august monarch's face from close quarters. To his consternation, he found that she had had exactly the same idea, and was fixing him with her beady eye. This ocular confrontation, between the Matriarch of Obscurantism and the harbinger of relentless scientific truth, somehow symbolizes the growing suspicion with which scientists see the world and the world sees scientists. The chasm has widened since those days. Margaret Gowing, the historian of science in the Second World War, tells the story of Churchill's meeting, on 16 May 1944, with the celebrated nuclear scientist Niels Bohr. The latter was terrified at the ultimate consequences of man's using atomic energy for war, and had gone to immense trouble to get the interview with Churchill to impress on him the seriousness of the step he was about to take. When he reached Downing Street he was almost quivering with excitement at the opportunity to voice the fears of science to the great statesman. But '. . . practically the whole of the time was consumed in argument between [Lord Cherwell] and Mr Churchill on irrelevant points. . . . The main point was never reached.' When Bohr, frustrated, asked on leaving if he could send Churchill something in writing, Churchill agreed but 'hoped it would not be about politics'. Bohr said afterwards: 'We did not speak the same language.' Churchill, too, 'retained disagreeable memories of the occasion'.

If, as we saw in the last chapter, philosophy is inclined to abdicate intellectual leadership to science, it is handing over to men who feel themselves increasingly unpopular, misunderstood and travestied. George Eliot, in *Silas Marner*, records the superstition, common among the farmworkers of her youth, that weavers were to be feared, because they worked indoors and used 'inhuman' appliances. The masters of the arcane will always be held in dread if they cannot explain their mysteries; especially if, like scientists, they are thought to possess growing power. Bacon thought the ideal scientist should be 'sober, chaste and severe', also humble and innocent. But his definition of the ideal scientist's aim – 'to establish and extend the power and dominion of the human race itself over the universe' – is neither humble nor innocent, and the awesome image of the modern scientist is projected back by public opinion from his aims and achievements. Baron Frankenstein, Dr Moreau, Professor Moriarty, Dr Mabuse, Dr Strangelove – the gothic personality of the fictional scientist is increasingly hostile.

Much of the blame lies with what one historian of science, Jerome R. Ravetz calls 'the tragedy of modern physics' – the appalling historical accident which transformed the most aristocratic, pure and philosophical branch of science into a new technology of mass destruction, and so brought hatred and ignominy not only on physics but the whole profession. 'I am become as Death, the Destroyer of Worlds,' quoted Dr Oppenheimer as he watched the first test-explosion of the H-bomb; his tone was not exultant but infinitely melancholic. Ravetz compares the disgrace of physics, which led the aged Einstein to wish he had spent his life as a watchmaker, to the pitiful mess of the Galileo Affair. Yet it is only fair to add that Galileo's defence – 'The conclusions of natural science are true and necessary, and the judgement of man has nothing to do with them' – while directed against ecclesiastical censorship, can also be seen as a demand that scientists must be licensed to pursue truth wherever it leads, and irrespective of the consequences to man's estate. Those who campaign against nuclear research have now been joined by the environment lobby in ranging themselves, as it were, alongside pope and cardinals and inquisitors, by insisting that science is too destructive to be allowed total freedom.

Then too, distrust of science is almost certainly a factor in the decline in the numbers of able children, in the West at least, willing to specialize in it, with physics the worst victim. The unpopularity of physics coincides with a crisis in its own internal development. 'Nuclear physics now finds itself at a dinosaur stage,' Ravetz writes; 'unable to evolve further, it awaits extinction unless some happy accident rescues it.' One Manchester physicist, Dr H. S. Lipson, thinks that physics, having exhausted its obvious lines of inquiry, and deprived of innovatory talent, may share the fate of Latin. This sad predicament of the queen of the specialist sciences has deepened the crisis in morale which has overtaken the entire profession. Non-scientists do not generally realize that the present hostility is comparatively recent, and all the harder to bear in that scientists see it as completely misconceived and unjust. Scientists were traditionally credited with the highest ethics, and were generally seen as wholly philanthropic in their efforts and aims. Men like Humphrey Davy and Michael Faraday were treated as popular heroes, almost as secular saints. Scientists had generally assumed that they would erect their own ethical monitoring system. Bacon took it for granted, in the *New Atlantis* (1626), that scientists would keep some of their secrets from the state. In his *Discourse de la méthode* (1637), Descartes put forward a professional oath: 'I will not engage on projects useful to some only by being harmful to others.' Galileo, as we have noted, would not allow that the judgement (or 'will') of man had any bearing on scientific inquiry; but his own ethics were none too scrupulous, since he tried to sell methods of determining longitude both to Spain and to the Netherlands during the Thirty Years War. In any case, ethical codes, drawn up from within or imposed from without, were bound to break down once the magnitude of science's bounty, for good or ill, was perceived. As Ravetz gloomily notes: 'In the longer perspective of history, the moral innocence of academic science appears as a temporary feature, a happy accident of circumstances.'

Faced with their new unpopularity, scientists often react with fury and exasperation. Hence the anger with which many of them greeted James D. Watson's *The Double Helix: a Personal Account of the Discovery of DNA*, which cast new and unwelcome light on the grubby motives which sometimes lie behind discoveries of the first magnitude. There was a similar reception for D. S. Greenberg's *The Politics of Pure Science*, which is frank about the fallible reactions of scientists when faced with the temptations of money and power ('Wherever there's a system, there's a racket to beat it.'). This new form of scientific literature has provoked a conflict of values within the profession. The *Bulletin of the Atomic Scientists*, deploring the worldly-wise and cynical tone of

The Scientist: an Anthology of Partly-Baked Ideas, edited by I. J. Good, called its publication 'nothing less than a crime against the ethical code, unwritten but vital, of the community of scientists. . . . Uncompromising, indefatigable pursuit of truth, then, is the hallmark that distinguishes the scientist from the charlatan. It constitutes the indispensable ethic of science.' Such rigour, however, is widely seen as old-fashioned, the hallmark of the older generation. On the other hand, it is the younger members of the profession who tend to take direct action in pursuit of ethical standards, as for instance in the abortive 'strike', in protest against the misuse of science, at the Massachusetts Institute of Technology in March 1969. Between the seniors who believe in standards as a moral force, and the juniors who concentrate on messy direct action, nothing effective is done. Most scientists heap the blame on the politicians, while resolutely holding aloof from the political process: the number of qualified scientists who present themselves for election in western representative assemblies is minute. Many of the misunderstandings would be cleared up if scientists devoted more time to studying, and publicizing, the history and philosophy of science. But good scientists are prejudiced in such matters. 'A great many highly creative scientists,' writes Sir Peter Medawar, '. . . take it quite for granted, though they are usually too polite or too ashamed to say so, that an interest in the history of science is a sign of failing or unawakened powers.' It is also true, Professor Gowing points out, that scientists do themselves no professional good by writing about the philosophy of science, especially if they have something new to say.

Politicians and scientists are at cross-purposes because each group feels it is dealing with the 'real' reality. Oddly enough, the same mutual belittlement has tended to make for frosty relations between artists and scientists (or 'natural philosophers' as they were called until the nineteenth century). Sir Philip Sidney, in *An Apologie for Poetrie* (1595), claimed the poet 'yieldeth to the powers of the mind an image whereof the philosopher bestoweth but a wordish description, which doth neither strike, pierce, nor possess the sights of the soul.' There was, and is, a feeling among the self-consciously creative and imaginative that the scientific approach tends to miss something essential. 'And now philosophy calls all in doubt,' complained Donne, 'The element of fire is quite put out.' 'Do not all charms fly,' asked Keats, 'At the mere touch of cold philosophy?' Among laymen, the association of isolation and coldness with science persists. Thus Wordsworth, though admiring the natural philosopher and, above all, Newton, wrote of

> ... his prism and silent face,
> The marble index of a mind for ever
> Voyaging through strange seas of thought, alone.

Bagehot, in *Physics and Politics* (1872), affirmed 'there is coldness in their fame. We think of Euclid as of fine ice; we admire Newton as we do the Peak of Teneriffe.' Bertrand Russell, in his essay 'The Study of Mathematics', admits as much: 'Mathematics possess not only truth, but supreme beauty – a beauty cold and austere, like that of sculpture, without appeal to any part of our weaker nature, sublimely pure and capable of a stern perfection such as only the greatest art can show.' The association of science with cruelty and inhumanity long predates the nuclear age. Goethe, who accused the scientist of the sin of isolating elements of perception from the whole, wrote of 'the pathology of experimental physics', and of Newton's 'empirico-mechanico torture-chamber'.

Yet at least there was, until comparatively recently, no absolute gap of understanding between scientists and the rest; there was in fact a good deal of overlap. Sir John Herschel translated the *Iliad*; Goethe studied plant morphology and optics. The central body of Newtonian principles was readily understood by ordinary intelligent men who took the trouble, and they lent themselves to illuminating explanations by analogy with machines, clocks and so forth. Creative writers could, and did, assimilate the latest scientific advances and interpret them for the public – Pope, Shelley, Tennyson, Whitman, Emerson, Sandburg, Hart Crane: the list could easily be much longer. The difficulty about the technical foundations of modern science, by contrast, is not only that they are hard for the ordinary layman to grasp, they often seem at odds with the logic of everyday practical experience. Physicists, at least, will now admit that a great deal cannot be understood by the non-scientist. As Robert Oppenheimer put it (1959): 'The deep things in physics . . . are not things you can tell about unless you are talking to someone who has lived a long time acquiring the tradition.' The imaginative writer can no longer cope. Hence scientific concepts and discoveries are no longer transferred to the humanist and religious areas. It is no use the scientist complaining: as a rule, the poet can no longer help. In fact, the scientists themselves are increasingly bewildered and depressed by the quantitative growth of science and its specialities. A second age of Babel has seemed to disintegrate the unity of natural philosophy. There are now more than 50,000 specialist scientific journals, publishing at least 40,000 learned articles a week. Lord Rutherford used to say: 'This is the heroic age of science! This is the Elizabethan Age!' But the buccaneering individualism his remarks reflected has been buried under the sheer weight of scientific effort: all the gross quantitative indices of scientific work have shown steady growth over many decades. Peter Kapitsa, the celebrated Soviet scientist, revisiting England in 1966, complained: 'Science has lost her freedom. Science has become a productive force. She has become rich but she has become enslaved and part of her is veiled in secrecy. I do not know whether Rutherford would continue nowadays to joke and laugh as he used to do.'

Nevertheless, it is not only defeatist but quite unnecessary to dismiss science as incapable, because of its very nature, of making the prime contribution to the advance of understanding, and so to the defence of civilization, that the moral philosophers, in their self-doubt, would assign it. It is still possible to make unified sense of the scientific contribution, and of its relationship to our values. But we can do this only by realizing that scientists are not a separate group of people, doing work which is essentially different from that of any other kind. There are not, there never have been, two 'realities'. In fact, there is no such person as 'the scientist'. It is a pity, in a way, that the celebrated nomenclator, Dr William Whewell, Master of Trinity, Cambridge, saw fit to replace the term 'natural philosopher' by coining the expression 'scientist' in 1840. It has served to dig a ditch between them and the rest of mankind. One of the merits of that notorious book, *The Double Helix*, is that its large and infinitely diverse cast of characters gives the lie to the belief that men engaged in scientific work have a great deal in common.

The truth is, as Sir Peter Medawar has pointed out in *The Art of the Soluble*, that most scientists could have easily been something else. They are composed of types common to all humanity: some are collectors, others classifiers, compulsive tidy-uppers, detectives and explorers, artists and artisans, poets, philosophers and mystics. While the volume of scientific knowledge expands continually, scientists are not necessarily becoming more narrowly specialized: 'One of the distinguishing marks of modern science is the disappearance of sectarian loyalties.' What is true, however, is the broad distinction between the creative and the analytic types of scientific work. This was first recognized by Bacon:

'It is an error of special note, that the industry bestowed upon experiments hath presently, upon the first access into the business, seized upon some designated operation; I mean sought after *Experiments of Use* and not *Experiments of Light and Discovery.*' He rightly argued that the understanding of nature is more important than the power over nature, at any rate in the long run. But it was not Bacon who made a snobbish distinction between 'pure' and 'applied' science: that came later. The use of the word 'pure' is particularly unfortunate, because it implies moral and intellectual superiority. Both forms of work are means to an end. As Medawar says, it is 'our humanist brethren who have taught us to believe that, while pure science is a genteel and even a creditable activity for scientists in universities, applied science, with all its horrid connotations of trade, has no place on the campus . . .'

It is only when we dismiss such false concepts as 'the scientist' and 'pure' and 'applied' science, and examine how the scientist actually works, that we begin to see how closely related scientific understanding is to the nature of civilization, as we have defined it, and to its defence. For the scientist, in a true sense, exercises creative imagination. He tells stories, as a creative act, and then seeks to discover, by a process of scrupulous testing, whether they are about the real world or not. A facility in devising hypotheses is essential to scientific work. Constructing a hypothesis is not essentially different from story-telling; both are creative acts; the empirical nature of the scientist takes over only when the stage of verification, or falsification, begins. As Medawar notes, the way in which scientists work at the creative stage, what they actually do, tends to be carefully concealed; for scientists are judged by their scientific papers, and these must be written in the conventional manner. What they say they do varies widely enough to accommodate any hypothetical description. But someone who made secret tapes of laboratory conversations would discover the storytelling element, and the fact that the preconceived idea – supposedly 'unscientific' – must nearly always be there.

We are now getting to the heart of the matter. We have argued that the pursuit of truth in freedom (the two are inseparable) is the essence of civilization. The first glimpse of truth is an imaginative act, in science – as we have seen – no less than in the arts. What distinguishes the true scientist from the false one, is how he proceeds *after* he glimpses, or thinks he has glimpsed, that spark of truth. The correct methodology of science is the correct methodology of civilization, too.

For the guidance towards this discovery we have to thank Sir Karl Popper, who first set out the line of reasoning in his *The Logic of Scientific Discovery*. This book, one of the truly original works of the twentieth century, was first published in German in 1934, but did not get English publication until 1959, and has only very slowly come to exercise the influence it merits. This is because Popper's method is not merely critical but, at first appraisal, apparently negative and destructive. He accepts the insistence of Medawar, which we have already noted, that scientific hypothesis is essentially creative or intuitive; a position confirmed by Einstein, who agrees 'that theory cannot be fabricated out of the results of observation, but that it can only be invented'. Having intuitively framed his hypothesis, what should the scientist then do? Popper was very struck by the dazzling scientific event of his youth, when the apparently impregnable system of Newtonian laws was suddenly upset by Einstein's theory. Nothing could have seemed truer than Newtonian physics, since they were constantly being confirmed not merely by observation but by creative use in 'normal' science as the basis of our modern technology. What followed from this? Popper noted David Hume's argument that inductive proof of a scientific law was logically inconclusive. If we look for evidence that water boils at 100 degrees centigrade, we will find confirmatory instances without number; but this will not prove it; nor will it increase the probability of its being true. What is more important, 'confirmatory' work of this kind will never give us any reason to doubt or to replace, to enlarge or qualify or improve the law. This applies to all so-called scientific laws. But the Einstein episode suggested that even one of the strongest of them needed revision. And, as a result of this apparently falsifying step, we had in fact enlarged the area of knowledge. Hence, the true scientist is not a man who looks for evidence to confirm his hypothesis, but one who looks for evidence to disprove it.

Once we adopt this highly critical falsification procedure as a methodology, we enlarge the area of the knowledge instead of keeping it static. We admit that all our knowledge is permanently provisionary; but with each falsification of the law, we reformulate it in a way preferable to the previous one. Popper's is a harsh doctrine: 'We cannot identify science with truth, for we think that both Newton's and Einstein's theories belong to science, but they cannot both be true and they may well both be false.' Or again: 'The wrong view of science betrays itself in the craving to be right.' Science is not truth; it is, rather, the pursuit of truth, the 'so-far-as-our-knowledge-goes truth'. Scientists should publish their hypotheses without fear that their destruction will be a personal disaster, since falsification, in whole or in part, is the anticipated and even necessary fate of all hypotheses; falsification is, in fact, constructive, because it adds to the provisional truth: 'It is not truisms which science unveils. Rather, it is part of the greatness and the beauty of science that we can learn, through our own critical investigations, that the world is utterly different from what we ever imagined – until our imagination was fired by the refutation of our earlier theories.'

Hence it follows that hypotheses or theories should be formulated to provide the highest informative content, because that makes the process of enlargement by falsification easier. This is one test in choosing between possible rival theories. Another is the degree of corroboration. Popper defines this in *Objective Knowledge: an Evolutionary Approach*:

... By the degree of corroboration of a theory I mean a concise report evaluating the state (at a certain time, *t*) of the critical discussion of a theory, with respect to the way it solves its problems; its degree of testability; the severity of tests it has undergone; and the way it has stood up to these tests. Corroboration (or degree of corroboration) is thus an evaluating *report of past performance*. Like preference it is essentially comparative: in general, one can only say that the theory *A* has a higher (or lower) degree of corroboration than a competing theory *B*, in the light of the critical discussion, which includes testing, *up to* some time, *t*.

Nature itself operates in the same way: 'The tentative solutions which animals and plants incorporate into their anatomy and behaviour are biological analogues of theories. . . . Just like theories, organs and their functions are tentative adaptations to the world we live in.' Since the object of the methodology is to enlarge by falsification, for most scientific purposes, a clear-cut statement which is slightly out is much more useful than one which is true but vague. We must therefore formulate our theories as clearly as possible so as to expose them as unambiguously as possible to refutation. We should not continually reformulate theory to evade refutation. Falsifiability is the criterion between science and non-science. A genuine scientific theory puts itself continually at risk. If all possible states of affairs fit in with a theory then it is useless since it cannot be tested; as there is no observable difference between its being true and being false, it conveys no scientific information. Only if some imaginable observation would refute it is it testable. Particularly obnoxious are theories which contain built-in defences against refutation.

Einstein's formulation was a classic case of true theory because it exposed itself to refutation by predicting observable effects no one had hitherto expected – for example, the deflection of light by gravitational pull; Einstein had no means of knowing that Eddington's observations in Africa on 29 May 1919 would back him up. A true scientist always leads with his chin, as it were; it is the phoney who makes it difficult to hit him.

Popper's methodology is a devastating weapon because it enables us to detect the pseudo-scientist straightaway, even if we are not very familiar with his subject. And it extends itself over the whole range of disciplines which claim to have a truth-content: none can escape it. The false betray themselves instantly by their unwillingness to risk the verification process, and still more by their evident anxiety to prove themselves. If then, we identify civilization with the pursuit of truth, we can say that a theorist, or a society, which cannot identify itself in some way with Popper's approach is not civilized. Of course, Popper, when he wrote, had not only in mind the true example of Einstein, but the false of the Marxists, and the followers of Freud and Adler. It is the Marxists and the psychoanalysts who continually reformulate their theories to avoid creeping refutation. Again, no conceivable observations could contradict the propositions of Freud or Adler, whose theories have built-in mechanisms to meet and absorb criticism. Popper points out that the secret of the appeal of Marxism and Freudianism is precisely their ability to explain everything. The Marxist knows in advance that, whatever happens, he will be able to fit it into some part of the theoretical edifice, and explain it. The Marxist is never stumped; the true scientist is always being stumped – he would think there was something wrong with him if he were not.

In *Conjectures and Refutations*, Popper draws attention to the similarity between such pseudo-sciences and religion (the Christians, it might be noted, have their own technique for reformulating theory, known as 'progressive revelation'). All-purpose theories, like Freudianism and Marxism, have

the effect of an intellectual conversion or revelation, opening your eyes to a new truth hidden from those not yet initiated. Once your eyes were thus opened you saw confirming instances everywhere: the world was full of *verification* of the theory. Whatever happened always confirmed it ... unbelievers were clearly people who did not want to see the manifest truth ... because it was against their class interest, or because of their repressions which were still 'unanalysed' and crying aloud for treatment. . . . A Marxist could not open a newspaper without finding on every page confirming evidence for his interpretation of history; not only in the news, but also in its presentation – which revealed the class bias of the paper – and especially of course in what the paper did *not* say . . .

Naturally, such theories as Marxism may tell us things. But they tend to describe facts in the manner of myths. They contain interesting psychological suggestions, but not in testable form. Most scientific theories, too, originate in myths – the scientist begins by telling a story. But they only become *scientific* theories at the point when it is possible to test them. Marxism and Freudianism remain in the witchdoctor stage of myth because they dodge refutation by reformulation, osmosis and imprecision. They could be useful; what is absurd and dangerous is that political and physical therapies should be based on them.

A good example of the all-purpose theory of the type Popper warns against is the medium-is-the-message hypothesis of Marshall McLuhan. McLuhan, an old-style literary critic, with various anti-urbanization nostrums culled from a variety of writers ranging fom G. K. Chesterton to F. R. Leavis, published *The Gutenburg Galaxy: the making of Typographical Man* in 1962. The theory is that man 'communicates' most effectively when he employs a multiplicity of senses. Hence primitive man lived in a highly imaginative atmosphere, and was more happy and fulfilled in consequence. The invention of writing made vision the chief channel of communication; printing made it virtually the only one. Man is not only limited, and so impoverished, in consequence, but the nature of the printing medium conditions him to strictly linear patterns and so to ideas which conform only to formal logic. The invention and popularity of TV broke the linear-pattern monopoly, and so has opened up life's riches again. McLuhan's theory, of course, was rapturously received by the mass-media, which instantly made him into a best-seller and a world figure. He also became popular among some young people, because he seems to be saying that it is not important to reach rational and logical conclusions by serious thinking – sensations are all that matter; hence, the student drop-out is living more fully, and getting more out of life, than the first-class honours graduate.

A section of mankind is always anxious to find new reasons for rejecting the 'modern world' especially if, as in McLuhan's case, its members are nevertheless allowed the benefits of modern mass-entertainment – a return to nature plus colour-TV. What is surprising is that McLuhan should ever have been taken seriously by the educated. His theory bears all the hallmarks of a pseudo-science in their most unmistakable form: the feverish search for 'confirmatory' evidence culled from every possible context, however irrelevant; and a parallel blindness to the multitude of facts which contradict it. It also has the giveaway built-in defences against criticism, since when falsifying facts are brought to McLuhan's attention, or rather thrust unavoidably under his nose, he feels himself able at any point in the argument to drop an example or 'proof', on the grounds that it was a 'scientific probe' that has not survived empirical experiment. His methods, in fact, are a travesty, almost a caricature, of the way in which the real scientist works.

Yet the success of McLuhan among very large numbers of young people helps to explain the continuing, indeed growing, influence of various forms of Marxist millenarianism among the young in the West, and in the Third World. The real attraction of Marxism, at any rate in its modern debased versions, is that it is an all-purpose explanation of the universe together with a construction-kit for an earthly paradise. But its veneer of intellectual respectability is established by its claim to be a 'science'. The very essence of Marxism proper is its claim to be scientific. Marx denied he was a 'Utopian Socialist' – he despised the breed. He claimed he was a scientist, accurately predicting the future. Just as the physical world was governed by Newton's laws, and the living world by Darwin's, so the development of human societies proceeded according to laws, which he had discovered. All such laws worked 'with iron necessity' towards inevitable results: a scientist like himself could predict and describe the results, but not alter them. He claimed he had discovered 'the Natural Laws of capitalist production'. We lived in a pre-determined world:

. . . even when a society has got upon the right track for the discovery of the Natural Laws of its movement – and it is the ultimate aim of this work to lay bare the Economic Law of Motion of modern society – it can neither clear by bold leaps, nor remove by legal enactments, the obstacles offered by the successive phases of its normal development. . . . It is a question of these laws themselves, of these tendencies working with iron necessity towards inevitable results. The country that is more developed industrially only shows, to the less developed, the image of its own future (*Capital*).

The propositions embodied in this approach are as rigorous as Newton's laws. This was deliberate, since Marx drew no distinction between himself and other empirical scientists. He wrote to Lasalle in 1861: 'Darwin's book [*The Origin of Species*] is important and serves me as a natural-scientific basis for the class struggle in history'; and in 1880 he wrote to Darwin himself, asking if Chapters 12–13 of the English translation of *Capital* could be dedicated to him. Darwin declined, on the grounds that he had not read the work and that he was now too old and weak to cope with proofs: 'Although I am a keen advocate of freedom of opinion on all questions, it seems to me (rightly or wrongly) that direct arguments against Christianity and Theism hardly have any effect on the public; and that freedom of thought will best be promoted by that gradual enlightening of human understanding which follows the progress of science' – a good example of a true scientist giving a mountebank the polite brush-off.

However, Marx is best dealt with on his own terms, as a scientist. It is not enough to say that Marxism is false because the Soviet Union has failed to create the stateless, perfect and classless society. Marx is not to be judged by 'Utopian Socialism' or what is now termed 'Vulgar Marxism'. It is a wise element in Popper's methodology that, just as a valid-seeming theory should be constantly tested at its weakest point, so a pseudo-scientific theory should be tested at its strongest. If Marx's scientific theory of socio-economic laws is treated with intellectual seriousness, a number of factual predictions emerge, all of which can be tested, and all of which prove to be false. Thus: only fully developed capitalist countries can go Communist; the revolution would have to be based on the industrial proletariat; the industrial proletariat must get poorer, more class-conscious, more numerous and more revolutionary under capitalism; Communism can only be brought about by the masses; ownership of the means of production must become concentrated in fewer and fewer hands; the classes must shrink into two, and so forth. Virtually all Marx's predictions of what must happen, on the basis of his 'laws of iron necessity' have been falsified by events. Hence, his theory is not scientific at all but a form of prophecy.

Moreover, Marx's claim to predict particular processes 'scientifically' is itself based on a wider fallacy that history is somehow pre-determined. Marxism is an example of what Popper calls 'historicism', that is, an 'approach to the social sciences which assumes that *historical prediction* is their principal aim, and which assumes that this aim is attainable by discovering the "rhythms" or the "patterns", the "laws" or the "trends" that underlie the evolution of history'. The approach is characteristic both of Judaism and of Christianity, seen as 'time' religions; but also of such secular and deterministic nostrums as 'the inevitability of progress' or Hitler's 'Thousand-year Reich'. Like many of his contemporaries, Marx got hold of the wrong end of the Darwinian stick, and thought that the pseudo-theories of 'social Darwinism' implied an inevitability of human development which he could collectivize into an economic and political prediction. In fact he ended up as just another Old Testament prophet, whose prophecies did not come true but none the less helped to alter events – for history is shaped not by pre-determined forces but by our own efforts to change it.

Marxism, being a 'science', had to have a 'philosophy of science'. But Marx could not find time to master the subject, and wrote nothing about it, other than dropping a few elliptic remarks, which have been endlessly glossed by generations of Marxist theologians. He left such matters to Engels, who spent eight years producing his *Dialectics of Nature* after he retired from business. This was a genuine example of Marxist logic and, as such, a characteristic specimen of pseudo-science. Engels argued that, since Man was a part of Nature, the most general principles of Nature must apply to him. Hence also scientists, consciously or not, were influenced by the prevailing philosophy: 'Natural scientists may adopt whatever attitudes they please, they will still be under the domination of philosophy' – so much for Galileo. They had to choose 'whether they wanted to be dominated by a bad, fashionable philosophy [i.e. capitalism] or by a form of theoretical thought which rests on acquaintance with the history of thought and its achievements [i.e. Marxism]'. In science-nature, 'the same dialectical laws are in motion which in history govern the apparent fortuitousness of events'. This would suggest that the only 'true' form of science is a dialectical one, a proposition susceptible neither of proof nor disproof and almost meaningless; again, Engels insists that 'Mind is secondary, derivative [to matter] since it is a reflection of matter, a reflection of being . . .'; or, again: 'The motion present in the world is explained by internal factors, and therefore no external mover is needed.' Engels produces many such laws, most of them based on absolute materialism, sometimes with an element of 'dialectic' added. They are not, of course, scientific laws, since hardly any of them are susceptible of empirical proof; they cannot be verified or falsified by logic or by the advances of science. Or, where there is a danger that science may subsequently overtake them, they are purposely left vague. This cautious approach was followed by Lenin, who also dabbled in science, notably in his *Philosophical Notebook*, and in his attack on idealism published as *Materialism and Empirico-Criticism*. Take, for instance, Lenin's definition of matter, vital for his materialism: 'Matter is a philosophic category for the designation of objective reality which is presented to man in all his sensations, an objective reality which is copied, photographed, or reflected by our sensations but which exists independently from those sensations.' The interesting thing about this definition, on which Lenin evidently spent some considerable thought, is that it does not actually define matter but rather the relationship of matter to the subject. The proposition was left sufficiently vague to allow for it to be updated, as it has been, in the light of scientific advances; it is thus a classic example of an unverifiable, or unfalsifiable, statement, and as such scientifically useless.

Despite, therefore, a veneer of scientism, Marxist theory and its derivatives are no more scientific than the writings of the Jewish apocalyptics, or St John's *Revelation* or Joachim of Flora's *The Harp with Ten Strings*. Their popularity attests to the continuing, perhaps increasing, credulity of mankind, the ability of millenarians and intellectual mountebanks to adjust to whatever level of popular education they work among, and the extraordinary impact on history of irrational modes of thought. Let us note one final piece of conjuring from the Marxist, or Vulgar-Marxist, bag of tricks, because it is important. As these theories are constantly being reformulated to meet awkward new evidence, they usually at any one moment are sufficiently rubbery to explain everything and justify anything. But in any case they have a foolproof, or fail-safe, device, in addition – the doctrine of crisis, used to explain aberrant behaviour or suspension of the rules. As Isaiah Berlin has pointed out, 'It is one of the strategems of totalitarian regimes to present all situations as critical emergencies, demanding ruthless elimination of all goals, interpretations and forms of behaviour save for one absolutely specific, concrete, immediate end, binding on everyone, which calls for ends and means so narrow and so easily definable that it is easy to impose sanctions for failing to pursue them.' Here, for instance is a Marxist using the crisis-mechanism to justify political censorship of art, a nice piece of intellectual effrontery: 'Stupid people often accuse Marxists of welcoming the intrusion of politics into art. On the contrary, we protest against the intrusion. The intrusion is most marked in times of crisis and great suffering. But it is pointless to deny such times. They must be understood so that they can be ended: art and men will then be freer. Such a time began in Europe in 1914 and continues still' (John Berger, *The Success and Failure of Picasso*).

One prominent sub-Marxist 'scientist' who constantly uses the crisis-mechanism, to justify, among other things, the use of positive censorship, when possible, is Herbert Marcuse. Marcuse is a German Hegelian, born in Berlin in 1898, who studied under Heidegger and fled to America from Hitler in the 1930s. He became a pop-idol of the Marxist student body in the West following the publication of his book *One-Dimensional Man*, and his personal identification with the 'student revolt' of the late 1960s. It is not difficult to understand his appeal. One of the weaknesses of the Marxist corpus has been that it is pre-Freudian. It described the hostile, collective capitalist world, but left out the individual human being and the element of personal alienation. Marcuse was clever enough to locate this gap in the appeal of Marxism, and to graft over it a Freudian membrane. The merging of Freud and Marx, as interpreted by Marcuse, proved emotionally satisfying; of course, from a scientific point of view it is peculiarly distasteful, since it compounds one variety of all-purpose theory with another. Thus the knowing face of Freud pops up wherever there are holes in Marxist theory, and vice versa. And, to make his argument still easier, Marcuse uses a crude debating device, culled from sub-Hegelianism, by which he converts concepts (and facts) into their opposites by a mere verbal adjustment. Thus freedom, when inconvenient to his thesis, becomes 'oppressive freedom'; violence, when necessary, becomes 'defensive violence'.

Given, however, that Marcuse has loaded all the dice in his favour, the result is extraordinarily unimpressive, except at a purely emotional level. His theme is that the whole of life is dominated by the social control of technical processes. What is his evidence of social control? Not very convincing; and this is because 'the power of the given facts' is itself an 'oppressive power'. Social control thus maliciously prevents him from 'proving' his thesis empirically. And this, he says, is typical of how modern society works. Its technology allows it to eliminate opposition by assimilating all those who in earlier times provided the dissenting elements. Freedom from material want has thus been transformed into an agency for producing slavery. But wasn't the freeing of people from want the whole object of political progress? No, because there are false needs and true needs. How come? Because there is false happiness and true happiness. Thus, the supposed leisure of modern society is not free, for leisure 'thrives in advanced industrial society, but it is unfree to the extent to which it is administered by business and politics'. Even so, aren't people free to accept it or not? No, because, for example, the permissiveness of modern society is an instrument of domination, since commercial sexuality saturates the surface of social life and 'satisfies' men without restoring to them the enjoyment of their own sexuality. All advanced industrial societies are essentially alike; there is no real difference between Hitler's Germany and Nixon's US. But in Nixon's US, didn't Marcuse and his friends escape this fearful conditioning? Yes, because they are special. And how did he escape social control to write this book? Because there are now forces in society which run counter to the tendencies he describes.

Marcuse is insistent that the elements of what we call civilization have been perverted to assist the controlling and conditioning process. Culture has been flattened out into a one-dimensional monstrosity. Language has been degraded into an instrument of totalitarian domination. Philosophy, which he chiefly identifies with Wittgenstein, has become corrupt and acquired an 'intrinsically ideological character'. Thus it helps to 'coordinate mental operations with those in the social reality'. What is particularly wicked is the way philosophers have devised formal logic to help social control; indeed, logic is the key to control: 'The idea of formal logic itself is a historical event in the development of the mental and physical instruments for universal control and calculability.' The same line of argument applies to science: 'The principles of modern science were *a priori* structured in such a way that they could serve as conceptual instruments for a universe of self-propelling, productive control . . .'

Here is Popper's definition of a pseudo-scientist reduced almost to the point of ridicule and absurdity. Marcuse not only looks avidly for anything which, by the remotest stretch of the imagination, might prove his thesis, and desperately averts his gaze from anything which refutes it, but he also insists on changing the rules of logic, science and verbal meaning to suit any purpose he sees fit. The 'dialectical logic' he produces is not logic at all. Indeed, it is clear that he does not understand what logic is, what it can do and what it can't do – hence he misunderstands Wittgenstein and denounces him for the wrong reasons. His attack on science reveals that he does not comprehend what science is for, or how it actually works. As he understands neither science nor logic, it is not surprising that he sees them as personal and political enemies, instead of what they are: neutral as nature itself. As for language, as one of Marcuse's critics, Alistair MacIntyre, has noted, among the worst of the evils befalling it in advanced societies is 'the taste for pretentious nostrums described in inflated language which induces excitement rather than thought'. This is one malady Marcuse does not note, since he is a conspicuous victim of it. Being a pseudo-scientist, a myth-maker, he uses language like a witchdoctor or high priest, as a magical incantation. He is not interested in the objective facts, as he is putting forward a conspiracy theory, into which all human phenomena must be squeezed; but, of course, once the essential suspension of rational disbelief has been achieved, all conspiracy theories work, all the time, and in all circumstances. In reality, advanced modern societies are, rather, distinguished by their lack of control – in *that* sense it is true Hitler's Germany had much in common with Nixon's America, for the last days of Hitler, like the last days of Nixon, witnessed a total loss of control. Nor is it true that advanced society only creates needs it knows it can satisfy; on the contrary, it is constantly encouraging materialist aspirations it cannot fulfil; it is characterized by the unkept promise. One mark of the pseudo-scientist is his imprisonment in his time: Marcuse's writing is essentially the product of the culmination of the long post-war boom in the 1960s; by the later 1970s, events had conspired to make his assumptions seem remarkably dated.

Where Marcuse is on more permanent, though still irrational, ground, however, is in marrying Freud to Marx. It may be that the idea was not original to Marcuse, for the weird offspring of this union of irrationals are already alive, grown and rampant: modern, all-purpose psychology and sociology. These are examples not so much of false sciences, like historicism, as of what Jerome Ravetz calls 'immature and ineffective sciences'. Thomas Kuhn, in *The Structure of Scientific Revolutions*, points out that one characteristic of a weak science is the lack of an agreed theoretical base: '. . . the practice of astronomy, physics, chemistry or biology, normally fails to evoke the controversies over fundamentals that often seem endemic among, say, psychologists or sociologists.' A second characteristic, particularly marked in psychology and sociology, is that the basic materials of such sciences consist of intuitive generalities which are presented as empirical laws, and, as Ravetz puts it, 'insecure speculations masquerading as fundamental explanations'. A third characteristic is the instability of achievement: instead of a steady accumulation of new facts, there is a succession of 'leading schools', each moving from manifesto to obscurity. A fourth characteristic, by contrast, is the sinister stability of the founding-fathers: the classics of the social sciences do not become obsolete in teaching: thus psychologists still study Freud and Adler, and the most influential voice among sociology students is still Max Weber – by comparison, the study of history can claim to be much more 'scientific'.

Immature sciences attempt to bolster up their self-esteem by seizing eagerly on any scientific instrumentation they can possibly use. Hence the fondness among social scientists for the computer, and for the elaborate tables and graphs which can be compiled with its assistance. But this weakness in methods of inquiry helps to perpetuate ineffectiveness, since the mechanism for processing 'results', and the degree of quality control, cannot obviously be stronger than the materials they are given. Worse, for social and academic reasons it is usually necessary to give the accolade of publication to innumerable sets of results, and propositions built on them; so the professional journals are useless in creating workable standards of quality. In psychology, for example, it is notorious that 'results' used to confirm hypotheses are often no better than random data because significance tests would validate almost anything. Sociology is often no better; indeed, both these 'disciplines' usually fail Popper's falsification test since their custom is to look only for evidence which validates theory.

It may be that an immature science could progress into a mature one. After all, all valid sciences have had to advance from the stage of myth by applying increasing rigour of proof. But the trouble with these weak sciences is that they feel they have to stand comparison with established ones. They cannot publicly debate their immaturity, or even admit it at all, without disastrous loss of academic status. Both sociology and psychology already have armies of ferocious academic enemies, who would like to see them expelled from the campus. Yet by pretending to be mature, they aggravate their problem. They may lose their moral sense, keep the real state of their discipline a shameful secret, and so become prey to every conceivable kind of blackmail and charlatanism. Worse still, such sciences are tempted to legitimize themselves by taking on practical work. This has been particularly true of sociology, which has tried to conceal doubts about its shaky theoretical foundations by embarking on a stupendous mass of field work. The result has been a mass-production of graduates, and their unleashing on defenceless populations, whether as part of domestic welfare programmes or (as in the case of the United States and Vietnam) as part of foreign and military policy. We shall come to the woeful public consequences of this policy later; for the moment, we simply note that this forced academic growth leads to an inevitable collapse of quality-control. These disciplines, then, tend to remain at the level of cliché-sciences. As Ravetz puts it: '. . . the genuine insights at their base, which may well be valuable in the education of students whose previous experience is utterly foreign to the area of inquiry, become reduced to clichés as teachers and researchers in the field rub them together in an attempt to produce a plausible facsimile of scientific argument.' This is one unanswerable reason why neither psychology nor sociology, still less a combination of both, is a safe basis for social engineering, or any form of executive action.

Of course, where science comes under political control, not only will pseudo-science and cliché-science flourish, but there is a risk that genuine sciences will be reduced to the level of what Ravetz calls 'folk-science' – that is, science which seems to 'fit in' to the non-scientific conceptions of the political elite. In the Soviet Union, for instance, there can be no doubt that scientists are obliged to work within an ideological framework, according to basic guidelines laid down as long ago as 1930, in an editorial printed in *Natural Science and Marxism*: 'Philosophy and the natural and mathematical sciences are just as politically partisan as the economic and historical sciences.' It is a basic assumption of the state ideology, dialectical materialism, that explanations of nature and natural events must be based on the sole existence of matter or matter-energy. Hence the Soviet scientist is under pressure to explain the unknown in terms of materialistic knowns, which may be quite inadequate. And, as we have noted, materialism, like its denial, is a philosophical position which can neither be proved nor disproved in any strict sense. Hence, Soviet scientists have been obliged to create intellectual *schema* within the prevailing dialectical materialism, rather as innovatory schoolmen of the fourteenth century operated within the Thomist–Aristotelian system. According to Loren R. Graham, in *Science and Philosophy in the Soviet Union*, 'There is even a category of Soviet philosophers and scientists who take their dialectical materialism so seriously that they refuse to accept the official statements of the CP on the subject; they strive to develop their own dialectical materialist interpretation of nature, using highly technical articles as screens against the censors.' All Soviet scientists are familiar with the relevant texts, and know the rules of the game. The best can thus minimize the dangers to their work of political control, but they cannot prevent theory being debated in an ideological context. Since 1945, this has happened, in the physical sciences, with the problem of causality, the role of the observer in measurement, the concept of complementality, the nature of space and time, the origin and structure of the universe, and the roles of models in scientific explanation; in the biological sciences it has embraced the origins of life, the nature of evolution and the problem of reductionism; in physiology and psychology, the nature of consciousness, the question of determinism and frce-will, the mind-body problem and the validity of materialism in the approach to psychology; in cybernetics, the nature of information, the universality of the cybernetic approach, and the potentiality of computers. This list, compiled by Loren Graham, indicates the extent to which major scientific issues in Russia must be approached with political limitations in mind. In some cases, as for instance the discussion on quantum mechanics in 1947 and later, the debate was profoundly influenced by dialectical materialism.

Oddly enough, Soviet political nostrums had little to do with the Lysenko Affair, the best-known fiasco of Communist science. But the rise and triumph of Lysenko is evidence of a more profound failing of doctrinaire science – the fact that the imposition of political controls makes it much harder, or even impossible, for ordinary scientific quality controls to detect fraud. Lysenko was a classical example of the pseudo- or folk-scientist. Defending one of his scientifically invalid propositions, he said: 'It would be against the great laws of organic life if members of the same species competed with one another, and did not help one another . . . nothing is worthy of being called true science unless it exhibits the great underlying order of the cosmos in general.' This is not, strictly speaking, dialectical materialism at all; it is much closer to orthodox Russian theology, with God left out; or peasant-lore. Lysenko moved on the same plane of intelligence as Teilhard de Chardin, and it is interesting that both these mountebanks were able to flourish, for a time, in the twentieth century, one in a closed, the other in an open society. The Marxists can point out, in their defence, that Lysenkoism is now dead, whereas the Tcilhardists still preach in the West; the West can reply that at least Father Teilhard was never entrusted with public policy, and it is true that folk-science cannot, as a rule, acquire official status in free countries where objective scientific quality controls operate. It is impossible to imagine a western democracy embracing the various forms of folk-science which dominated the Chinese 'Cultural Revolution', from back-garden blast-furnaces, an endearing but impracticable idea, to the abolition of western-style academic research, and the substitution of acupuncture for standard medical practice.

On the other hand, western governments make constant use of pseudo-science and immature sciences, and sometimes accord them the status of a folk-science. Agreed economic theory is notoriously unreliable, and its statistics full of every conceivable trap, but both are commonly used to determine not the minimal, inescapable decisions of government but ambitious exercises in national planning. Ravetz compares government economists and Treasury officials to witchdoctors urging choices on a tribal king. Then, too, governments employ futurologists, who are little better than astrologers, and (at any rate in the 1950s and 1960s) academic experts in nuclear strategy, a new kind of military wizard or soothsayer. Sociology has become the folk-science of liberal reformers and it is hurled into action whenever they get their hands on power, and on every conceivable 'problem'. As one leading American quantitative sociologist puts it: 'There's nothing in any day's issue of the *New York Times* that doesn't belong in the field of sociology.' At various levels, too, psychology and sociology have become the pop-science, or folk-science, of the western urban masses. A young woman, interviewed in New York during a rape-outbreak, and asked if she was frightened, replied: 'Yes, and I only hope I'm on the right side of the statistics.' But was she any more scientific than the justices of the US Supreme Court, who employ sociological arguments for their rulings on such central issues as racially segregated schools?

It is right that great reliance should be placed on true science to take the lead in that pursuit of truth which is both the object of civilization and its best defence against its enemies. And it is fortunate that we have easily understood tests to distinguish between valid science and its proliferating imitations and perversions. Everyone should know how to conduct these tests. But the main work of monitoring must, of course, lie with the higher seats of learning. In the last resort, the health of a civilization is no better, and no worse, than the health of its universities.

CHAPTER 12

Ivory Tower
or Knowledge Factory?

The prime function of a university in society is to serve as the monitor and custodian of its culture. In his *The Idea of a University*, John Henry Newman characterized it in a noble sentence as 'the high protecting power of all knowledge and science, of fact and principle, of inquiry and discovery, of experiment and speculation; it maps out the territory of the intellect, and sees that . . . there is neither encroachment nor surrender on any side.' But precisely because the university has this central role in guiding the intellectual movement of society, it has a multitude of eager enemies, anxious to appropriate it and pervert its powers for their own sordid or immoral purposes. The danger was noted over three hundred years ago by Thomas Hobbes, in the last section of his *Leviathan* (1651): 'For seeing the universities are the fountains of civil and moral doctrine, from whence the preachers and the gentry, drawing such water as they find, use to sprinkle the same upon the people, there ought certainly to be great care taken to have it pure, both from the venom of heathen politicians and from the incantation of deceiving spirits.'

'Heathen politicians' have always kept a close eye on the universities; and dons, alas, have never been backward in seeking political masters to serve. From their twelfth-century inception universities have responded avidly when princes and pontiffs sought their help. Oxford itself owes its origin to the dispute between Henry II and Archbishop Becket; the infant Bologna sought to arbitrate between the popes and the Hohenstaufen, as did Paris between Plantagenet and Capet – helping to burn Joan of Arc in the process; Prague from its earliest days was a partisan in the religious struggles of Bohemia; and all the universities of Christendom busied themselves in Henry VIII's marital difficulties. No one who troubles to read the accounts of Tudor royal 'progresses' to Oxbridge can have any doubt that the ancient universities were entirely at the beck of the government. Heads of houses owed everything to royal favour, and grovelled accordingly. The first universities in the United States were nominally independent, but in practice they were closely linked to civic purposes, and expected to play a dutiful role in strengthening the approved characteristics of the society around them. In France and Germany universities openly served the purposes of the state.

Like many other good things, academic autonomy was essentially a nineteenth-century invention. In Britain, for instance, the Victorian solution was to resurrect the parliamentary statute as a last-resort method of control and reform, but otherwise to let the universities get on with the pursuit of excellence, and the training of elites, in their own way. When public funds were first made available for university development, two great liberal statesmen, Lord Haldane and H. A. L. Fisher, were at great pains to lay down principles to ensure that the universities were protected from political pressures. These eventually crystallized into six basic freedoms, which guaranteed universities the right to select their own students, appoint their own staff, control their syllabuses and degree standards, determine their own size and rate of growth, fix their own balance between teaching and research, and decide themselves how government money should be spent.

Unfortunately, as in the past, those who run universities itch for a wider role. Pedagogues tend to indulge in a recurrent fantasy in which they not only instruct the young but rule the world; inside most dons a benevolent despot is struggling to get out. What may be termed academic triumphalism takes many forms: in the Middle Ages and the Renaissance, the triumphalists proclaimed that their caste alone could authoritatively interpret the law of God and nations; now the emphasis has switched to the university as the progenitor of power and wealth – the brain behind the GNP. This new phase was born in the great Allied research programmes of the Second World War (notably the Manhattan Project), gathered pace during the 1950s and came to a resounding climax in the 1960s. It was adumbrated a generation earlier by the late-Victorian scientific professoriate, imbued with Darwinian survival-of-the-fittest nationalism, who saw in embryonic university technology the key to world power. Alfred Whitehead, writing in 1916, warned: 'In conditions of modern life, the rule is absolute: the race which does not value trained intelligence is doomed . . . there will be no appeal from the judgement which will be pronounced on the uneducated.'

The tone of the argument was set in the late 1950s by C. P. Snow, who urged that it was Britain's neglect of higher education – both in quantity, in terms of the total output of graduates, and in quality, by an undue bias towards the arts at the expense of science and technology – which chiefly explained her poor economic performance and her geopolitical decline. By contrast, he added, it was the United States' unprecedented investment in universities which had made her the world's first superpower. Now, two decades later, there is a good deal of scepticism about the evidence behind Snow's basic assertions. As long ago as 1970, for instance, the Organization for Economic Cooperation and Development reported that the United Kingdom, compared with other west European countries, Canada, the United States and Japan, had (in 1964) 'the greatest concentration on science and technology in higher education and the biggest proportion of qualified scientists and technologists (graduates, diploma- and certificate-holders) in relation to population and labour-force' – the exact opposite of the conventional Snovian thesis. But at the time, Snow's *The Two Cultures and the Scientific Revolution* (1959) quickly received statistical underpinning on both sides of the Atlantic. In Britain, the Robbins Report of 1963 produced a staggering mass of figures to show the reserves of brainpower waiting to be tapped by new and expanded universities, and so ultimately (it was argued) turned into higher production and increased productivity. The year before, Edward F. Denison, of the US Committee for Economic Development, published *Sources of Economic Growth in the United States*, showing that in the thirty years up to 1960, half of US economic growth had been due to the expansion of the education system, above all to the multiplication of universities. It was generally assumed that this trend would continue and reinforce itself. The same year, 1962, Fritz Machlup, in *The Production and Distribution of Knowledge in the United States*, calculated that production, distribution and consumption of knowledge accounted for 29% of the US Gross National Product, and that the 'knowledge industry' was growing at twice the rate of the rest of the economy.

In this triumphalist atmosphere, academic *exaltés* saw the universities not merely as harbingers of progress but as its central dynamic. A typical grandee of the period, Clark Kerr of Berkeley, devoted the 1963 Godkin

Lectures at Harvard to showing how the campus was taking over the leadership of society. 'Knowledge' was now 'the most powerful single element in our culture, affecting the rise and fall of professions and even of social classes, or regions and even of nations'. Hence 'what the railroads did for the second half of the last century and the automobile for the first half of this century may be done for the second half of this century by the knowledge industry: that is, to serve as the focal point for national growth'. Kerr claimed that the siting of universities now determined the shape of conurbations, the planning of new motorway systems and the physical spread of industrial development. Trade no longer followed the flag, but the mortarboard. He based what he called 'the rise of Ideopolis' on the maxim that 'university centres have a tendency to coalesce'. In advanced societies, the campus dominated economic geography: hence the galaxy of star universities which formed the vertebrae of the super-technological East Coast, or the glittering necklace of research institutes which adorned western California and caused a dazzled C. P. Snow to exclaim: 'There is nothing like this concentration of talent anywhere in the world!'

University expansion was linked not merely with a bigger GNP but with a reinforcement of democratic freedom. The 'wave of the future', Kerr thought, was likely to be 'middle class democracy . . . with all its freedoms', since the campus of the West, with its 'better use of intellect in all intellect's many dimensions' would prove far more efficient in promoting growth than the 'dictatorship of the proletariat'. Investment in the university would create not only wealth beyond the dreams of avarice but military security and political stability.

Hence during the 1960s, most western nations doubled or even trebled their university places, Britain for once being among the foremost in setting the trend. It is true that Lord Robbins, chairman of the committee whose recommendations recast the higher education system, later testily claimed in his autobiography that he never fell for the central fallacy of academic triumphalism: 'I cannot believe that it is at all convincing to attempt to establish crude correlations between higher educational statistics and the GNP.' But he was sure that 'in general, society is likely to be more efficient, more progressive, more humane, the larger the proportion of people who have the opportunity of developing their intelligence in this way'. Moreover, since 'elsewhere in the modern world public policy is based on these assumptions', he felt that 'we should have to be very sure indeed of the contrary before we took the risk of not doing likewise.' This shaky argument, of the type which convinced the rear echelons of the Gadarene swine, carried the day. In any case, as Robbins noted, the real impulse towards gigantism came from the universities themselves. When he put his diagnosis to them he found they 'responded with suggestions for expansion far exceeding anything that had been suggested to us in evidence'.

As a result, higher education joined electronics and natural gas as Britain's leading growth industries during the 1960s; twenty new universities and thirty polytechnics were opened; the number of students and the budget both more than doubled; educational expansion, led by the universities, turned the pedagogue into a new mass-element in the population, planned by 1981 to number around two million, 8% of the entire employed population. These figures were paralleled, or even exceeded, in all the advanced democratic states. Where, one wondered, would the Snovian afflatus end?

As a matter of fact there was a loud hiss of escaping air even while the expansion was still gaining force. The spring of 1968 marked the beginning of massed student revolts, first in France and the United States, later all over the world. These outbreaks were first greeted with a degree of approval, but as they persisted and revealed their essentially destructive and irrational nature, public opinion swung against the student community and with it against the whole idea of university expansion without limit. Rioting and disruption devalued the appeal of university, not least among working-class aspirants and their parents. The growth of equality of opportunity in higher education, by bringing graduates into more plentiful supply, strengthened already strong tendencies to equalize earned incomes. By the early 1970s, the Confederation of British Industry, for instance, calculated that the average graduate would be thirty-five before he equalled the earning-power of the manual labourer. Similar figures emerged in France and West Germany. Moreover, the production of more sophisticated figures showed that some at least of the statistical evidence on which the expansion was based had been misinterpreted, as we have already noted. On a world scale, the university afflatus of the 1960s and early 1970s was followed by the worst economic depression for forty years. What, then, became of the supposed link between the numbers of graduates and the size of the GNP? Britain's example seemed even more destructive of the theory, since despite her huge efforts to expand university output, her economic decline continued and accelerated. Thus university education was shown to be index-linked neither to the GNP nor individual earnings. What, then, was the point of it?

At the same time, more detailed efforts at graduate manpower-planning were shown to be misleading and sometimes positively disastrous. France found herself with a huge surplus of graduates, especially in the social sciences, during the 1970s. Most western countries proved unable to provide the right number of doctors, supposedly the profession most susceptible to accurate manpower projections. Of course, such 'planning' is based on demographic projections (as well as economic ones), which notoriously bring the best statisticians to grief. Thus the British planners grotesquely overestimated the number of teachers required; in this field, all the experts were hopelessly confounded by events over quite a short period, and confident ministerial estimates were proved inaccurate by factors of 50% or more; by the mid-1970s, Britain was shutting down surplus Colleges of Education while still building new ones.

The final blow was the revolution in the price of oil in the winter of 1973, and the cuts in public expenditure which followed. If academic triumphalism was undermined by hirsute students, it was finally demolished by oleaginous sheiks. All over the world, plans to expand higher education were ruthlessly revised and scaled down. In America, the 1973 *Final Report* of the Carnegie Commission on Higher Education recorded a general loss of public confidence in higher education, the failure of the economy to absorb even the present output of graduates, a drying-up of private donations, and a tendency of universities to assume what it termed 'a stationary state'. It concluded: 'Higher education has moved from genteel poverty to genteel poverty in one generation.' In Britain, the 1970 projection of a rise to 900,000 or even one million places in higher education was revised downwards to 640,000 (end-1974) and subsequently to 600,000 and then to 550,000. In Australia, plans for three new universities were simply cancelled. Agnosticism towards higher education became one feature of a general belief that research and development was a grossly overrated form of national investment. Everywhere, the number of unfilled places in science and technology faculties rose sharply. The proportion of GNP flowing into research dropped in every OECD country, and the head of the organization's science policy division, Jean-Jacques Salomon, declared the 'golden age of R & D' to be 'over for good'.

The rise of academic triumphalism damaged the university ethic because it devalued its sense of intellectual individualism, and flew in the face of Newman's wise observation: 'A university is an *alma mater*, knowing her children one by one, not a foundry, or a mint, or a treadmill.' Unfortunately, the new and malignant forces which triumphalism conjured up outlived its downfall, and the damage threatens to be permanent. Despite the demonstration during the last decade that the universities cannot help governments, to anything like the degree that had been claimed, in their pursuit of economic and political objectives, the 'heathen politicians' show no inclination to abandon their attempt to control academic strategies. In France, for instance, the year 1976 saw the beginning of a wide-ranging government plan to bring university curricula into line with what it conceived to be its needs for science and technology graduates. The logic behind the plan, which met with fierce resistance from dons and students, was that the government, rather than the universities, was the right agency to decide how many students were accepted by which faculties, together with what they should be taught. Academics were to become mere *fonctionnaires* of the state, as *lycée* teachers had long been.

In Britain, the process of government take-over has been less spectacular, but the University Grants Committee, the quasi-governmental body which distributes state cash, has steadily encroached on university autonomy, not least by imposing forms of accountancy which reflect the government's desire to produce the maximum number of graduates at the lowest possible unit-cost. Announcing, for instance, the 1975–6 grants, the UGC issued an unblushing warning that universities with slow growth-rates would in future receive less money. Most of the six freedoms once guaranteed to the universities have been eroded; and a senior Ministry of Education official has asked openly 'whether the government could continue to debar itself from what has been termed "the secret garden" of the curriculum'. 'It simply will not do,' snapped one of the education ministers in 1975, 'to allow universities and polytechnics to recruit whatever people they fancy'; the universities should become 'less research-intensive' and their research (if any) should be 'geared' to 'economic and social needs'. The universities, he added, were too 'elitist', and paid far too much attention to the more brilliant pupils, especially those educated to the age of eighteen with good examination results; instead there should be a 'fundamental shift' to 'less exacting' courses for sixteen-year-olds.

'Elitist', of course, is now one of the prime hate-words in the Vulgar

Marxist vocabulary, and government pressure on universities in France, Britain and elsewhere to become more 'populist' and 'relevant' undoubtedly coincides with the Marxist aim to destroy the traditional university as an independent centre of freedom, and drag it bodily into the system of state-planned education. The Marxists welcomed the post-1973 financial crisis because, as one of them, Martin Jacques, put it in *Marxism Today*, 'The state has begun to subject the university sector to much greater pressure which, though taking a largely financial form, seems designed to effect major changes in the nature of the sector.' The direction these changes should take was set out in 1968 in a remarkable study of 'anti-elitist planning', *The New Polytechnics*, by Eric Robinson, a leading Labour Party 'adviser' on education:

> Sooner or later, this country must face a comprehensive reform of education beyond school – a reform which will bring higher education out of the ivory towers and make it available for all. This will be achieved through a bloodier battle than that for the comprehensive reform of secondary education . . . the process of narrowing the gap between the haves and the have-nots will, for reasons of economic necessity, mean that there must be some levelling down of the haves as well as levelling up of the have-nots.

He went on to demand 'draconian measures against the universities, to bring them under direct government control', to 'compel them' to put teaching before research, and to 'force them' into 'closer association' with other institutions already controlled by political forces.

This assault by government from without on university autonomy and standards of excellence has become all the more formidable in that it coincides with the aims of the fifth column within the university perimeter: the new student Fascist Left. Clark Kerr, in extolling 'Ideopolis', had foolishly supposed that, by expanding student numbers, the forces of reason and freedom would thereby be strengthened. In fact the very opposite happened, as might have been foreseen by Kerr's accompanying characterization of the university as the key part of 'the knowledge industry'. For, if knowledge were to be 'industrialized' and the university turned into a 'knowledge factory' related to 'output' and the GNP, then it followed its internal relationships would cease to be primarily academic, that is hierarchical, and would become industrial and based on class-conflict. As a knowledge factory, the university ceased to be an *alma mater* and became a kind of employer. The huge increase in numbers greatly assisted this shift towards industrialization, and a parody of union-management conflict. Worst of all, as the greatest beneficiaries of the expansion were the social sciences, especially sociology, it created cadres in every university whose training, such as it is, makes them peculiarly fitted to lead student agitation. For a great deal of contemporary sociology is precisely the offspring of the marriage between the pseudo-science of Marxism, and the pseudo-science of Freudianism, which produced the writings of Herbert Marcuse; and it was only natural, therefore, that Marcuse became the tutelary deity of the student Fascist Left. Everywhere the sociology students, bred in the so-called 'discipline' nurtured by the union of two irrational philosophies, assumed the leadership of the student unions. Freudianism is a throwback to pre-scientific myth descriptions of mysterious natural phenomena; Marxism is a system of quasi-religious prophecy. Both, though rationally quite unsound, have undoubtedly insights which prove useful in the management of people; and Marxism, in addition, has a methodology of power-seeking. The combination is almost uniquely qualified to produce twentieth-century witchdoctors, using the language of modern technology but in reality playing on some of the deepest and darkest human emotions. Here, then, was the second evil force Hobbes warned against – 'the incantation of evil spirits'.

The activities of the student Fascist Left at universities all over the free world have been often described but rarely understood. Externally, they are summed up by the greeting to new students in the *Handbook* published by the students' union at the North London Polytechnic, at the opening of the 1975–6 academic year: 'If you get a kick out of street-fighting and agitation, then you've certainly come to the right place.' Seen from the inside, however, the object is not random violence but a carefully thought-out plan to destroy the academic standards and the autonomous freedom of the University. The way in which the plan operates has been variously set out in booklets sold or distributed to incoming students. In one version, *Student Power*, edited by Robin Blackburn and Alexander Cockburn, the object is stated plainly:

... to turn the tables on the system by using the universities and colleges as base-areas from which to undermine key institutions of the social order. No advanced capitalist state can afford to maintain a permanent police occupation of all colleges and universities, nor can it act like a Latin-American military thug and simply close down the universities, which after all are necessary in the long run to the productive process. So long as the universities and colleges provide some sort of space which cannot be permanently policed, they can become red bases of revolutionary agitation and preparation.

The same volume provides a practical blueprint, 'Campaigning on the Campus', written by Carl Davidson. The activists, he advises, should first capture the 'internal media', including all meetings; then they should hold lecture-series, to 'de-sanctify and de-legitimise the authority of the institution'; union funds should be taken over for political purposes. Next, they should begin 'encroaching control' by gradually taking over direction of the form and content of the academic syllabus and staff appointments; they should persuade the staff to move against the administration, or at least to remain neutral when it is attacked. He adds: 'Criticise classes in the classroom. Constantly criticise course-structure, content, class sizes, the educational system and corporate capitalism. . . . Ultimately we have access to only one source of power within the knowledge factory. And that power lies in our potential ability to stop the university from functioning . . .' The object, in fact, is not reform but destruction. Indeed, the Fascist Left ideology assumes that the characteristics of the university – the use of reason and logic, the insistence on absolute standards of scientific proof – are themselves evils to be overthrown. We have already met the same irrational hatred of objective knowledge in Marcuse's theories. The point was made with naïve bluntness by a student leader at Essex: 'Reason is an ideological weapon with which bourgeois academics are especially well armed.' Another student leader, at Kent, added: 'There is no one truth in which the university can educate us. We have to find our own version of the truth for ourselves, and what may be true for one person may well be untrue for another.' Here, as we noted when discussing language, is an example of the way in which an essential word like 'truth' is de-gutted of meaning and turned into an empty carapace. For the student Fascist Left, truth is indivisible, but some truths are more divisible than others.

Such a view, of course, makes the university itself superfluous, and indeed once it has been taken over it has only a small part to play in the future plans of the Left. But for the moment, attention is focused on what it teaches, and here the student agitators have powerful allies among the academics. Thus Steven Rose, professor of biology in the Open University, writes: 'Scientists must understand and struggle against the undemocratic nature of science as an institution (its hier-archy – all power to the professors; its elitism – all power to the experts; its sexism – all power to the men; and its racism – all power to Western modes of thought).' Another prime object is to destroy any examination system based on what is termed 'conventional knowledge'. Hence,

Knowledge and Control, edited by Michael F. D. Young, notes: 'One can
. . . see . . . research possibilities . . . which might examine . . . the
process of negotiation between examiners and students about what
counts as a "sound answer".'

One of the objects of destroying the 'conventional' examination
system is to control the awarding of degrees, and especially of first-class
honours degrees, so that the Fascist Left can get its own members into
academic positions of power. The number of these donnish supporters,
or 'aggro-dons', is growing constantly. They are not, as yet, numerous
enough or well-organized enough to topple the system of higher education
unaided. But they are helped by the indifference or cowardice of many
academics who normally have no sympathy with the aims of the Left.
It is not always fair to blame the 'neutral' dons, since one of the tactics
of the Fascist Left is to mount campaigns of virulent personal abuse, in
leaflets, student magazines, posters and so forth, against any members
of the staff who offer them the slightest opposition. In nearly every case
the accusations they hurl are complete fabrications; but, as with the
Goebbels 'big lie', they are often half-believed, and a distinguished
academic can have his reputation permanently muddied in consequence.

Then, too, there are many in higher education and politics who drift
with what they imagine to be the progressive tide simply because they
do not wish to be classified, however mistakenly, as 'anti-student'. All
over the world, some of the key decisions which have played straight
into the hands of the agitational Left have been taken by Centre or even
Right-wing politicians. This is particularly true of France and Britain.
In Britain, for instance, it was Shirley Williams, the Right-wing Labour
Minister of State for Higher Education, who forced through the decision
to grant student activists a much higher percentage of places on the
governing bodies of polytechnics, which enabled the aggro-Fascists to
wreck several of them. It was Edward Short, the Right-wing deputy
leader of the Labour Party, who threw the weight of the Ministry of
Education behind the view that student disruption was caused by
excessively severe rules (a view disproved by the example of North
London Polytechnic, the worst case of all, where the disruption programme was drawn up before the new institution came into existence, or
anyone knew what the rules were). Again, it was Margaret Thatcher,
later to become the Right-wing leader of the Conservative Party, who, in
the winter of 1970–1, changed the wording of the official regulations to
allow public money to be handed over to the Student Unions, and thus

to finance the campaign of disruption. The road to student revolution has been paved with the good intentions of moderate- or even conservative-minded people anxious to be trendy.

The second half of the 1970s has, it is true, seen the beginnings of a powerful reaction against the trends we have just examined. Many university presidents and vice-chancellors are now openly and vociferously opposed to government direction, even if they can only rid themselves of it by accepting less cash and curtailing expansion programmes. There is, too, a move against bigness among academics, and a new determination that authority in the university must be protected from intrusion both by the 'heathen politicians' and by the 'deceiving spirits' of the student Left. The latest study of the subject, Graeme C. Moodie and Rowland Eustace's *Power and Authority in British Universities* takes the elitist (or what they call the 'republican') line that power should be diffused among varying groups of experts: 'Decisions on any issue should be taken by those who know most about it. . . . The supreme authority, provided it is exercised in ways responsive to others, must . . . continue to rest with the academics.' This view is now the prevailing one on both sides of the Atlantic, and there is evidence that it is shared by a substantial proportion of the students themselves.

The observable trends, therefore, appear to be moving, just perceptibly, back in the direction of reason and truth. The tragedy, though, is that at a time when the university should have been concentrating on its chief task of monitoring and guiding our culture it has had to fight a desperate defensive battle to protect its very existence. The battle is by no means over, but it will have served a positive purpose if it persuades a sufficient number of academics that they cannot abdicate from the power struggle which is engulfing our civilization. It may, indeed, seem strange for them to regard themselves as in the front line. But in a sense this has always been part of their role. It seems strange, too, to discuss academia in terms of military analogy. But the comparison has already been forced upon us by the university's enemies. One thing is clear: if the university now stands in the front line of civilization, it is urgent to point out that this defensive work should not be a Maginot Line, lost for ever once penetrated. It should, on the contrary, constitute a defence in depth: every kind and variety of institution where higher education is available, while linked indeed in one huge defensive confraternity, should each pursue, within wide limits, its own self-determined course. The independence and autonomy of each separate university and college, each controlled by its academic elites, is the best fighting posture for academia to adopt today. One is reminded of the sixteenth-century image of John Foxe, who referred to every printing-press in the country as a 'block-house against the enemies of truth and reason'. So, too, the university today is not an ivory tower, but a real one; the prime need is to keep its independent walls in constant repair, and above all to ensure that it is not betrayed from within.

But preserving the autonomous university as a fortress of truth and reason is not enough. Dons are quick to point out that the habits of mind of the men and women they receive are already, to a great extent, formed – or malformed – before they set foot on the campus. As a moulder of culture the university cannot be protected in isolation from the schools. And it is in the schools that the enemies of civilization are now mounting an attack of great ferocity.

CHAPTER 13

Schools for Attilas

One of the lessons driven home by the phenomenon of student aggression against the university system is the close connection between arguments over education and arguments over ethics. Like the followers of most quasi-religious ideologies, the aggro-students have never doubted that the end justifies any means employed, or hesitated to employ lies, violence and theft (of student funds) to promote their political objectives within the university system. The Marxist–Freudianism which forms the prevailing religion of the many Western students exercises a powerful emotional appeal to the young. What concerns the university authorities is that schoolchildren arriving on campus to begin their university career are subjected to the ceaseless attentions of the proselytes of this new secular religion, and lack sufficient training in ethics to examine its claims critically. They are more worried, that is, by the quality of the moral background provided in the schools than by their academic proficiency – which in many respects is higher than ever before.

Nor are dons the only people who worry about ethical and moral teaching in state schools. So does everyone else, not least schoolteachers. The problem is not exactly new. For two centuries, ever since the foundation of the United States, American educationalists have been debating what moral system ought to be taught in their schools. Some American colonies were founded for religious purposes; and their first schools were built to further these purposes. But the United States itself was created as a secular, non-denominational federation; and its public schools were, *ab initio* and almost by definition, non-sectarian. But should this mean they were non-religious, that is non-Christian? Not at all, replied Horace Mann, who effectively created the American state school in the early nineteenth century. He favoured religious instruction 'to the extremest verge to which it can be carried without invading those rights of conscience which are established by the laws of God and guaranteed by the constitution of the state'. Thus the US schools got non-denominational religion, that is a kind of generalized Protestantism, based on the Bible. Mann's twelfth and final report on the public schools movement stated: 'That our public schools are not theological seminaries is admitted. . . . But our system earnestly inculcates all Christian morals; it founds its morals on the basis of religion; it welcomes the religion of the Bible, it allows it to do what it is allowed to do in no other system, *to speak for itself.*'

Hence in America, the teaching of religion in schools was treated as primarily a moral business – as opposed to a doctrinal one – directed to 'character training'. The sectarian trimmings were supplied at home, and this gradually allowed Jews and Catholics to avail themselves of the public school system for their children. Gradually, too, the religious element was first reduced, then eliminated, as illogical. As the Presbyterian educationalist Samuel T. Spear put it in 1870: 'The state, being democratic in its constitution, and consequently having no religion to which it does or can give any legal sanction, should not and cannot, except by manifest inconsistency, introduce either religious or irreligious teaching into a system of popular education which it authorizes, enforces and for the support of which it taxes all the people in common.' However, he added, there must be *some* spiritual foundation; and since the state was not Christian but republican, then republicanism should constitute it. This view prevailed, and in time the American way of life functioned as the operative moral creed of US state schools. Horace Mann Kallen, writing on 'Democracy's True Religion' in the *Saturday Review* (July 1951), sets out the official philosophy: 'For the communicants of the democratic faith, it is the religion *of* and *for* religion. For, being the religion of religions, all may freely come together in it.' The point is made even more strongly by a leading religious teacher, J. Paul Williams, in *What Americans Believe and How they Worship*:

Americans must come to look upon the democratic ideal . . . as the Will of God, or if they please, of Nature . . . Americans must be brought to the conviction that democracy is the very Law of Life . . . government agencies must teach the democratic idea as *religion*. . . . Primarily responsibility for teaching democracy might be given to the public school. . . . The churches deal effectively with but half the population; the government deals with all the population. . . . It is a misconception to equate separation of church and state with separation of religion and state.

This approach has been generally adopted in the United States, and variations of it are to be found in state schools run by democracies all over the world. But it is open to the objection that it confuses religion and politics, and in particular associates morality with a particular ideology. This, indeed, is to play straight into the hands of the Vulgar Marxists, who teach that all systems of ethics or morals are derived from political and economic postulates and are therefore inseparable from the ideological form of society. As Mao Tse-tung puts it: 'In every society everyone lives as a member of a particular class, and every kind of thinking, without exception, is stamped with the brand of a class.' Morals, therefore, depend upon the class perspective, and are to be taught accordingly. Lenin argued that many virtuous concepts which we tend to treat as moral absolutes are merely class assumptions. Hence:

Freedom is a bourgeois prejudice. We repudiate all morality which proceeds from supernatural ideas or ideas which are outside the class conception. In our opinion, morality is entirely subordinate to the interests of the class war. Everything is moral which is necessary for the annihilation of the old exploiting order and for uniting the proletariat. Our morality consists solely in close discipline and conscious warfare against the exploiters.

In theory at any rate, Lenin preached the intrinsic moral righteousness of the working class, and gave this fantasy its classic formulation in *State and Revolution*: 'Freed from capitalist slavery, from the untold horrors, savagery, absurdities and infamies of capitalist exploitation, people will gradually *become accustomed* to observing the elementary rules of social intercourse.' Whether he really believed this is to be doubted; even in the same book he admits the need to maintain 'the *strictest* control by *society and by the state*' so long as the 'ordinary run of people, who like seminary students in Pomyalovsky's stories, are capable of damaging the stocks of public wealth "just for fun" and of demanding the impossible'. It is interesting that Lenin should regard seminary students as archetypes of anti-social behaviour; and very characteristic that, when in doubt, he urged the greatest possible moral severity. Certainly, the society he created, and its imitations or replicas imposed elsewhere, teaches and enforces the strictest Victorian standards on its citizens; moral relativism is permitted only to the state and its rulers, moral absolutes being retained for the emancipated proletariat. And in all essentials, these moral absolutes, universally taught in all Vulgar Marxist states, are based on the Ten Commandments. The system, therefore, is unsuccessful because it is inconsistent; the moral injunctions, religious in origin, conflict with the denial of God, and the citizen knows that the theoretical and actual behaviour of the state is in violent and perpetual conflict with the behaviour it commands of him.

Even in modern secular society, in fact, it is very difficult to escape from the mesh of the Mosaic Law, at any rate if you insist on absolutes. Some have argued that secular and absolute moral codes can be derived from scientific standards of conduct. Thus in *Science and Human Values* Jacob Bronowski thought that a system could be built up around the virtues of independence, tolerance, freedom of speech, and so forth, which scientists practise in their work. He argued that the scientific code was a good one because such virtues were professionally necessary – they 'have grown out of the practice of science because they are the inescapable conditions of its practice'. A great many scientists would accept this. Some would go further, like Ernest Nagel: '. . . . the organisation of science as a community of free, tolerant, yet alert critical inquirers embodies in a remarkable measure the ideals of a liberal civilisation' ('The Place of Science in a Liberal Education', *Daedalus*, 1959). But many other scientists (and most non-scientists) are more sceptical. They point to the achievements of Nazi and Soviet science, which refute the view that liberal virtues are the 'inescapable condition' of professional practice. They point, too, to the kind of moral behaviour among western scientists, as revealed by *The Double Helix* and similar recent glimpses within the ivory tower. In any case, the kind of virtues which Bronowski lists are not necessarily scientific, and have been taught for a very long time in the best liberal academies; classicists would claim them as Graeco-Roman, with as much (or as little) justice.

The dominant modern tendency is not to search for absolute moral standards at all, but to insist that all codes are relative and subjective. A. J. Ayer argues strongly in *Language, Truth and Logic* that moral judgements are incapable of rational or objectively valid justification, and are purely emotional. There have been innumerable attempts to show that moral codes evolve as a result of linguistic structures, geographical or racial factors (or both), or even through the dominance of certain media of communication. Among the social scientists, especially the anthropologists, there is a positive suspicion of any code which claims universal validity. The approach was epitomized by Dr Edmund Leach, Provost of King's, Cambridge, in the 1967 Reith Lectures:

Beware of moral principles. A zeal to do right leads to the segregation of saints from sinners, and the sinners can then be shut out of sight and subjected to violence. Other creatures and other people besides ourselves have a right to exist. . . . So long as we allow our perceptions to be guided by morality we shall see evil where there is none, or shining virtue even when evil is staring us in the face, but what we find impossible to see are the facts as they really are.

This anti-moral doctrine is ironic coming from the head of a college founded by an Anglican saint, and in a Lecture named after a man who created the British Broadcasting Corporation and who had inscribed on the Portland stone of its headquarters that he had 'dedicated this Temple of the Arts to Almighty God' to lead its audience 'in the paths of virtue and wisdom'. In fact Leach and Lord Reith are not so very far apart, as any undergraduate who attempted to set fire to King's College, or steal its silver, would quickly discover. Leach's point, in reality, is that being consciously moralistic is socially undesirable. But even this is open to the objection that, if moral principles are deliberately and consciously discarded, value-judgements simply become covert and unavowed.

This, indeed, is precisely what has happened among thousands of young social scientists, especially sociologists, in every advanced western country today. Most, if questioned, would agree with Leach that moral systems are relative and moral principles, regarded as absolutes, should be avoided. But most of them, in practice, are searching for a moral anchorage, and took up sociology precisely because they thought it would enable them to find one. Therein lies a contemporary tragedy. Professor Alasdair MacIntyre has made the point that young sociologists, seeking through their spurious discipline a view of the world which would orient their inner moral convictions, and give them hope in the work of social reform they want to carry out, are the same sort of people who once turned to varieties of religion and, a generation later, to the sort of German-style idealist philosophy taught by T. H. Green and his contemporaries. They are people born to believe, searching for an activist secular faith:

. . . a great many of the young coming into sociology wish for a theory of society that will legitimise belief in certain sorts of changes in social life. In fact what we have to learn from the social sciences as they now exist is how little understanding [they] can give us beyond the everyday understanding of social life that we have anyway . . . there is going to be a disillusionment with sociology just as there was a disillusionment with religion and with philosophy. We are going to see people racked with guilt because they have lost their sociological faith.

In this confused argument between absolute moral codes which no longer command the intellectual consensus, and a relativistic view of morality which in fact conceals a whole series of value-judgements, western society has tended to adopt a utilitarian approach. But as John Barnsley points out in his exhaustive treatment of the subject, *The Social Reality of Ethics: the comparative analysis of moral codes*, a utilitarian approach has an inherent defect exposed by the nagging question: 'Utility for whom?' or even *cui bono*? The Marxist 'who-whom' argument makes utilitarian morals difficult to defend unless one can feel morally satisfied with the society in which they are taught.

Indeed, utilitarian morals are particularly exposed to the kind of attacks on institutionalized society, and its moral underpinnings, mounted by the post-Marcusians of the sociological Left. They oppose not only the teaching of any set of morals or ethics in school (since such will be the morals and ethics of bourgeois society) but even the act of compelling children to go to school at all, which is itself a form of bourgeois morality. 'Childhood is a bourgeois invention,' states Ivan Illich in his book *Deschooling Society*, which emanates from a multinational pseudo-scientific workshop, established in Mexico, and called the Centre for Intercultural Documentation. Illich was trained as a Roman Catholic priest, and he epitomizes the covert value-judgements and the almost desperate but unavowed search for absolute morality which underlies fashionable moral relativism. Illich has evolved a methodology for attacking virtually all the institutions, even the most (apparently) well-meaning, of bourgeois society, though he is perhaps best known for his efforts to destroy the state system of education.

Illich's arguments are a farrago of sub-Marxist clichés, false analogies, non-sequiturs, false or bent facts and weird prophecies; and he makes abundant use of Marcuse's linguistic technique for disposing of awkward realities which do not fit in with his thesis. He also consciously misuses words, like 'pollution' and 'obscene', by adapting them to the demands of his abusive rhetoric. His language, indeed, strongly recalls the 'theological Billingsgate' of the Dark-Age Christian controversialists, with whom he has a great deal in common; and his version of *odium theologicum* makes his work painful to read. His argument is difficult to summarize, as it is neither continuous nor sticks to the point, being more a series of ejaculations. Essentially, Illich insists that we tend to confuse the substance of what we want to do with the process whereby we do it:

> Medical treatment is mistaken for health care, social work for the improvement of community life, police protection for safety, military poise for national security, the rat race for productive work. Health, learning, dignity, independence and creative endeavour are defined as little more than the performance of institutions which claim to serve these ends . . . the institutionalisation of values leads inevitably to physical pollution, social polarisation and psychological impotence: three dimensions in a process of global degradation and modernised misery.

This passage, very characteristic of Illich's preaching style, illustrates the low standard of proof he demands of himself, and his tendency to generalize himself off-balance by an endless pursuit of analogies ('public education would profit from the deschooling of society just as family life, politics, security, faith and communication would profit from an analogous process'). What he says contains an element of truth, but it is really no more than the assertion, with which all would agree, that human societies, whatever their political complexion, are better at defining agreed desirable objects than at devising the institutions to attain them. The message is not new, since Illich is essentially an old-fashioned egalitarian, angered by the almost ineradicable tendencies in nature and society to produce inequality. He wishes to extend to the schooling process the anti-elitist levelling we have already described at work in the universities; but, unable to design a school system which produces, or even promotes, equality, he argues that the very act of schooling, by grading achievement, necessarily produces social hierarchies, and so should be opposed. Hence, in Latin America, he writes, 'the majority is already hooked on school, that is, they are schooled in a sense of inferiority towards the better-schooled'. He believes that the very existence of the school 'discourages and disables the poor from taking control of their own learning'. Thus school has an 'anti-educational effect on society'. Recognized as the institution which specializes in education, its failures 'are taken by most people as proof that education is a very costly, very complex, always arcane and frequently almost impossible task'. Enforced schooling not only polarizes society, 'it also grades the nations of the world according to an international caste system'.

Illich colours his diatribes by employing a quasi-technical and 'precise' vocabulary, and he weights his pages with a ponderous apparatus of footnotes and references to give the impression of academic scholarship. But, as with Marcuse, very few of his statements will bear even cursory examination, and Illich's evident lack of humour forbids us to take them in a spirit of paradox or hyperbole. It is clear he is not interested in truth as such, but rather in righteousness. 'The escalation of the schools is as destructive as the escalations of weapons, but less visibly so'; '. . . preventive concentration camps for pre-delinquents would be a logical improvement on the school system.' 'School has become the world religion of a modernized proletariat, and makes futile promises of salvation to the poor of the technological age.' In practical terms, he favours a combination of traditional teaching-by-rote and street-corner political indoctrination: 'The Brazilian teacher Paulo Freire . . . discovered that any adult can begin to read in a matter of forty hours if the first words he deciphers are charged with political meaning'; '. . . only the mobilization of the whole population can lead to popular culture.' Schools are counter-productive, comparable to 'social agencies which specialize in the manipulation of their clients', such as gaols, mental hospitals, nursing homes and orphan asylums. The best course to pursue is a break-out from institutional schooling into popular education:

> The risks of a revolt against schools are unforeseeable, but they are not as horrible as those of a revolution starting in any other major institution. Schools are not yet organised for self-protection as effectively as a nation-state, or even a large corporation. Liberation from the grip of schools could be bloodless. The weapons of the truant officer and his allies in the courts and employment agencies might take very cruel measures against the individual offender, especially if he or she were poor, but they might turn out to be powerless against the surge of a mass movement.

So far there has been no evidence Illich has detonated a mass-movement on the lines of the campus revolts. But the practical influence of his, and similar, lines of argument should not be underrated. Illich is merely the best-known and most articulate of a host of sociologists and educationalists who wish to recast the whole system of primary education in a new, non-academic mould. The tragedy is that western society is careful to ensure that their actual experiments are only permitted in the city slum schools catering for the very poor, and in the world's more backward countries. Here, occasionally, a form of deschooling takes place, in that Marxist or sub-Marxist teachers substitute forms of social activism for inculcation of the basic skills, and turn out pupils with the 'right' political orientation but who cannot read or write. Thus by a crass process of ideological arrogance, some of the poor and the under-privileged are deprived of their only chance – a good state education – to escape from their predicament. These experiments have been violently repudiated by the working-class parents who see their children's futures squandered, but they often have the support of educational experts and authorities both geographically and socially removed far from the slum arenas.

'Deschooling' and similar theories of moral education illustrate the danger of indulging in intellectual adventurism at the expense of inno-cent human beings. Of all the discoveries man should be humbly chary of announcing, that of a new system of ethics is the most hubristic. Only in periods of tremendous change, when ethics are discussed in both absolute and relative terms, do effective novel systems of ethics emerge. One such time was in Greece of the fifth century BC; not only ethics but the whole philosophical system of Socrates and Plato was profoundly influenced by the desire to meet the challenge of ethical relativism. The trouble with ethical relativism is that it tends to drift into nihilism, since it presents ethical systems as arbitrary and thus treats them with scep-ticism. Relativism must weaken the sense of moral unity of mankind, since, as Alasdair MacIntyre puts it, 'Between the adherents of rival moralities and between the adherents of one morality and the adherents of none, there exists no court of appeal, no impersonal neutral standard . . . [not even] a shared interpretation of the vocabulary.'

The fact is that some moral systems are intrinsically superior to others. A moral system can be useless; or even evil. No one ever doubted this until comparatively recently. Observation confirms the existence of a hierarchy of moral codes. One example is provided by Edward Banfield's study of a poor south Italian village, *The Moral Basis of a Backward Society*. 'In the Montegrano mind,' he writes, 'any advantage that may be given to another is necessarily at the expense of one's own family. Therefore one cannot afford the luxury of charity, which is giving others more than their due, or even of justice, which is giving them their due. The world being what it is, all those who stand outside the small circle of the family are at least potential competitors and therefore also potential enemies.' Yet this debased system of morals does not neces-sarily spring from economic conditions. The whole point of morals is that they are not determined by the environment but can be raised or lowered by human agency, whether individual or collective. This can be seen throughout southern Italy and Sicily, where some towns and villages are dominated by the Mafia and other secret societies, while their neighbours, enjoying similar economic fortunes, are morally free Exactly the same moral differentials can be observed historically in, say, the Italian Renaissance, where the moral climates of the various city states varied enormously; or among the new townships of the American West during the second half of the nineteenth century. There is no evidence that shortage economies inevitably produce defective moral codes. Nearly all the great religious systems, notably and above all Christianity, sprang from subsistence societies. Christianity is precisely a rejection of 'the world being what it is' argument; it is also a rejection, specifically, of the family-comes-first morality, which leads directly to Mafia-type codes.

Where there is clearly a connection is between the absolute level of the moral code, and the absolute level of civilization, since civilization is the pursuit of truth, and truth is central to moral elevation. The fact that history is undetermined, and that events will proceed as we allow them, or force them, to happen – must, indeed, be shaped largely by human efforts – does not mean that values should be arbitrary. Here, as usual, Karl Popper has some wise observations:

> Nearly all misunderstandings can be traced back to one fundamental misapprehension, namely, to the belief that 'convention' implies 'arbitrariness'; that if we are free to choose any system of norms we like, then one system is as good as any other. It must, of course, be admitted that the view that norms are conventional or artificial indicates that there will be a certain amount of arbitrariness involved, i.e. that there may be different systems of norms between which there is not much to choose (a fact that has been duly emphasised by Protagoras). But artificiality by no means implies full arbitrariness. Mathematical calculi, for instance, or symphonies, or plays, are highly artificial, yet it does not follow that one calculus or symphony or play is as good as any other.

Granted, then, that any moral or ethical code in a civilized society must contain an artificial element as well as an absolute one, and granted that it is necessarily related to the general performance of civilization, it is likely to be directly associated with the forces which have created that civilization. And so we find that it is in our case. The standard ethical and moral code of our civilization is the product of

Christian religious teaching, as modified, selected and emphasized by the dynamic middle class responsible for its main economic and cultural achievements. Need we be surprised, then, to discover that it is precisely 'middle-class morality' that is under ferocious attack from the enemies of civilization?

CHAPTER 14

The Assault on Value

We have already noted the role a middle class, and especially an urban middle class, plays in the creation of a civilization, notably in the establishment of those economic and political freedoms which make it possible. It would not be correct to say that there is an absolute law which associates the emergence of a middle class with the flowering of civilization. All one can say is that, pursuing the technique of proof by falsification, it is impossible to produce a case in which the necessary freedoms have been established without the assistance of such a class. What seems equally established is that, when the status and power of the middle class is eroded or destroyed, political and economic freedom is lost, and civilization is in consequence diminished. For the only alternative to a social structure in which a middle class can survive and prosper is the harsh division, familiar to all totalitarian states, between rulers and ruled, between the *honestiores* and the *humiliores*. In such a society, there can be no sharing or diffusion of power, for the gap between the two halves is too abysmal, and the ruling faction cannot experiment with devolution without risking its own extinction; nor can there be social mobility across the chasm, for such a brutal division can only be maintained by laws of status and privilege – a nobility by birth, or by party card. Indeed, without the bridge of a middle social group, the distinctions between the two halves of society must become more fundamental, and the legal rights of the *humiliores*, whether in the Roman empire or in modern Fascist-Communist systems, gradually approximate to those of slaves.

It is highly likely, too – and certainly there is no historical example to disprove it – that a middle class is essential to prolonged economic dynamism, for otherwise there is no social index of success or failure. The point was made, with characteristic bleakness, by Thomas Malthus in his *Essay on the Principles of Population* (1798): 'If no man could hope to rise, or fear to fall, in society, if industry did not bring its own rewards, and idleness its punishment, the middle parts would not certainly be what they are now.' The middle class, implying a social continuum right across the spectrum from highest to lowest, is a conduit whereby ability can acquire commensurate opportunities, and the defective members of privileged groups can be appropriately degraded. Hatred of social mobility, and the economic dynamism it makes possible, was the prime emotion of the Marxist ethic, heightened, as it was, by a gross misunderstanding of Darwin's analysis of nature. Thus Marx to Engels, 18 June 1862: 'It is remarkable how Darwin recognizes among beasts and plants his English society with its division of labour, competition, opening up of new markets, "inventions", and the Malthusian "struggle for existence".' Engels re-stated the point more fully in his *The Dialectics of Nature* (1873):

Darwin did not know what a bitter satire he wrote on mankind, and especially on his countrymen, when he showed that free competition, the struggle for existence, which the economists celebrate as the highest historical achievement, is the normal state of the *animal kingdom*. Only conscious organisation of social production, in which production and distribution are carried on in a planned way, can lift mankind above the rest of the animal world as regards the social aspect, in the same way that production in general has done this for mankind in the specifically biological aspect.

One should not be too surprised by the depth of misunderstanding of what Darwin was actually trying to teach, betrayed by these remarks. Engels and Marx fell into the common fallacy of Social Darwinism, perhaps the most influential misconception in history, since it produced the Marxism of *Capital*, the imperialism of Joe Chamberlain, and the racialism of Adolf Hitler. Indeed, the confusion between evolutionary and social competition persists to this day. We hear constant appeals that human beings must escape from 'the rat-race' of free-enterprise society. Here is a case of verbal prestidigitation obscuring manifest reality, since it is a matter of universal knowledge that neither rats, nor any other animals, take part in races, unless compelled and trained to do so by men. Men, unlike animals, are immensely competitive, ambitious and aggressive creatures. The 'rat-race', or rather 'man-race' is a normal and necessary part of human existence. If social and other restraints are removed, human societies will tend to organize themselves into infinitely graded hierarchies, always moving, always changing, whose minute distinctions are marked by that most flexible and accurate of all indices – money. Thus, as human beings progress, and attempt to realize their capacities, the middle grades of society must and will develop, unless massive and deliberate steps are taken to restrain them. The evolution of a middle class seems to be both a cause and a measure of the development of civilization.

Moreover, all the evidence that is available confirms the common observation of social commentators over many centuries, that the development of a middle class leads to an improvement in collective and personal morality. The emergence of so-called 'middle-class values' is a characteristic of mature and civilized society. This is an awkward fact which the most objective social scientists have been obliged by their data to concede. William Kay, in the most comprehensive recent survey of the subject *Moral Education: a sociological study of the influence of society, home and school*, concludes:

There is an abundance of evidence to confirm that culture determines morality . . . a child sensitised to people's feelings, made aware of first-order moral principles, and linguistically and intellectually equipped to conduct himself according to these insights, has the potential to become a morally mature man; while the child deprived of some, or of all, has not . . . Moral values are the internalised component of a common culture. Hence cultural and moral deprivation, or privilege, are positively correlated.

It is possible to break down the elements of moral behaviour into five distinct but interrelated responses, which are both skills and expressions of value. These are: the ability to make moral judgements; a preference for deferred benefits to immediate gratification; the capacity and willingness to see others as persons, with a consequent consideration for their feelings; flexibility in interpreting general principles; the ability to apply such principles creatively, and so make morality dynamic. Of course it is possible to make a breakdown on other lines, but this one will serve. Surveying the innumerable analyses and studies of how human beings measure up to these five categories, Mr Kay finds 'on irrefutable evidence' that 'high social status is correlated with a high moral reputation'. He adds hastily (his italics): '*However, if any deduction is to be drawn, it is not that the middle classes are a superior breed. It is that the economic, educational and cultural privileges which they enjoy should become the property of all.*'

The observation is eminently sensible; and until the last quarter-century would have received almost unanimous assent from the free societies of the western world, and indeed from many others. The *embourgeoisement* of the great mass of the working people was regarded as a desirable, and attainable, objective. Now, however, the climate of opinion has greatly changed. With the rise of trade-union power, and in particular with the spread of varieties of sub- and Vulgar Marxism in the West and the Third World, there has been an exaltation of what are now termed 'working-class values' and the positive denigration of middle-class ones. The switch of approbation is, of course, based on the Leninist assumption, which we have already examined, that the morals of the working class are deterministically superior to those of any other. As we noted, Lenin was not sufficiently confident of the truth of his theory to allow it to influence the manner in which he governed Russia; and no sociological evidence has ever been produced to justify it – on the contrary, we now know that the evidence goes all the other way. But such judgements of the moral worthiness of different groups in society in general tend to reflect changes in their relative economic and political power. And, in the western democracies, the economic and political power of the middle class has declined steadily during the quarter-century in which its moral values have been challenged and scorned.

The economic decline of the middle class has been brought about by a combination of progressive taxation, inflation and the power of the industrial unions. The phenomenon is universal in the West, though the pace and scale of the decline vary considerably. We may take the case of Britain for illustration because there the incidence of all three factors is particularly marked, and the consequences correspondingly spectacular. Moreover, in Britain the relative decline in middle-class incomes is accelerating very fast. G. Routh, in *Occupation and Pay in Great Britain, 1906–1960*, has shown that average earnings of higher professional workers fell from four times the average for all men, in 1913–14, to three times the average in 1960. By a neat stroke, the extreme example not only of relative but of absolute economic decline were those traditional exponents of middle-class values, the Anglican bishops, whose average income in money terms did not rise over forty years, during which prices rose four-fold. But 1960 was only the beginning of the great inflation and of the triumph of industrial unionism in Britain. The changes over the last fifteen years have been far more destructive of middle-class status. Thus, if we take the case of university professors, we find that in 1914 they earned eight times the national average. By the early 1960s this had fallen to four times. By the early 1970s it had fallen to twice, and it is still falling fast. Indeed, many academics below professorial rank are now actually earning less than huge groups of skilled, semi-skilled and even unskilled industrial workers. In a paper on professorial salaries presented by Professor G. D. Newbould in November 1975, it was shown that a professor would have had to be given a salary of £19,411 in 1975 if he had received an average share in the real growth of the economy since 1965; in fact he received £8,968, less than half the notionally equitable figure; simply to restore his 1965 purchasing-power, he would need a salary increase of 40%. What is more, although the professor, even after tax, still had more to spend than the average industrial worker, Professor Newbould demonstrated that, over a lifetime, the professor might well be worse off:

Assume the salary of the manual worker is put into a building society share account and likewise the Professor's salary, and each account is left to accumulate. Building society share accounts pay interest at 7 per cent. The question is: 'How long is it before the balance in the two accounts is equal?' Obviously, the manual worker's account will be ahead for some time because of his earnings starting at the age of 16, but the Professor will be able to add larger amounts in later years. I think many will be surprised to find that the age of the Professor, before his balance catches up with the manual worker's, is 47. . . . If the interest-rate rose to 9 per cent, the balance in the Professor's account would *never* be as large as that of the manual worker.

By the mid-1970s in Britain there was a general, and growing, awareness among the middle class that not only had they failed to benefit at all, in terms of real incomes, from the growth of the national income over the ten years 1965–75, but that, with one or two exceptions (hospital administrators and bank executives) their purchasing power had actually fallen during the same period, often by as much as 20% or more. During the same decade, real incomes of industrial workers had risen by 13%. By contrast, differentials *within* the manual working class not only remained stable during the same period, up to the imposition of flat-rate wage restraint, but in fact had been relatively stable since the fifteenth century (see A. R. Thatcher, 'The distribution of earnings of employment in Great Britain', *Journal of the Royal Statistical Society*, 1968). The realization that British industrial unions, while totally unsuccessful – indeed counter-productive – in terms of the international wages structure, had achieved a tremendous and cumulative series of victories over

middle-class workers, set up what can only be called a wave of syndical-
ist panic among the bourgeoisie. Some fled under the umbrella of
industrial and white-collar unions. The more general trend was the
revitalization, or rather militarization, of existing but ineffective middle-
class unions and associations. The leading Nuffield College study on
middle-class unionism, G. S. Bain's *The Growth of White Collar
Unionism*, had concluded forcefully that '. . . the future growth of white-
collar unions in Britain is largely dependent upon government action to
encourage union recognition', and so had predicted 'a significant
increase in the degree of white-collar unionism in Britain during the
1970s'. This proved accurate; if anything an underestimate. For not
only did the government constantly increase the share of power and
influence allocated to all unions in the direction of the national economy,
by legislative changes in 1976 it effectively compelled firms to recognize
unions across the whole social spectrum, and virtually imposed by law a
closed-shop structure on the whole country.

In these circumstances, the middle classes felt they had no alternative
but to unionize themselves efficiently, and even to assume the behav-
ioural characteristics of the working class in a situation of industrial
conflict. They took up the weapons of the strike, official and unofficial;
of banning overtime and working to rule; of disruption and sabotage; of
demonstrations, parades, direct action and sometimes even violence.
Doctors and nurses, schoolteachers and dons, journalists, dentists, civil
servants, office workers and the like began to behave with all the group-
selfishness and social irresponsibility of their erstwhile social inferiors,
and to wage the sectional wages war with all the savagery and blindness
in their power. Professional workers of all kinds, with exceptionally
high codes of conduct, who had hitherto placed their obligations to
society above financial rewards, were now driven by rapid impoverishment to abandon their traditional ethics. Those in exceptionally strong
negotiating positions, such as the higher civil servants, simply forced the
government to allow them to raid the public till. Everywhere there was
the sound of falling masonry as the cathedral of middle-class values,
that great monument to nineteenth-century rectitude, honesty and public
service, came crashing down in ruin. The proletarianization of the
British middle class, that leading creator and custodian of western
civilization, is one of the most significant social changes of our times.
Not only was the policy of promoting the *embourgeoisement* of society
abandoned, not only was the effort to raise the moral code by intro-

ducing all to middle-class cultural privilege scrapped as impractical, but the whole process was put into reverse. The educated and cultured elite was positively stampeded by government policy into embracing the social morality of the industrial ghetto.

The consequences have begun to appear very rapidly, and they are ominous indeed. Any government which conducts a deliberate assault on standards of moral conduct is asking for trouble, not least in the economic field. The successful working of a modern economy in a free society, where government must respond to public pressures, and trade unions are privileged under the law, must depend to a large extent on the degree of self-restraint exercised by powerful groups within society. When self-restraint is lowered, that is, when large groups of workers with economic power lay claim to the national product, in such a way that the sum total of those claims exceeds the capacity of the economy, the result must be inflation. When this abdication of a sense of responsibility spreads from the industrial unions to the middle class, and so becomes general and collective, the result can only be hyperinflation. The level of social morality is directly linked to the performance of the economy. Hence it follows, as night follows day, that the proletarianization of middle-class morality leads to economic catastrophe.

For inflation, especially in its acute form, is, as Keynes noted, one of the most insidious and destructive evils which can overcome society, an enemy of civilization almost without peer. The sort of wage-inflation Britain was forced to undergo in the mid-1970s inflicts the kind of damage which it takes a generation to repair. It makes social planning almost impossible. It means more overcrowded schools, underpaid teachers, under-equipped and understaffed hospitals, rebellious nurses, bankrupt universities, lecturers who cannot afford to study or buy books, students without textbooks, slum public housing, despairing social workers, dismal hells for the mentally sick, and miserably inadequate pensions and welfare benefits of every kind. It means the poor have to argue more to get help, and traipse around from office to office as the rules are tightened. It means more 'problem families' and so more crime. It means more old people dying secretly in extreme privation. It means libraries without money to buy books; and so fewer books; and fewer writers. It spells disaster for the theatre, music and the arts. Indeed, hyperinflation is a mortal enemy of civilized living in any form. It means drab buildings and poor craftsmanship, ill-kept public parks, fewer and poorer TV and radio programmes, less public or private sponsorship of talent, less risk-taking on genius, and much, much more rounding down to the lowest commercialized level.

What is perhaps even worse is that hyperinflation sets up a voracious moral corruption eating out the heart of society. It is the very antithesis of the communal ideal. Where social morality teaches us to see ourselves as part of a whole, members of a human society based on comradeship, mutual help, friendliness, trust, magnanimity and hope in the future, wage inflation sets group against group and makes self-interest the guiding principle of life. It makes money seem the only social nexus and the only criterion of well-being. It forces on all of us the aggressive posture of comparative envy. It turns money and its ever-changing value into the chief preoccupation not only of the miser and the banker but of every human being, the dominant topic of conversation, the source of all anecdote, the ever-present, ever-nagging worry behind every plan and move. It makes the young predatory, the middle-aged mean and acquisitive, the old fearful. It penalizes not just the poor, the old, the sick and the weak, but the decent, the diffident, the unselfish, the reasonable, the temperate, the fair-minded, the loyal and the generous. It allows the social mood to be determined by the rapacious, the unscrupulous, the anti-social and the bully. Uncontrolled inflation creates a world of blind materialism, where ideals cannot be realized, where force, power and selfishness are the only dynamics, and where charity is dead.

It also has a further consequence, which is destructive of the very essence of a civilization. Civilization, we have argued, is the rational pursuit of truth within a framework of order. The discovery of truth, of course, is part of this ordering process, the way by which man locates himself in the universe. This is a very long, complicated and cumulative process. Man needs to orientate himself in time, by discovering and perfecting chronology; in space, by acquiring geographical and astronomical knowledge; in nature, by discovering its laws and using them to master his environment. He is also engaged in a continuous effort of moral and social orientation, reflected in his attempts to improve his designs for civil government, for legal and ethical codes, and his image of what a just society should be. There is, likewise, a process of moral ordering, in which man seeks to discover his worth in relation to other men, and to the potentialities of his surroundings. Human beings need to know where they stand in all these matters, for such knowledge is an essential element in their security, and so their happiness, such as it is. So we surround ourselves with systems of orientation, as truthful as we can make them. The readers of this book will have begun to gather by now that the consistent strategy of the enemies of our civilization is the attempt to destroy these systems, or replace them with false ones; for, when truth is undermined, man becomes disorientated and lost, and so a prey to those who wish to reconstruct society on a basis of force, savagery, magic and the base passions. Hence, as we have observed, the attacks on language and logic, on science and reason, on the schools and universities; hence, too, the avid promotion of pseudo-sciences, irrational quasi-religions, and phantasmagoric utopias. Now economic self-location is by no means the least important of these systems of truth by which men seek reassurance. Indeed, for the mass of mankind it may well be the one to which they refer most frequently in the common business of life. And stable money is essential to economic orientation, for money is not merely a medium of exchange, but a standard of value. If the meaning of money is destroyed, one of the great locating certitudes – one of the central physical pillars of civilization – is removed, and the balance of man is disturbed. That is why inflation, if acute enough and continued long enough, is always destructive of civilized society, and why its promotion is always the object of our enemies. But it is not, of course, the only way in which the dislocation of civilized man is sought. We must now look at the assault on less tangible concepts of value.

CHAPTER 15

Crime, Madness and Savagery

The campaign to disorientate civilized man by his enemies takes two broad and connected forms. The first is the attempt to destroy the intellectual legitimacy of science; the second is the undermining of certain key distinctions which allow civilization to function, and which science endorses. To achieve these twin objectives, all the resources of the new pseudo-sciences are systematically and laboriously deployed.

As usual, we find that the key to the strategy was forged by Marx. Seeking to make his ideology proof against the assaults of reason, logic or empirical demonstration, he built into it a safety device which in effect transforms it into a closed system, invulnerable on its own terms to any falsification – the true mark, as we have seen, of a pseudo-science. The safety device consists in arguing that, since class is the determining factor in society, it also determines intellectual procedures and criteria:

> The ideas of the ruling class are in every epoch the ruling ideas: i.e. the class which is the ruling *material* force of society, is at the same time its ruling *intellectual* force. The class which has the material means of production at its disposal, has control at the same time over the means of mental production, so that thereby, generally speaking, the ideas of those who lack the means of mental production are subject to it.

There is, therefore, no such thing as science, reason, logic; what we suppose to be objective, and therefore valid, disciplines are in fact bourgeois science, bourgeois reason and bourgeois logic. And so forth: like most of Marx's pivotal ideas, it is capable of almost indefinite extension by analogy. Marx set up this protective device to defend his dialectical materialism from bourgeois critics. It automatically invalidated their arguments, rather as, in science fiction, mysterious 'force-fields' are used to repel enemy rockets. But of course it is also capable of aggressive use, to destroy the certitudes of true science and replace them with ideologically convenient fantasies.

In fact, it is at this point that all the pseudo-sciences tend to come together, to establish that the development of science, and the 'scientific revolution' which began in the seventeenth century and continues today at accelerating pace, are not essentially phenomena in intellectual history as all true scientists suppose, but the guided products of social and economic forces. For of course, once this point is conceded, there is no objective way of distinguishing between a true science and a false one. It is notable that the radical sociologists, who dominate this form of activity, regard *The German Ideology*, which Marx wrote with Engels, and in which he set out his theory of class knowledge, to be by far the most important Marxist text – as, in a sense, it is now becoming. Moreover, thanks to Freudian 'insights', the argument discrediting scientific objectivity can be made far more powerful than in Marx's time, for it can be urged that those practising a class science may do so unconsciously. For an excellent example of the way in which the Marxist thesis has been updated and streamlined, let us look at a long essay by Robert Young, 'The historiographic and ideological contexts of the 19th-century debate on Man's Place in Nature' in *Changing Perspectives in the History of Science: Essays in Honour of Joseph Needham*. Discussing Darwin's very understandable refusal to get mixed up with Marx, Young writes:

> If one is studying the writing of town-planners, political scientists, socio-logists, anthropologists, economists, psychologists, ethnologists, physio-logists, geneticists, molecular biologists, chemists, physicists or mathemati-cians, one finds oneself at different points on a continuum between writings which obviously reflect socio-political assumptions and those which do not (obviously). In studying disciplines which are near the beginning of that list, ideological assumptions appear, as it were, on the surface of the page. At the other extreme, a student of the history of physics or mathematics – or indeed of recent molecular biology – would be very incredulous if faced with an interpretation of his data which stressed ideological assumptions which appeared to play no part in the data before him.

The approach is ingenious, is it not? For the supposition, here, is that all sciences, however abstract and remote from politics 'on the surface', are in fact susceptible to ideological bias; and that this bias is all the more insidious in that it is hidden. A mathematician, then, cannot protest his innocence of class assumptions, for the answer is that they have been there all the time even though he has been unaware of them: he is, as it were, an unconscious 'carrier' of the class disease, and his work is thereby poisoned. The point, of course, is familiar to readers of Marcuse, who is concerned to attack the objectivity of nature, and the concept of 'the nature of things'. 'Glorification of the natural,' he writes in *One-Dimensional Man*, 'is part of the ideology which protects an unnatural society in its struggle against liberation.' The idea of objectivity and truth in science is dismissed by Robert Young as 'this colossal confidence trick'. He adds: 'If we are to understand why men defer to experts about how they can and should live, and to biology for the limits of human nature and society, we must understand the historical process which produced this set of abstractions and led them to become common-sense and to replace outrage, sapping men's faith in the ability to transform society for the benefit of all.' Or again: 'The advancing edge of objectivity must be replaced by a revival of radical consciousness which is developed concomitantly with the growth of radical will and action.'

In this last sentence, Young abandons the posture of a historian of science, and rants like a political huckster; and it is a fortunate fact that the intellectual poverty of this type of argument is often illuminated by the strident tone of the language used. Thus Trent Schroyer, in 'Towards a Critical Theory for Advanced Industrial Society' in *Recent Sociology Number Two*, uses the type of assertion-by-cliché 'argument' we came across with Illich: 'Contemporary science and technology have become a new form of legitimating power and privilege ... the scientistic image of science has become the dominant legitimating system of advanced industrial society . . . the scientistic image of science is the fundamental false consciousness of our epoch.'

Indeed, it is improbable that the present Marxist attack on scientific objectivity would have been at all effective if those who mount it had not also been able to draw on the techniques of mystification discovered by Freud and his followers. For Freudianism, and the procedures of psychoanalysis, are the kind of pseudo-science which deal with a concept of truthfulness akin to imaginative literature. This is not the same as scientific truth, but it appeals to human minds because it strikes them – often quite wrongly – as a form of archetypal truth. In his critique of psychoanalysis, Sir Peter Medawar points out that it cannot escape its Freudian roots, and that Freud himself has been overtaken by the advances of true science: many of his basic concepts were formulated before the recognition of inborn errors of metabolism, before the chromosomal theory of inheritance, and before the discovery of Mendel's laws; the existence of hormones and the mechanism of the nervous impulse were unknown when Freud began to create his system. Hence, adds Medawar, many of the central ideas of psychoanalysis are profoundly unbiological – the death-wish, the assumption the mind is very fragile, the depreciation of the genetic contribution to human diversity, and the interpretation of dreams as abnormal psychical phenomena. Psychoanalysis is therefore akin to Mesmerism and phrenology, in that it enshrines elements of truth in a false general theory; those who practise psychiatric medicine are in the position of early-nineteenth-century doctors, trying to get round as yet unsolved difficulties by witchdoctoring.

But if psychoanalysis is almost entirely barren of true concepts, it displays a terrific facility for explaining things. It is this which makes it a mythology rather than a science, but it is this which also gives it such a powerful appeal. There is nothing it cannot explain, neatly, and (at a certain intellectual level) convincingly. As an example of what he terms 'the Olympian glibness of psychoanalytical thought', Medawar summarizes a paper on anti-semitism, given at the 23rd International Psychoanalytical Congress, Stockholm, 1963: 'The Oedipus Complex is acted out and experienced by the anti-semite as a narcissistic injury, and he projects this injury upon the Jew who is made to play the role of the father. . . . His choice of the Jew is determined by the fact that the Jew is in the unique position of representing at the same time the all-powerful father and the father castrated. . . .' Moreover, the technique of all-purpose explanation is completed by another safety-mechanism, which even explains why some people disbelieve in it. As with Marxism, it has achieved complete intellectual closure, and once someone allows his mind to get lost in this maze, it is very difficult for him to get out.

Here, then, is the theoretical basis on which the attack on science is conducted. How is it carried out in practice; and, in particular, how is it used to destroy what I have termed certain key distinctions, which enable civilization to function, and which science endorses? Let us examine three of these distinctions in turn: between the criminal and the law-abiding, between the mad and the sane, and between the civilized and the savage. All these are areas where true science has had to struggle hard to evolve in a permanently satisfactory manner from what might be called universal common-sense assumptions. In the case of crime, all civilized societies have assumed there is such a person as a criminal, and have punished him, even if their criteria for identifying him have varied. Classical criminology, first fully expounded in Cesare Beccaria's *Essay on Crimes and Punishments* (1804), is a branch of social contract theory derived from Hobbes and Locke, and updated by the principles of late eighteenth-century utilitarianism. It assumed that the present division of property had a moral sanction, and that all law-breaking behaviour after the contract was struck was irrational or pathological. It was the duty of society to reward useful activity and punish damaging activity; hence its right and obligation to punish the lawbreaker. Classical criminology is attacked by Marxist social scientists on the grounds that it embodies the bourgeois notion of utility, which merely replaced one false theory of property, the feudal or aristocratic standard that rights came from birth, by another, the middle-class assumption that rights come from the ability to make money.

In fact the real objection to classical criminology is that it embodied an exact scale of punishment for equal acts without reference to the individual, or the circumstances of the act. This basic inadequacy arose from the fact that it could not define exactly what a criminal was, or why he acted as he did. And attempts to enlarge classical theory to meet this objection ran into blind alleys. Thus Cesare Lombroso, acting on a misunderstood hint from Darwin's *Descent of Man* (1871), conceived the idea of an atavistic man, a criminal archetype or throwback, which he set out in *L'Uomo Deliquente* (1876), after examining the skull of the notorious brigand Vihella. Lombroso claimed atavistic man could be recognized by 'physical stigmata' – abnormal dentition, asymmetry of face, supernumerary nipples, toes or fingers, by large ears, eye defects, inverted sex-characteristics, and by human additions such as tattooing. In investigating the anatomical characteristics of anarchists, he found that 31% in Paris, 40% in Chicago and 34% in Turin had stigmata; whereas members of other extremist movements averaged only 12%. Lombroso later had to modify his theory to include such groups as epileptics, the insane, and occasional criminals with only traces of atavism and degeneration; and in time the whole idea was abandoned as without scientific foundation. More modern attempts to discover a physical basis to explain crime and the criminal include investigation of body shapes, and the so-called XYY chromosome theory, based on the apparent fact that the extra 'Y' (the 'normal' male is XX, the normal female XY) was positively linked to increased height and psychopathic tendencies. But all these theories are crude and open to a variety of objections.

Criminology, therefore, has tended to rest in the domain of the social sciences, or the immature physical sciences. Its predominant form, known as Radical Positivism, operates from a number of 'common-sense assumptions', such as that there is such a person as a criminal, that a moral consensus does exist, and that a crime occurs when a criminal infringes the consensus. But it is highly critical of the way this situation is dealt with. Thus, it rejects the assumption that crime is an overwhelmingly youthful, masculine and working-class activity; it accuses police and judiciary of using non-scientific criteria in operating the system, and urges reform to ensure that social control operates more effectively and scientifically in accordance with the objective interests of all concerned. It argues that not all acts defined as crimes are anti-social, and that not all anti-social acts are defined as crimes. Its concern, therefore, is primarily with the operation and enforcement of social control, and with the definition of the moral consensus – hence it studies 'conduct norms' rather than crimes as defined by law. Above all, it accepts the distinction between the great mass of normal people, who create the moral consensus, and a minority of deviants existing at the margins of society, who challenge it.

Positivism is the nearest we can get, so far, to a true science of criminology. Hans Eysenck, perhaps the most impressive of the positivists, summarizes his position thus:

Criminality is obviously a continuous trait of the same kind as intelligence, or height or weight. We may artificially say that every person either is or is not a criminal, but this would be so grossly over-simplified as to be untrue. Criminals vary among themselves, from those who fall once and never again, to those who spend most of their lives in prison. Clearly the latter have far more 'criminality' in their makeup than the former. Similarly, people who are not convicted of crimes have committed crimes for which they were never caught or, if they were caught, perhaps the court took a rather lenient view. Others have never given way to temptation at all. From a rational point of view, therefore, we cannot regard criminals as being completely distinct from the rest of the population. They simply represent the extreme end of a continuous distribution, very much as a mental defective represents the extreme end of a continuous distribution of intelligence, ranging upwards through the average to the very high IQ of the student or even the genius (*Crime and Personality*).

Here, then, the scientific approach is very close to the traditional view even down to the terms used: 'fall', 'give way to temptation' and so on. Eysenck adds that, because of modern technology, society is becoming more closely knit together, and that the problem of crime is therefore becoming more acute, and more in need of radical scientific solutions. Writing in *New Society* ('The Technology of Consent', June 1969), he asked:

... how can we engineer a social consent which will make people behave in a socially adapted, law-abiding fashion, which will not lead to a breakdown of the intricately interwoven fabric of social life? Clearly we are failing to do this: the ever-increasing number of unofficial strikes, the ever-increasing statistics of crime of all sorts, the general alienation on which so many writers have commented, are voluble witnesses to this statement. The psychologist would answer that what was clearly required was a technology of consent, that is a generally applicable method of inculcating suitable habits of socialised conduct into the citizens ...

Eysenck believes that the technology necessary to achieve this consent is already in process of being created, through Pavlovian science and behaviourist techniques; and he argues that, since the methods exist and the need is admitted, they will eventually be used. His view is very likely correct, for at the moment true science not only has no other answer to the problem of crime but not even a promising alternative line of inquiry.

It is at this point that the pseudo-scientists intervene, and claim a solution by, in effect, dissolving the problem. They deny the existence of objective crime and repudiate the distinction between the criminal and the normal member of society. Actually, it is a source of great grief to them that Marx was plainly not very interested in crime as such, though a section of *The German Ideology* does deal with rights, crime and punishment. Engels thought the crime he observed in Manchester was a form of demoralization brought about by capitalist oppression. Marx, in so far as he troubled to analyse crime, took an old-fashioned view, which he dressed up in his own inimitable manner. Crime was concentrated in the *lumpenproletariat*, among the unproductive, and therefore unorganized workers. They were doubly parasitical, since they not only failed to contribute to the production of goods but created a livelihood for themselves out of the goods produced wholly by the productive workers. Marx therefore did not have to face the awkward question, as Lenin did, as to why the workers continued to behave badly even under non-capitalist conditions, since he did not regard criminals as true workers at all. It was left, therefore, to William Bonger (1876–1940), the only notable Marxist criminologist, to pick up the hint Engels dropped, and argue, in *Criminality and Economic Conditions*, that 'criminal thoughts' arise from a lack of 'moral training' which is denied to the proletariat in an industrialized capitalist society. Hence capitalism causes crime. It has developed 'egoism at the expense of altruism', and crime is positively encouraged in an egotistic environment.

These Marxist approaches do not, therefore, repudiate the distinction between the criminal and the non-criminal; they merely provide an economic explanation for the criminal's existence. It was the early sociologists who first began to destroy the concept of criminality itself. Emile Durkheim cited the case of Socrates to 'prove' that yesterday's criminal is often today's philosopher. He argued that crime is persistent precisely because it is the work of men with ideas defined as illegitimate within the existing collective conscience. Hence a flourishing crime-rate is an indication that the systems and ideas of social control are out of date. 'Crime,' he urged in the *Rules of Sociological Method*, '. . . must no longer be conceived as an evil that cannot be too much suppressed. There is no occasion for self-congratulation when the crime-rate drops noticeably below the average level, for we may be certain that this apparent progress is associated with some social disorder.'

From this initial 'insight', as we may term it, sprang the first modern 'sociology of crime', the so-called 'Chicago School', which analysed crime a product of 'social ecology', or part of the environment. A community, wrote Robert Ezra Park in 1936, has 'something of the character of an organic unit. It has a more or less definite structure and a life history in which juvenile, adult and senile phases can be observed'. Crime was not abnormality but a normal part of the ecology and the life-history. This first 'explanation' of crime as a necessary part of social progress has been followed by a multitude of others, too numerous to describe, which differ not only in important details, but in their most fundamental aspects. Thus there is the 'ecological pluralism' set out by Edwin H. Sutherland and Donald R. Cressey in *Principles of Criminology*. A person 'becomes delinquent because of an excess of definitions favourable to violation of law over definitions unfavourable to violation of law'. These definitions are learnt in a normal learning process. Hence crime is not a product of lack of social training, as Eysenck maintains, but is acquired in an identical fashion to non-criminal behaviour. It is learnt in groups. Individual pathology, therefore, is not a cause of crime.

Then there is a series of schools, associated with the Americans H. S. Becker and Edwin Lemert, known variously as social-control theorists, social-reaction theorists, transactionalists or labelling theorists. Lemert argues that social control actually creates deviance, which has no objective existence. As Becker puts it: 'The act of injecting heroin into a vein is not inherently deviant. If a nurse gives a patient drugs under a doctor's orders, it is perfectly proper. It is when it is done in a way which is not publicly defined as proper that it becomes deviant. The act's deviant character lies in the way it is defined in the public mind' (*Sociological Work*). This formulation, of course, ignores the realities behind the two acts; if we substitute 'amputation of a limb' for injections, the realities can no longer be ignored. Such pseudo-science can nearly always be exposed by rejecting its preferred analogies and replacing them by others. The sociologies of crime which deny its intrinsic existence are invariably distinguished by crumbling logic; they are also inherently unstable as is indicated by constant osmosis, and an alarming oscillation between confidence and perplexity.

Thus one master of the school, David Mazda, asserts, 'The process of becoming deviant makes little human sense without understanding the philosophical inner life of the subject as he bestows meaning upon the events and materials that beset him' (*Becoming Deviant*). The delinquent 'represents not a radical opposition to law-abiding society but something more like an apologetic failure, often more sinned against than sinning in his own eyes'; the delinquent is not alien to society but a disturbing reflection or caricature of it. On the other hand, Mazda, in an interview about this book with *Issues in Criminology*, winter 1971, concedes:

I think that *Delinquency and Drift* is a jumbling of conservative, liberal and radical views. Different chapters have different philosophic and political implications. I think *Becoming Deviant* is sort of liberal and radical, maybe a little conservative too; but I think somewhat more consistent than *Delinquency and Drift*. So the view of society that I had, if I had one, in *those* books . . . what in Hell *did* I think when writing those two books? Actually, my view of society is much more evident in something I wrote called 'Poverty and Disrepute' and in an essay on poverty I'm working on now. I'm not sure that I have a view of society.

The tone here is much closer to that of a demoralized creative writer discussing works of imagination than of a scientist reviewing his performance. Such a leading theoretician could only operate in a discipline which has no effective control over quality and no common agreement on fundamentals – in short, not a true discipline at all, but, to use a phrase of Medawar's, a salon science rather than a laboratory science.

The real danger of the sociologies of crime is that, though they argue at the salon level, they operate in the real world; they form part not merely of a theoretical pseudo-science but an applied one. Ralf Dahrendorf and other 'conflict-theory' advocates argue, as in his *Essay in the Theory of Society*, that legal norms are necessary to prevent the disintegration of the collectivity into individual warfare; sanctions are needed to ensure normative compliance; social conflicts are inevitable in modern society; indeed, legal systems do not reflect public opinion and the moral consensus, or spring from any hedonistic calculation; they are simply arbitrary systems of social control, shaped by whatever are, at any moment, the most powerful interests. It follows from this, therefore, that the sociologists of crime feel no moral obligation to identify themselves with the law, even in principle; on the contrary, they argue that their professional obligation may be to frustrate the law. Nils Christie, in 'Scandinavian criminology facing the 1970s', published in *Scandinavian Studies in Criminology*, maintains:

We have now made it clear that our role as criminologists is not first and foremost to be received as useful problem-solvers *but as problem-raisers* . . . our situation has a great resemblance to that of artists and men of letters. . . . Together with other cultural workers we will probably have to keep a constant fight going against being absorbed, tamed and made responsible, and thereby completely socialised into society – as it is.

Thus the criminologist joins the 'deviant' in trying to destroy/change society. In Scandinavia, indeed, social workers trained in the new criminological 'science' not only identified themselves with what they term 'the defences of the weak' but sought to organise them by forming KRUM, the prisoners' trade union, which was able to coordinate a prison strike across three national boundaries in 1972. In the most comprehensive analysis of these new trends by three enthusiastic adherents, Ian Taylor, Paul Walton and Jack Young (*The New Criminology: for a social theory of deviance*), the authors claim:

. . . the politicisation of crime and criminology [is] imminent . . . a criminology which is not normatively committed to the abolition of inequalities of wealth and power, and in particular to inequalities in property and life-chances, is inevitably bound to fall into correctionalism. . . . For us, as for Marx and other new criminologists, *deviance* is normal – in the sense that men are now consciously involved (in the prisons that are contemporary society and in the real prisons) in asserting their human diversity.

At this point then, the distinction between crime and legality is totally abolished and the criminal is presented as the normal member of society -- with the added implication that the law-abiding are the real deviants. The threat this presents to civilized behaviour can be grasped when it is realized that these 'scientists' define Solzhenitsyn's account of the Gulag Archipelago as an excellent description of 'social control' in action – that is, they draw no distinction between, say, the English and United States systems of criminal law, with their infinity of safeguards for the individual, and their adherence to the principles of equity, natural justice and equality of access and treatment, and the Soviet terror-system which is based not on jurisprudence at all, but on force and fraud. And in terms of their argument there *is* no distinction: to this extent, their attempt to disorientate is complete.

The same desire to obfuscate characterizes the attempts of some sociologists and psychologists to remove, or even reverse, the distinction between madness and sanity, with the added complication that in this field the dividing line is necessarily an ambiguous one. Madness has always been difficult to define; for most of human history, the best men could do was to describe it, or rather identify certain physical signs of insanity. When David broke with Saul, he went to Achish the Philistine, King of Gath, and pretended to be mad: 'So he changed his behaviour towards them and feigned himself mad in their hands, and made marks on the doors of the gate, and let his spittle run down his beard. Then said Achish to his servants: "Lo, you see the man is mad; why then have you brought him to me? Do I lack madmen that you have brought this fellow to play the madman in my presence?"' (I *Samuel* 21:13–15.) Or again, Ben Jonson's Volpone, when the lawyer Voltore feigns madness in Act V, cries:

> see, see, see, see!
> He vomits crooked pins! His eyes are set,
> Like a dead hare's hung in a poulter's shop!
> His mouth's running away!

But though certain signs were commonly identified with 'ordinary' madness, all pre-modern societies found it hard to distinguish between the mad, the possessed, prophets, 'speakers with tongues', and ecstatics and epileptics. Democritus characterized forms of beneficial, or divine, madness as *enthusiasmos*; and Socrates, in the *Phaedrus*, says: 'The greatest blessings come by way of madness, indeed of madness that is heaven-sent.' With the rise of an authoritarian Christian church in western society, the idea of divine madness was progressively discounted, and there was an increasing tendency to place all seemingly disturbed persons under constraint.

This is the situation modern science inherited; and it cannot be said to have made spectacular progress in tidying it up. Modern society has an unreasonable appetite for scientific definitions and categories. And the fact is that, while the old categories of madness have been discredited, they have not been replaced by agreed formulae. We cannot agree on an accurate definition of madness; nor can we define mass-phenomena, psychic epidemics, collective psychoses, mass delusions, and the like; we do not even know whether individual and collective disturbances are related. All we can really do is to devise a variety of therapies, which work increasingly well with certain types of disturbance. Here is a case of science progressing empirically without a universal theory.

But of course the absence of satisfactory theory is a standing invitation to the pseudo-scientist, and madness has become a tragic arena for the display of tenuous explanations, or myths. Social scientists have been invading the subject since the 1920s, and it is notable that the first issue of *Psychiatry*, in 1938, carried an article 'Mental Hygiene and the Class Structure', which claimed that traditional work on madness 'hides its adherence behind a scientific façade, but the ethical premises reveal themselves on every hand, partly to a blindness to scientifically relevant facts'. The social scientists brought forward class, environment, culture and other non-physiological factors in analysing mental health, and the tendency, as with crime, is to blur the distinction between normal and abnormal. Thus J. W. Eaton and R. J. Weil write in *Culture and Mental Diseases*: 'The concept of mental health is not a scientific but a value-judgment.'

The last, of course, is an arguable proposition. Much more dangerous are the activist and anti-rational theories propagated in recent years, and widely disseminated among young social workers and social scientists by best-selling books. One such is Michel Foucault's *Folie et deraison*, translated as *Madness and Civilisation*. This work is organized in the fashionable style of Fernand Braudel, the French 'total' historian, and treats discursively of the old 'lazar-houses' and the origins of madhouses. Foucault's intellectual pedigree, on his own admission, centres on

Nietzsche and the Marquis de Sade, and his argument marks a return to the ancient thesis that lack of balance can be a form of genius or divinity. Indeed, Foucault holds that madness is not a disease but a form of knowledge. In a historical discussion of attitudes to madness, he claims that we were once able to speak with and listen to the mad; then the dominant cultures of the seventeenth to eighteenth centuries, based on burgeoning science and the supremacy of reason, lost the capacity to understand the knowledge of the insane, and dialogue was succeeded by silence. Hence, from the time of the Age of Reason, madmen were expelled from society and locked up, as the Middle Ages had done with lepers. Next, in the nineteenth century, the idea of guilt was injected into madness, which was reduced to the status of a mere disease, often incurable, and madhouses became places of punishment. Foucault's main contention, therefore, is that reason has no objective privileges over unreason.

Of course, such a book is not a work of science but rather a series of unproved, and indeed unprovable, assertions. But it has the fascination of an all-purpose explanation-myth, and the real danger arises when it begins to influence those actually concerned with the mentally sick. Cultural psychiatry, almost by definition, repudiates the idea of an organic cause of mental abnormality. The true scientist, as Sir Peter Medawar points out, wants the organic explanation to be the correct one, because then there is a possibility that he can cure it. *Madness and Civilisation* reached the English-speaking world with an introduction by Dr David Cooper, who writes: 'The true significance of [this book] resides most precisely in the terror that it may produce in a significant few of us.' And it was Dr Cooper who was responsible, at Shenley Hospital, for the development of what he called an 'anti-hospital' in a villa accommodating about twenty young male schizophrenics. In this villa, according to Cooper's friend R. D. Laing, a 'subculture' developed; and 'as staff–patient role distinctions became blurred, Villa 21 became more of a household, without "staff" putting patients to bed, getting them up, drugging them, and so on. It became no longer clear who, if anyone, was "treating" whom for what, since it was no longer discernible, or even an issue, who was sane and who was crazy.'

Laing himself is by far the best known and most influential of this group of writer-psychiatrists, chiefly because he is also a poet, and has an abundance of the imaginative skills necessary for successful myth-weaving. He argues that there is a clear parallel between so-called madness and so-called crime, since in his view it is the treatment which transforms an unusual situation into madness, just as the law makes a deviant into a criminal. In *The Politics of the Family and Other Essays* he writes:

> If A and B are incongruent, the mind police (psychiatrists) are called in. A crime (illness) is diagnosed. An arrest is made and the patient taken into custody (hospitalisation). Interviews and investigations follow. A confession may be obtained (patient admits he is ill, displays insight). He is convicted either way. The sentence is passed (therapy is recommended). He serves his time, comes out, and obeys the laws in future. Some people are refractory to such methods, as their prognosis is regarded as poor. The psychiatrist, who is a specialist in these matters, can see one of these refractory cases coming.

Hence Laing regards 'formal psychiatry' (that is, psychiatry which has some kind of scientific basis) as the enemy of the 'mad'; he objects to its 'vocabulary of denigration'. Those it defines as sane, he writes in *The Divided Self: a study of sanity and madness*, may well be 'radically unsound' and 'dangerous', whereas 'the cracked minds of the schizophrenic may *let* in light which does not enter the intact minds of many sane people whose minds are closed.' A patient's 'mad' behaviour often reflects his situation *vis-à-vis* the psychiatrist: 'I am quite sure that a good number of "cures" for psychotics consist in the fact that the patient has decided, for one reason or another, once more to *play at being sane*.' In the closing words of this book, he writes of Julie, an active psychotic, 'there was something of great worth deeply lost or buried inside her, as yet undiscovered by herself or by anyone.'

In *The Politics of the Family* Laing generalizes his assault on the psychiatrist-policeman into a destructive analysis of all the orderly, rule-making elements in civilization, which he sees as springing from the family unit, which begins repressive training at the earliest age. He argues that many adults are, in effect, in a hypnotic trance, induced in infancy. 'Attempts to waken up before our time are punished, especially by those who love us most.' Hence: 'If anyone in a family begins to realise he is a shadow of a puppet, he will be wise to exercise the greatest precautions as to whom he imparts this information to [*sic*].' If someone does wake up (i.e. become 'mad'), the psychiatrist-policeman is called in by loving relatives; he 'treats them for waking up, and drugs them asleep again (increasingly effective as this field of technology sharpens its weapons), and helps to drive them crazy'. Laing argues that we create a whole system of falsehoods and defence-mechanisms from the beginnings of our lives, in order to adapt socially. We make a 'holocaust of our experience on the altar of conformity', become empty in consequence, seek to fill the hole with material accomplishments, crack, then turn to psychiatry. The essay, then, is an attack on rules and values, and such concepts as 'good', 'bad', and so forth. It has proved, without question, attractive stuff for any young person at odds with society. The myth-making 'explanations' are ingenious and, as usual with these pseudo-scientific theories, we come across a cunning safety-mechanism which magically repels criticism, and gives the system complete intellectual closure. In Laing's case it is contained in the sentence: 'There are rules against seeing the rules, and hence against seeing all the issues that arise from complying with, or breaking them.' Thus he does not have to prove that there is an elaborate plot by society to destroy the individual, to make the sane mad, the mad sane and so forth, because secrecy about the details of the plot is a key part of the plot. One can't prove the existence of rules because one of the rules is that you don't know what they are, and are not supposed to know they exist; that's the whole point – don't you see? Laing's whole success rests upon the fact that he has composed an exciting conspiracy-theory, not about politics, but about life itself.

But politics, as one might expect, do come into it in the end. Laing refuses to define schizophrenia, except tautologically: 'Schizophrenia is the name for a condition that most psychiatrists ascribe to patients they call schizophrenic.' (This sentence, incidentally, is in italics; fondness for italic emphasis is a characteristic of Laing's, as indeed it is of members of the purple-and-green-ink brigade.) But he goes on to say:

> The concept of schizophrenia is a straitjacket that restricts psychiatrists and patients. . . . The whole of our civilisation may be a captivity. But the observations upon which psychiatrists and psychologists have drawn in order to build up the prevailing picture of schizophrenia have, almost entirely, been made on human beings in double or even treble captivity. . . . Marx said: under all circumstances a Negro has a black skin but only under certain socio-economic conditions is he a slave. Under all circumstances a man may get stuck, lose himself, and have to turn round and go back a long way to find himself again. Only under certain socio-economic conditions will he suffer from schizophrenia.

But of course! Here Laing exposes the barrenness of his intellect by trying to have it both ways. Not only does madness not exist, but it is caused by capitalism! Yet oddly enough, and in actual sober fact, it is only under the radically different 'socio-economic conditions' of the Soviet Union, that the sane really are incarcerated in lunatic asylums.

The attack on systems of morality, by destroying the concept of crime, and on reason, by removing distinctions between sanity and madness, is closely linked to the deliberate devaluation of established knowledge, especially scientific knowledge, by the exaltation of the thought-processes and the scientific culture of primitive savages. Here the assault on civilization is at its most open and audacious because the object is to remove its claim to privileged status, and to show, in effect, that there is no such thing as high culture. The tragedy about this particular line of aggression is that it is able to draw upon the work of distinguished anthropologists, such as, for instance, Mary Douglas, Professor of Social Anthropology at University College, London. Her excellent study, *Purity and Danger: An Analysis of the Concepts of Pollution and Taboo,* has been seized upon by the cultural relativists and obfuscationists as ammunition for their campaign. Thus Robert Young, in an essay we have already quoted, claims that her work serves to undermine western concepts of rationality, or at least to treat them as relative, on a par with irrational concepts in other societies: 'Beginning with her study of pollution and taboo in *Purity and Danger,* she has, with increasing boldness and imagination, applied the approach of the anthropologist to the economic, technological and scientific cosmologies of her own culture'; she has, he asserts, 'however little she may wish to set in train politically radical thinking', suggested ways of freeing ideological analysis from the restrictions which have kept it away from the domain of natural science.

It is obviously important for the relativists to succeed in appropriating the work of someone of the consequence of Professor Douglas, because those anthropologists who are emotionally and intellectually committed to their line of argument do not, on the whole, carry much weight, at any rate among the predominant Anglo-Saxon branch of the science. By far the most prominent of them is the Belgian Claude Lévi-Strauss, Professor of Social Anthropology at the College de France, and author of the international best-seller *La Pensée sauvage,* translated as *The Savage Mind.* Lévi-Strauss is a lawyer and philosopher by training, and came to anthropology somewhat late in life, via sociology. His mental pedigree is not impressive, since he describes geology, psychoanalysis and Marxism as his 'three mistresses'; and, as Edmund Leach points out in a pointed brief analysis of his writings, Lévi-Strauss does not appear to have done very much field-work, and what he has done is of 'only moderate quality'. According to his autobiography, *Tristes Tropiques*, he made brief visits to the interior of Brazil, 1934–7, but only accumulated three months' field-work; and he was in central Brazil in 1938–9, but seems to have been on the move all the time, with little opportunity to do work on the spot. Leach comments: 'A careful study of *Tristes Tropiques* reveals that, in the whole course of his Brazilian travels, Lévi-Strauss can never have stayed in one place for more than a few weeks at a time and that he was never able to converse easily with any of his native informants in their native language.' There was also a short trip to Bangladesh in 1950. But if his field-work is slight, his quantity of publications is prodigious, and, as Leach says, he clearly owes his advancement to publications rather than academic work.

Lévi-Strauss writes obscurely, and it is not easy to summarize his basic argument, or indeed to understand it in places. But his prime object would seem to be to discredit the prevailing view that the myths of savages are primitive absurdities, representing a rudimentary stage in the development of scientific thought. He argues, on the contrary, that myths make sense; magic and science should not be contrasted, but seen as two parallel methods of acquiring knowledge or 'two scientific levels at which nature is accessible to scientific inquiry'. Both are 'equally valid'. He 'proves' this proposition by pointing out that Neolithic Man was 'heir of a long scientific tradition' because he discovered, by a scientific process of reasoning, all the basic arts, pottery, weaving, agriculture, the domestication of animals, smelting and so forth. Why, then, was there a period of stagnation of several thousand years between the Neolithic revolution and modern scientific thought? In Chapter 1 I have given the historian's answer: social and political restraints, arising from the absence of freedom. Lévi-Strauss thinks differently: 'There is only one solution to the paradox, namely, that there are two distinct modes of scientific thought.' The original science is very close to sensible intuition. Savage thought is a kind of do-it-yourself science, which he characterizes by the untranslatable French term *bricolage*: '. . . it is important not to make the mistake of thinking that [mythical thought and science] are two stages or phases in the evolution of knowledge. Both approaches are equally valid. . . Mythical thought . . . acts as a liberator by its protest against the idea that anything can be meaningless with which science at first resigned itself to a compromise.' He contrasts the concrete knowledge of the savage to the abstract knowledge of the western scientist. Thus he quotes a Canadian Indian: 'We know what the animals do . . . because long ago men married them and acquired this knowledge from their animal wives. Today the priests say we lie, but we know better. The white man has been only a short time in this country and knows very little about the animals; we have lived here thousands of years and were taught long ago by the animals themselves.'

Lévi-Strauss argues that savages are better classifiers, inspired by an ingenious totemic logic, which operates in a number of dimensions, many of them symbolic. They have different intellectual structures, and make connections in radically different ways. The more isolated the savages are, the more sophisticated their mental alternatives to our thinking become; thus the Australian aboriginals have a delicately re-fined taste for erudition and speculation; they are philosophical dandies and intellectual snobs. Moreover, the apparently disorganized collections of beliefs and customs characteristic of the savage are not arbitrary; on the contrary, the whole system hangs together, and each aspect of his knowledge and society – though studied separately by ethnologists and fashioned by them into distinctive institutions – is part of the unifying structure. Thus so-called totemism is an aspect of classification. Lévi-Strauss caps his argument by 'showing' that modern information theory has helped 'to legitimise the principles of savage thought and to re-establish it in its rightful place', since such things as telecommunica-tions, computers and electron microscopes have allowed us, admittedly more accurately, to reach conclusions about the nature of the world already perceived by primitive man.

The theory must have an element of truth embedded in it, in that societies living in static isolation for thousands of years may well have acquired empirical glimpses of truth which civilized men obtain by other means. But this point, obvious in itself, was noted long ago by Comte, when he called the 'savage' mind 'spontaneous'. Lévi-Strauss's argu-ment fits in neatly with the pseudo-scientific critique of civilization, and the devaluation of its institutions, since he seems to accuse professional anthropologists of obscuring the qualities of the savage intelligence, rather as policemen are accused of creating criminals and scientific psychiatry of making sane people mad. There is, to use Blake's phrase, a 'fearful symmetry' in all these attempts to disorientate civilized man. Lévi-Strauss's contribution is, in a sense, the key one: he is producing not merely a myth but a myth about myths – what Medawar terms a metamythology. But his arguments bear all the hallmarks, with which

we are now dismally familiar, of a pseudo-science. His object throughout is to prove his theory up to the hilt. Hence, as Dr Leach says, he is
insufficiently critical of his source-material. Restlessly sorting through
the published evidence of anthropological field-work, he always seems
able to find exactly what he is looking for. Any evidence, however
dubious, is acceptable so long as it fits with his logically-calculated
expectations. But wherever the data runs counter to the theory, he either
ignores it, or summons up all his rhetorical powers to show why it is
inapplicable, irrelevant or false. He is not so much a scientist examining
a proposition, as a lawyer working to a brief – a relic of his early training.
What is more, as with the theories of other pseudo-scientists we have
examined, there is an irresistible tendency towards gigantism – that is,
indefinite expansion of the theory to include anything or everything, by
additions and analogy; so that, as Leach says, 'lately the whole system
seems to have developed into a self-fulfilling prophecy which is incapable
of test because, by definition, it cannot be disproved'. And, naturally,
Lévi-Strauss has his own safety-device to repel critical boarders. This is
a purely linguistic one, on the lines of the Marxist use of the phrase
'internal contradictions' to explain away evidence which does not fit any
of their propositions. Thus Lévi-Strauss embraces awkward and
invalidating facts by calling them 'supplementary dimensions', as for
instance: 'This remarkable inversion of a system which we have revealed
as occurring in a vast territory stretching from Venezuela to Paraguay
does not contradict our interpretation but enriches it by a supplementary dimension . . .'

There we may leave Lévi-Strauss and his colleagues in obfuscation.
Their object is to destroy certitudes, to infect the corpus of received
civilized knowledge with doubt, and so to dislocate western man, take
him away from his natural, familiar defences, and set him up again,
naked, on an empty and bewildering plain. This process of disorientation can be halted, as we have seen, by a careful and rational defence of
truth. Unfortunately, the obfuscators have received the assistance of
unconscious and unwilling allies in the realms of creative imagination –
and this because of an inherent defect in the civilizing process itself.

CHAPTER 16

'The Night of Unknowingness'

As we have already noted, the central characteristic of western civilization is dynamism. Some irresistible force – it may be the obsession with time inculcated by ethical teaching – impels continuous forward motion. Western man is a constitutionally restless creature. In his *Leviathan*, Hobbes likened existence in our society to a race. Felicity is the state of mind of those who are in front. But the race has no finishing-line; the whole point of life is simply to be in it: 'There is no such thing as perpetual tranquillity of mind while we live here, because life itself is but motion and can never be without desire, or without fear, no more than without sense . . . there can be no contentment but in proceeding.'

This dynamism explains why it was the West which fathered the scientific and industrial revolutions. But dynamism is also the identifying feature of western imaginative culture, and therein lies a very grave difficulty for our civilization. Dynamism implants an urge to perfectionism in the western artist, and compels him never to rest content with his modes of expression. There can never be any question, in western art, of the repetitive stability, the infinite variations on established patterns, which characterize most of the great art-systems of the world, notably in Asia. Western dynamism, then, creates extraordinary levels of achievement. But dynamism is also a destructive force, for it compels the artist to abandon or smash his creative moulds as fast as he creates them. He is constantly bursting through the artistic limitations and disciplines he himself has imposed at an early stage, and moving forward, like an uncontrollable machine, into unknown territory, often to aesthetic disaster. Nothing seems able to control, or brake, let alone reverse, the western cultural juggernaut, as it rolls relentlessly into the future.

Moreover, the speed of the monstrous chariot is quickening. When we speak of the crisis in western culture, that is essentially what we mean. Of course the artist is not, and must not be, the servant and defender of an ideology or way of life, as the Soviet authorities (and others) maintain But neither is he set apart from society; his activities, however motivated, can strengthen or weaken it. Today, it can be argued that the discarding of artistic modes created over centuries contributes precisely to that disorientation of man which we have examined in the previous chapter. Let us examine ways in which this tragedy occurs.

In Chapter 4 we saw how the visual arts evolved in primitive societies as a form of technology and education; that the realistic portrayal of life, and especially man in relation to his environment, is closely connected both to the development of other civilized techniques, and even perhaps to the concept of human freedom; and we saw how, in the case of one visual technique, the mastery of pictorial space, the key discoveries, lost in the collapse of the Graeco-Roman world, were developed again in the later Middle Ages as part of the technological process which prepared the western world for its economic and industrial take-off. The idea of a deep separation between art and science is a comparatively novel one, unknown to the ancients or the Renaissance, and moreover a fundamentally false one: for art is a form of knowledge.

The visual arts are part of the process whereby man orientates himself in the world of space. In antique times, the progress of art towards perfect imitation, or *mimesis*, was exactly like the progress of technology to modern minds – that is, the model of progress as such. Pliny told the story of sculpture and painting as a history of inventions: the painter Polygnotus was the first to represent people with open mouths, and with teeth; the sculptor Pythagoras the first to show nerves and veins in relief; the painter Nicias the first to paint light and shade effectively, and so forth. Vasari's biographies of Renaissance painters and sculptors use essentially the same criteria. Moreover, this approach to art history is correct; though it is not the only permissible one. A painter cannot paint realistically until he sees correctly; and seeing correctly is related to knowledge, which is acquired and cumulative. A primitive artist 'sees' so little because he knows no more. Images received by the eye are re-arranged by the brain in the light of experience and information derived from learning. Civilized writers have always known this. As Pliny put it, 'The mind is the real instrument of sight and observation, the eyes act as a sort of vessel, receiving and transmitting the visible portion of the consciousness.' Hence, as Constable said, 'The art of seeing nature is a thing almost as much to be acquired as the art of reading the Egyptian hieroglyphs.' Such insights have merely been confirmed by the evidence of photography, and by the work of modern visual psychologists.

But if we now know scientifically something about how the eye and the brain coordinate, we do not really understand the psychology of art at all, as those who have attempted to describe it admit. Thus J. J. Gibson, the greatest of the visual psychologists: 'Learning to attend to novel features of the world, to explore it, is something which psychologists do not understand at present.' D. O. Hebb, in *The Organisation of Behaviour*, concedes that 'the perception of size, brightness and pitch should be written down for the present as not yet accounted for by any theory'. Ralph M. Evans, in his *Introduction to Colour*, says that there is as yet no explanation, for instance, for the 'spreading effect' of superimposed colours, and the way in which it operates as a visual process.

Thus the scientist is, as yet, no help to the visual artist in his problems. And his problems are real. They spring not merely from his instinctive dynamism, but from the rapid diffusion and acquisition of his discoveries. Hence, as E. H. Gombrich writes in *Art and Illusion*, by far the most illuminating study of this whole subject, the inventions and effects of representation which were the prideful achievements of earlier masters have rapidly become trivial. 'Many a modest amateur,' he says, 'has mastered tricks which would have looked like sheer magic to Giotto . . . the victory and vulgarization of representational skills create a problem for both the historian and the critic.' But a problem, most of all, for the artist. If he is to preserve his separate existence as a specialist, how does he proceed? The scientist moves serenely on, happy to abandon his earlier discoveries to schoolchildren, confident in the knowledge that there is an infinity of new ones awaiting his specialist skills. The artist's instinct, of course, is to move on also. But where to? The problem first became acute in the nineteenth century, or at least was then recognized as acute, with the apparent exhaustion of the resources of representational art. Did painting, say, then face atrophy, as some scientists believe nuclear physics faces it today?

In the absence of true theory, artists and their critics attempted to solve the dilemma by adopting what turned out to be a false one, the 'theory of the innocent eye'. Here is a good example, as Gombrich shows, of a pseudo-science developing because its practitioners neglected to take the precaution of adopting 'proof by falsification'. In the eighteenth century, Bishop Berkeley created a new theory of vision, an extreme development of the insight familiar to Pliny and others. According to Berkeley, who held a general anti-materialist theory of nature, the world as we see it is entirely a construct, slowly built up by every one of us in years of experimentation. Our eyes merely undergo stimulation on the retina; it is our mind that weaves these sensations into perception, our conscious picture of the world based on experience. Berkeley's view, which of course is true up to a very limited point, had been generally adopted by the early nineteenth century; and, on top of it, John Ruskin imposed a theory of aesthetic psychology based on an analysis of J. M. W. Turner's paintings. According to Ruskin, in *Modern Painters* (1843), the progress of art is essentially the triumph over the prejudices of tradition. The non-artist, without an artist's specialist training, cannot see nature as it really is, because he cannot disentangle what he actually sees from what he merely knows. Hence 'the truth of nature is not to be discerned by the uneducated senses'. Educating these senses involved what he termed 'the recovery of the innocent eye'. The true painter had the eye of innocence, which he had learnt to detach from the clutter of knowledge. Turner's later work was the ultimate progress towards visual truth, because he had gradually discovered how to leave out what he merely knew, and only paint what he saw – the patchwork of colours in his canvases of the 1830s and 1840s.

Ruskin's theory, which created modern art criticism, and prepared the way for the Impressionists and all subsequent developments in painting, undoubtedly saved the artist as a separate caste. But is it true? Not only is it not true, but it is ultimately highly destructive. Gombrich calls it 'laying the explosive charge which was to blow the academic edifice sky-high'. In fact it destroyed more than the academic edifice; it demolished the theory, practice and values of humanist art. For it followed from Ruskin, that the artist, and only the artist, had the key, through his special gift and trained eye, to what things really looked like. Once this lurch forward was achieved, the juggernaut quickly became unstoppable, running over Ruskin himself in the process.

In fact the innocent eye is a myth. Here, at least, modern visual psychology can help to put the facts straight. According to J. J. Gibson, the eye's retina does not react to individual stimuli of light, as Berkeley thought, but to their relationships or gradients. So we cannot actually suppress conceptual knowledge. Laboratory experiments show that knowledge actually influences the way we see things, as well as causing us to readjust images. The stimulus patterns of the retina do not alone determine our picture of the visual world. Its messages are modified by what we know about the 'real' shape of objects – or, rather, their characteristic shape, that is the shape which gives the most information about the object. Primitive peoples, insisting on clear classification, usually paint an object in this shape – thus the human being is shown full-frontal, to convey the maximum information about him, irrespective of his true posture.

In general, our mind works on the information given by the retina in a series of expectations, guesses and hypotheses. The so-called optical illusion is not, in a sense, exceptional but normal; in psychology the concept of illusion is itself illusory since no experience actually copies reality. Perception, thus, is a relative business; mind and knowledge are at work all the time; there are no absolutes, so there can be no question of eliminating knowledge to get at the pristine, innocent eye. No such eye exists. And the idea that we ought just to see coloured patches is absurd. Ruskin was wrong to think there is an original sin of vision which has corrupted the way we see things, destroying the beauty given to us, and which only the artist can give us back. In fact, artists and non-artists alike see exactly what they ought to see. From his work on wartime problems of teaching naval pilots to land on aircraft carriers, J. J. Gibson formed a profound respect for the layman's visual equipment: human beings, he writes, 'to a marvellous extent are equipped to probe and learn by trial and error, by switching from one hypothesis to another until one is found that ensures our survival'. The visual field, he says, depends on attitude; it is 'the product of the chronic habit of civilized men of seeing the world as a picture. . . . So far from being the basis, it is a kind of *alternative* to ordinary perception.' What the artist does, argues Gombrich, is to take advantage of the ambiguity of civilized sight, by trying different visual readings; he learns to look critically and probe his perceptions by painting alternative interpretations. But if this process of interpretation is conducted on the basis of true theory, there are very real limitations to the painter's freedom.

Unfortunately, the theory of the innocent eye was not disproved until after the artistic juggernaut had demolished the whole structure of ideas underlying representational, or illusionist, art. Over many thousands of years, the traditions of illusionist art had been accumulating a multitude of symbols and conventions, ranging from the way to portray fur, perfected by Dürer, to an immensely complicated code of facial expressions;

these traditions, moreover, had been built up in continuous contact with the observer, so that the dialogue between painter and layman had been continuous. The destruction of illusionist art not only ended the dialogue but makes its resumption increasingly difficult.

The speed with which the visual arts have moved away from illusion and reality, into an entirely false world of imaginative perception, is a tribute to the power of the dynamic urge in western artists, and the eagerness with which they have seized on Ruskin's invitation to give way to it. There have been attempts to modify and update Ruskin's initial theory to accommodate this rapid progression. Thus Rudolf Arnheim, in *Art and Visual Perception*, maintains that different periods have different standards of lifelikeness, and that 'a further shift in the artistic reality level' will eventually make Picasso's people and objects 'look exactly like the things they represent'. But this theory has no scientific basis whatever. It is undermined, not least, by Picasso's repeated assertion that he did not see things as he painted them; for he was a clown, playing tricks on fools. Moreover, even if the theory were true, it would not accommodate the headlong movement away from any representation at all. As recently as 1921, Aldous Huxley, in his satirical novel *Chrome Yellow*, has the fatuous Mary Wimbush, the pseudo-intellectual, apostrophize the latest Parisian painter, Tschup-litski: 'He's getting more and more abstract every day. He'd quite given up the third dimension when I was there and was just thinking of giving up the second. So, he says, there'll be just the blank canvas. That's the logical conclusion. Complete abstraction. Painting's finished. He's finishing it.'

What was hilarious satire in 1921 had become humourless fact long before Huxley was in his grave. Thus, to quote only one of many examples, Morris Louis, by his own description a 'post-painterly abstractionist', simply painted streaks on the edge of the canvas, leaving the rest untouched; as one of his interpretative admirers put it, 'The dazzling blankness of the untouched canvas at once repulses and engulfs the eye, like an infinite abyss that opens up behind the least mark that we make on a flat surface' (Michael Fried, *Introduction to Morris Louis, 1912–1962*). Yves Klein, another well-known international figure, not only showed empty canvases but held exhibitions of emptiness, that is, white-painted empty galleries. 'The visual arts,' writes one of their most distinguished chroniclers, Edward Lucie-Smith, 'are showing distinct signs of weariness, as if we were approaching the end of something.'

Indeed: one may compare the passage quoted from *Chrome Yellow* with this analysis by a leading American critic of US sculpture in the 1960s:

The Minimalists appear to have realised finally that the far-out in itself has to be the far-out as an end in itself, and that this means the farthest out and nothing short of that. They appear also to have realised that the most original and furthest-out art in the past 100 years always arrived looking as though it had parted company with everything previously known as art. In other words, the furthest-out usually lay on the borderline between art and non-art. The Minimalists have not really discovered anything new through this realisation, but they have drawn conclusions from it with a new consistency which owes something of its newness to the shrinking of the area in which things can safely be non-art. Given that the initial look of non-art was no longer available in painting, since even an unpainted canvas now stated itself as a picture, the borderline between art and non-art now had to be sought in the three-dimensional, where sculpture was, and where everything material that was not art also was.

The point is put rather differently by Claude Lévi-Strauss, who is verbally resourceful if nothing else. Non-representational paintings, he writes, are 'realistic imitations of non-existent models. It is a school of academic painting in which each artist strives to represent the manner in which he would execute his pictures if by chance he were to paint any'.

Thus we see the visual arts joining the familiar pattern by which truth, reality and reason are denied, and man is deprived of certitudes, so that his values can be taken over and transformed. In the case of painting, the process of disorientation is not merely conceptual but physical too. Lucie-Smith, in what I take to be a defence-explanation of abstract art ('How Abstract Art Can Influence Thought and Vision', printed in *Thinking About Art*), writes: 'By discarding the particular references which are required by presentation, it leaves us to contemplate them in an almost pure state.' But what, in fact, is the actual perception obtained by an observer in the nearest possible approximation to an empty visual space? The answer is given by J. J. Gibson in *The Perception of the Visual World*:

[His eyes] will not focus or converge and he cannot fix or look on. He will see luminosity or colour but . . . it is unlocalised in the third dimension: its distance is indeterminate. The sea of light around him might vary from bright to dark and from one hue to another but the quality of colour would be neither that of a surface on the one hand nor would it be extended in depth on the other. It is neither near nor far. The space he sees is certainly not two-dimensional in the sense of being flat but it is also not three-dimensional in the sense of being deep . . . it has no texture, no arrangement, no contours, no shapes, no solidity, and no horizontal or vertical axes. The observer might as well be in absolute darkness so far as he can *see* anything.

Or, alternatively, have fallen into one of Morris Louis's 'infinite abysses'. Of course, here Gibson is analysing the observer *in* abstract visual space, assuming his environment consists wholly of atmosphere without any opaque objects: the disorientation is complete and unqualified. The analogy with the observer *of* abstract visual space is not complete, but the argument tends to suggest that abstract art, and indeed all forms of non-representational art, tend to disorientate the individual and induce intellectual confusion. Visual art ceases to be knowledge and education, and becomes destructive of truth and rationality.

The process can be seen at work even where forms of representational art survive, for it was a further consequence of Ruskin's doctrine of the innocent eye that the artist is accorded a special status – one might say a sacred one, since his individuality becomes central to the work of art, almost its subject. Dynamic movement in this direction received a tremendous impetus from Jean-Paul Sartre. Mary Wimbush, to return for a second to *Chrome Yellow*, 'was accustomed in London to associate only with first-rate people who liked first-rate things, and she knew that there were very, very few first-rate things in the world, and that those were mostly French.' Frenchmen, as we are seeing, play a notable part in all pseudo-intellectual and pseudo-scientific movements, and are exceedingly active in assaulting the civilization they helped so notably to create. One tremendously damaging blow was struck by Sartre in 1946, when he gave his notorious lecture at the Sorbonne, 'Existentialism is a Humanism', in which he effectively transplanted the Germanic doctrines of Heidegger to French soil. It is odd indeed that the French, who had just got rid of the Germans physically, should then have immediately embraced them intellectually, but the fact is that this lecture was perhaps the most influential since Ruskin's famous inaugural as Oxford Professor of Fine Art, in 1870. The lecture gave a powerful impulse to western cultural dynamism which, heaven knows, it did not need, since it insisted on originality at all costs. 'We must begin with the subjective,' said Sartre; the individual, especially the individual artist, must be 'man to the very limit, to the absurd, to the night of unknowingness'. Here, indeed, was an invitation to the intelligentsia to set about the disorientation of man – the 'night of unknowingness' might well serve to

categorize our epoch – and it is no coincidence that Sartre's writings
have been exceptionally influential in shaping various pseudo-sciences
we have examined; they keep popping up, for example, in the work of
Lévi-Strauss, rather like King Charles's head in Mr Dick's petition to the
Lord Chancellor. Sartre's image, in *Huis Clos*, of mankind imprisoned
in an abstract vestibule to eternity, recurs in various forms in all the
western arts of the post-war world.

Where painting clings to figurativeness, and its illusory skills, there is
the same effort to dislocate and confuse the viewer. Let us examine this
by taking two examples of terror, grief and pain, and the way in which
artists portray them. The first is Goya's painting *The Third of May 1808*,
which dates from 1814. We know a good deal about the background to
the painting, because it is the subject of a monograph by the distinguished historian of modern Spain, Hugh Thomas, published in 1972.
The painting deals with an incident during the Napoleonic occupation of
Spain – the rising of part of the population of Madrid on 2 May 1808,
and its brutal suppression, followed by mass executions the next day, by
Napoleon's viceroy, Marshal Murat. Murat's severity, it seems, had been
inspired by the emperor himself. He had written to Napoleon shortly
before, grumbling about his difficulties with the Spanish; Napoleon
replied contemptuously that he was tired of a general who, with 50,000
men under him, was in the habit of asking for things instead of taking
them; he added: 'If the *canaille* stirs, shoot it down.' The rebuke, said
Murat, stunned him 'like a tile falling on my head'. Hence his implacable
treatment of the rioters; in writing to Napoleon he even exaggerated the
numbers he had shot.

The painting of the event Goya gives us is a work of great artistry and
passion. But it is not a work of propaganda, and though highly imaginative the imagination behind it is in no way romantic. It is a masterpiece of
truth. We do not know if Goya actually saw the executions but he was
personally connected with the May events in a number of ways. In any
case, by the time he came to paint this picture, nearly six years after the
event, he was by way of being an expert on war and violence, on which he
had brooded, and worked, throughout the intervening period. What
strikes one about this painting is that Goya makes no attempt to conceal
the horror of violent death, or to redeem it by hints of heroism and
redemption. A man in a white shirt and yellow breeches is about to be
shot – the lantern of the execution squad is turned on him, and he
stretches out his hands in a despairing crucifixion. His expression is not

resigned but petrified. A friar, too, also about to be shot, is likewise afraid and looks at the ground rather than the executioner, his hands clasped in prayer. Another victim hides his eyes in his hands, a fourth looks despairingly up to heaven; a fifth clenches his fists in pointless rage, his face contorted with hopeless fury. The soldiers are brutal yet somehow elegant automatons. There is blood all over the corpse in the foreground. There is no doubt from the picture where Goya's sympathies lay, but he does not present the murdered men sentimentally, merely as different human beings facing death in various attitudes of fear. The painting must, and is meant to, inspire horror, fear, revulsion. But these drastic emotions are not meaningless or unlocalized. It is quite clear what the painting portrays. The actual executions took place on Madrid's Montana del Principe Pio, between the city and the River Mazanares; this area is now built over, but we know what it looked like then, and Goya has put in the background of buildings, though he did not greatly trouble himself to render them accurately. The background is there; the event took place; the men existed – indeed, we know the name of Goya's friar. Hence, there is a solid historical context for this painting which allows us to relate ourselves to it morally. Our reactions to this painting may vary greatly, but each of us knows where we stand; we are not disorientated. We are given information and draw conclusions, and the process of communing with the painting is not wholly unlike that *catharsis* which Aristotle claimed was the result of great dramatic art. Here is a work of visual tragic art in the finest tradition of western civilization.

Now let us turn to a painting, or rather series of paintings, by Francis Bacon, variously known as 'Screaming Popes' or 'Screaming Cardinals'. Bacon operates in what might be termed the modern figurative tradition, and he is a painter of outstanding gifts and accomplishment. Like Goya, he deals in violence and fear in their most extreme forms. Unlike Goya, it seems to me, he is not interested in the truth of the visual world; in fact, as often happens with painters, he prefers to see the world, in the first instance, through other paintings. This particular series of studies was inspired primarily by Velasquez's famous *Portrait of Pope Innocent X*, in the Doria Gallery in Rome. But, as Lawrence Alloway has pointed out (*Francis Bacon*), the series is also related to a weird portrait of Cardinal Filippo Archinto, who is shown partly hidden by a semi-transparent curtain, a feature which makes an appearance of sorts in Bacon's canvases. Thus, those who call the studies popes, and those who call them cardinals, may both be right (or wrong, as the case may be).

It is characteristic of Bacon's work, however, that we do not even know whether the subject of these paintings is a cardinal or pope. Innocent X was a helpless seventy-four-year-old, irresolute and dominated by his widowed sister-in-law, Olympia Maidalchini. His papacy was disastrous for the Roman Catholic church. He proved unable to influence the negotiations which led to the Peace of Westphalia and ended both the Thirty Years War and the period of religious conflict. Instead he issued a Bull deploring the peace treaty and denouncing the decision of the Catholic princes to grant heretics the right to exercise their religion. He thus got the worst of both worlds, and as a result the papacy ceased to influence European affairs for over a hundred and fifty years. In short, a tragic and memorable man. But no hint of this appears in Bacon's painting. The pope, or cardinal, is being subjected to the most intense torture, physical or mental, or perhaps both. His scream of prolonged agony is so intense that we can almost hear it; so intense is his pain, and his terror of more to come, that his physical personality is beginning to dissolve – in fact the body in one of the studies is in an advanced stage of dissolution.

Bacon conveys fear, pain and horror almost as powerfully as Goya. But that is all he does convey. There are no other facts or inferences the viewer can grasp to establish himself, morally, in relation to this series of paintings. Why is the pope screaming? Who is doing what to him, and why? Is it God, or man; are his torments real or imaginary, physical or mental? When did they start, and will they finish? Is this the real world or Hell? Are his enemies ours, or ought they to be our friends? Which side should we be on? Or should we be on neither? Are there in fact sides? None of these questions is answered. Indeed, they cannot be answered since the painter does not know the answer himself, and probably does not even feel qualified to pose the questions, since he declared, in a BBC interview with David Sylvester in 1968, that his work is similar to that of abstract painting: 'I think that you can make, very much as in abstract painting, involuntary marks on the canvas which may suggest much deeper ways by which you can trap the facts you are obsessed by. If anything ever does work in my case, it works from that moment when consciously I didn't know what I was doing.' Not only is the viewer disorientated but so is the painter, since he is not in intellectual control of his work at the critical moments. Unlike Goya's painting, where fear, horror and pain are firmly anchored to historical fact and moral certitude, the destructive emotions dominate and exclude any alternative and compensating ones. It is worth noting that Laing in *The Divided Self*, welcomes Bacon's work as examples of 'a world in which there is no contradictory sense of the self in its "health and validity" to mitigate the despair, terror and boredom of existence'. The viewer of Bacon's pope might just as well be in Louis's 'infinite abyss', since his dislocation from the universe of truth and value is complete until he removes his gaze from the tortured canvases, and rejoins the real world of civilization. Far from being purged by the tragedy, he is bewildered, confused and disquieted by his experience. Alas, these effects are produced by other forms of western art, as we shall see.

CHAPTER 17

Cultural Juggernauts

What is interesting about the age of dislocation in which we live is that all the arts contribute to this sense of homelessness, but each does so in its own way. Architecture, for instance, sometimes disorientates us in a physical, as well as a metaphorical, sense. There must be many travellers who have had the uneasy experience of waking, after a doze, in an international airport, forgetting where they are, and being totally unable for some moments to identify the place and country from their surroundings. The sheer geographical anonymity of many functional constructions, airports, motorways, hotels, and so forth, does not reflect a creative internationalism but, rather, betrays a poverty of ideas, an absence of regional emotions, and a dominant cost-accounting which knows no frontiers. Where an attempt is made to provide a local veneer, as for instance in Hilton hotels, it serves merely to draw attention to the barren uniformity beneath. What is impressive about the great historic schools of architecture is either their complete identification with an area, as with the temples and theatres of Magna Graecia, or the local variations on a predominant style, above all in the Gothic, where the modifications of the archetype are functional as well as aesthetic. The standardization of design which fills us with oppressive bewilderment is very much a feature of the last half of our century. In earlier epochs new technology was successfully regionalized, as, for instance, in the rich varieties of railway architecture (and even engineering).

Discussing artistic dislocation in his book *The Struggle of the Modern*, Stephen Spender asks whether it might not reflect the physical dislocations of the twentieth century caused by wars, the mingling of cultures, social and scientific change, and the increased mobility of man. Of course these are important contributory factors; and it is one of the themes of this book that, within the framework of a civilization, it is impossible to separate political and economic change from artistic development. Yet it is a fact that many of the structural changes in the arts began before 1914, the historic turning-point, and took place against a social background of unusual stability. These changes would have taken place whatever the external circumstances because they were impelled by the restless dynamism of western culture.

I do not propose to trace the pattern of these disorienting mutations in detail, because the reader can do that for himself, but merely to point out lines of inquiry. Art is a source not only of pleasure but of reassurance; it is not a luxury of civilization but a necessity. If art undermines the common certitudes, it lowers morale and makes external assault more deadly. And we are rendered unsure not only by what we see but by what we hear (and read). The tragedy can be seen at its most pitiful in the sphere of music. Music is the intellectual queen of the arts, the one whose theory and practice is closest to the workings of the sciences, and where the impulsions of logical dynamism are most forceful. But it is also much closer to our human essence than is usually supposed. Like speech, it is a characteristic of humanity even at the most primitive level. A study, for instance, of the Veddas, a pygmoid people of primeval hunters living in the interior of Ceylon at the very lowest layer of culture, reveals that, though they have no instruments of any kind, they possess a musical system, with intervals, rhythm, recurring melodical turns and characteristic terminal cadences. Such prototypes of music in its most elementary form bear no relation whatever to even the most complex bird-calls and other animal noises.

Professor Revesz, the Dutch psychologist who finally established this fact in 1941, argues, in his *Introduction to the Psychology of Music*, that music, like language, springs from the principle of communication, probably from the wordless shout or calling signal; only the singing voice has real carrying power. And, since the phylogenesis of music is communication, it must have a structure. The calling signals of primitive peoples, in fact, often have a distinct musical structure. Song and music, therefore, owe their origins to speech, and it is in their nature to convey meaning by structure. Western music is a comparatively late development; but its progress has been astonishingly rapid, comparable indeed in time as well as pace with scientific technology. With all music, but especially with highly developed music in the western manner, the decisive thing, as Revesz argues, is the structure or architecture, the multiplicity and unity of form. It demands not only knowledge and a feeling for style, but the ability to analyse: the phenomenological approach. When we enter a cathedral, and examine its various axial tendencies and its symmetrical, and asymmetrical forms, we perceive it phenomenologically; the approach to music is, in all essentials, the same.

It is precisely because music is grasped phenomenologically that its structural breakdown, since about 1900, is proving so serious. Perhaps its development was too rapid; at all events, by the beginning of our century the process seems to have reached its limits and was breaking out of the restraints imposed by the system. Consonance broke into dissonance; in tonality, evolution could go no further without fatally weakening the principle of tonality itself; hence, though logical harmony was fundamental to the western system, both went. The same difficulties arose in other forms of structure, and in rhythm, melody, timbre and texture, and were similarly 'solved' by abandoning the custodial restraints.

The tragedy became inevitable the moment when, as Aaron Copland put it, Arnold Schoenberg 'decided that tonality was not an essential element of serious music'. Civilization, as Yeats said, is a system of self-restraints. Not that one should impute any moral, or even artistic, blame to Schoenberg. His early work moved through phases of Brahms, Dvořák and Wagner, and his motive in smashing the system to bits was not destructive but, on the contrary, that irresistible urge towards novelty which is the creative glory of western culture. The tragedy of music that followed was a tragedy not least for himself. Schoenberg, Charles Rosen writes in his recent biography, continued to provoke, to the end of his life, 'an enmity, even a hatred, almost unparalleled in the history of music'. He was made painfully aware that much of the musical world held him guilty of a kind of ferocious artistic parricide. In 1945, in an atmosphere of undisguised hostility, the musical committee of the Guggenheim Foundation turned down his application for a grant to allow him to continue composing, one of many public slights he received. As he therefore had to go on taking pupils, he was able to write only one of the books he had planned, his *Structural Functions of Harmony*, and some of his large-scale musical works were never finished.

Schoenberg was so shocked by the fury his initial abandonment of tonality aroused that he deliberately moved from complete atonality

to the twelve-tone system to appease the musical public; but of course
it is a logical structure not of tonality but of atonality since the notes
are related not to a common centre but only to each other, and to the
public the new device seemed merely to be adding a sarcastic insult to a
fatal injury. For Schoenberg, one of the most knowledgeable and gifted
composers in the entire history of music, with a passionate attachment to
the art, professional life became an almost intolerable burden; he said
four years before he died: 'Personally I had the feeling as if I had fallen
into an ocean of boiling waters, and not knowing how to swim or to get
out in another manner, I tried with my legs and arms as best I could. . . .
I never gave up. But how could I give up in the middle of an ocean?' But
his artistic integrity allowed him no regrets, and no remorse. Once, asked
if he were Arnold Schoenberg, the famous composer, he replied: 'No one
else wanted the job, so I had to take it on.'

And of course the damage has now been done and we cannot retrace
our steps. One of the characteristics of western culture is that, once a
mould has been broken and replaced, it can never be effectively repaired
and used again. All the modern attempts to reintroduce the old musical
manner have been relative or absolute failures. But the public have been
equally obdurate about accepting the new. In the eighteenth century the
vast majority of musical works performed at concerts and in churches
were contemporary. In 1776, for instance, the organizers of the London
Concerts of Ancient Music explained that 'ancient' referred to pieces
more than twenty years old. The proportion of 'modern' music performed
remained high throughout the nineteenth century. But a statistical
summary, quoted by Roy McMullen in *Art, Affluence and Alienation: the
fine arts today*, suggests that over 90% of the music performed in the
third quarter of the twentieth century was composed before 1900. Wilfred
Mellers, a leading critic and composer who takes a pessimistic view of
the musical future, observes that 'the desire to listen exclusively to the
music of the past rather than to that of one's own time is a phenomenon
that has never happened before'.

Yet we should not be surprised, for since music is communication, and
needs structure to fulfil its purpose, it cannot work without a structure
perceptible to the listener. Thus, serialism does not provide a workable
order, at least for most listeners, because the structure is mathematical
rather than aural. The alternative of random or aleatory music, as
provided by such 'composers' as John Cage or Stockhausen, does not
work either; indeed it is not even random since the performers tend to

slip into patterns, even highly traditional ones, unless their 'randomness' is actually scored for them – so strong is the urge towards structural certitude of civilized western man. Moreover, modern musical works enjoy a limited degree of acceptability only in so far as they possess a comprehensible structure, often a hidden one. In an important book, *Tonality and Musical Structure*, Graham George argues that structure is essential to what he terms 'acceptable comprehensibility'; he uses the Kantian definition that structure is a concept imposed by the mind of its own necessity on its experiences: that it is the mind's subjective reduction to comprehensibility of its experience of objective reality, and that without this subjectively imposed structure there is no comprehension. George demonstrates that, where some form of structure is perceptible in modern works, it is in fact a form of tonality. Thus, the Second and Seventh Symphonies of Mahler are examples of juxtaposed tonality; Hindemith's *Mathis der Maler* is a case of interlocking tonality. He shows that the so-called 'progressive tonality', or non-tonality of Carl Neilsen, is in fact misleading, because genuine progressive tonality would be featureless, and he detects elements of a concealed structure in Neilsen's Second Symphony, *The Four Temperaments*, and indeed in his other symphonies.

The sad tale of twentieth-century music, then, illustrates not merely the disasters which flow from a loss of certitude but the almost desperate anxiety of most civilized people to cling on to it if they can. Of course, as we have seen, certitude can be expressed scientifically as well as structurally; and it can also take a variety of moral forms. Man needs to know where he is, and when he is civilized he acquires this knowledge through cultural and moral criteria, which are closely enmeshed. That acute observer of the animal world, Gavin Maxwell, makes the point as follows:

As soon as routine is broken a new element enters, in however minute and unrecognisable a trace – the fear of the unknown which is basic to the behaviour of all animals, including man. Every living creature exists by a routine of some kind; the small rituals of that routine are the landmarks, the boundaries of security, the reassuring walls that exclude a *horror vacui*; thus, in our own species, after some tempest of the spirit in which the landmarks seem to have been swept away, a man will reach out tentatively in mental darkness to feel the walls, to assure himself that they still stand where they stood – a necessary gesture, for the walls are of his own building, without universal reality, and what man makes he may destroy (*Ring of Bright Water*).

He may, indeed, destroy them; and it is part of the dynamism of
civilized western man that he is constantly altering or even demolishing
the moral and cultural landmarks. The critics call this 'weakened
reference', and sometimes the references to people and things known to
the reader are so weak that the work appears to be a private communication to unknown private persons, or elaborate messages in an uncrack-
able code. The master of this art *in vacuo* is of course Samuel Beckett,
whose novels and plays convey mood and atmosphere but virtually no
information; or, rather, the amount of information he conveys has
steadily declined throughout his writing career. The craftsmanship and
ingenuity he displays are admirable, and some claim him to be the
greatest writer of the twentieth century; but Beckett has reached the
stage of aesthetic dominance when those who cannot understand what
he is doing or why he is doing it are inclined to apologize for their own
lack of comprehension rather than blame his failure to convey his
meaning – an enviable position for an artist to secure for himself. In his
later works critical judgement must almost be suspended since the critic
has virtually no information on which to work, and must make it all up
for himself. Thus, of two of Beckett's latest works, *Comment c'est* deals
with a naked man crawling in mud; it is a subject rather than a theme or
a treatment; and *Lessness* is an abstract comparative, which induces a
vague but perceptible feeling of disquietude and failure but not in any
particular context or situation – the reader is in a similar predicament to
the man suspended in J. J. Gibson's empty visual spaces. As we have
seen in another context, there is an attempt to provide knowledge but
not knowledge *about*.

The difficulties which western cultural dynamism presents to original
and civilized artists can be seen in the cases of the two leading 'serious'
playwrights of the Anglo-Saxon world, Harold Pinter and Tom Stoppard.
Pinter is a major tragic writer in the tradition of Ibsen, whose compulsion to break out of the structural forms of post-Ibsen tragedy lead
him to weaken the references deliberately and systematically, so that the
spectator is never permitted to become fully orientated, though he is
painfully aware of tragedy being enacted. Therein lies an irony or contradiction, since Pinter is 'pretty well obsessed with words when they get
going', as he puts it. His plays hinge round success or failure to commun-
icate, and he draws constant attention to the fact that the vernacular, for
which he has an extraordinary feeling, is supposedly the speech of
ordinary people and understood by them easily, but in reality conveys

very little and serves more to demarcate the distances between individuals than their togetherness. In plays like *The Homecoming, The Caretaker, The Birthday Party*, the speech is drawn from the limitations or failure of language spoken by evasive, furtive or frightened people, or those seeking to menace or dominate them without apparent cause. There is never any explanation or motivation for the action. Here the fear conveyed is similar to that produced by indiscriminate terrorism; since no one in particular is a specific target, anyone might be; and the audience is at liberty to identify with the victims on stage since so many factual questions are left unanswered, indeed unasked, and their ordinariness strengthens the point.

Pinter has described his art as 'Two people in a room – I am dealing a great deal of the time with this image of two people in a room. The curtain goes up on the stage, and I see it as a very potent question: what is going to happen to these two people in the room? Is someone going to open the door and come in?' When asked by Kenneth Tynan what his two people in the room were afraid of, Pinter replied: 'Obviously they are scared of what is outside the room. Outside the room there is a world bearing upon them which is frightening. I am sure it is frightening to you and me as well.' (Interviews with Hallam Tennyson, BBC General Overseas Service, 7 August 1960; and with Kenneth Tynan, BBC Home Service, 28 October 1960.) Hence, in *The Birthday Party*, the two menacing men, Goldberg and McCann, are never explained. Pinter has theoretical and practical objections to plays which provide too much information; he deliberately rejects the 'progressive disclosure' of the Ibsen archetype. In a 1960 programme note he writes:

The desire for verification is understandable but cannot always be satisfied. There are no hard distinctions between what is real and what is unreal, nor between what is true and what is false. . . . A character on the stage who can present no convincing argument or information as to his past experience, his present behaviour or his aspirations, nor give a comprehensive analysis of his motives, is as legitimate and as worthy of attention as one who, alarmingly, can do all these things. The more acute the experience, the less articulate its expression.

Of course, we have been arguing throughout that civilized man believes, and must believe, that there are hard distinctions; that reality and truth are genuine and in most cases absolute concepts, not relative ones. Here again we see the artist, in his necessary pursuit of structural growth, in conflict with the social interest. The conflict can, and does, develop in other ways. Thus Tom Stoppard, our leading comic dramatist in the tradition of Oscar Wilde and George Bernard Shaw, breaks right through the referential structure not so much by withholding information as by providing it in prodigious quantities, but usually in elliptical or misleading form. Stoppard, like Pinter, has a positively Jacobean obsession with words, though not as patois; he, like Chomsky, is interested primarily in the deep structures beneath the brilliant verbal fireworks he contrives to explode. His method is the traditional comic one of the rigidly logical pursuit of ideas based on mad premises, one very familiar to Shaw; but in Stoppard's case the references or markers are all attached to booby-traps. *Rosencrantz and Guildenstern are Dead* is a vacuum play, because the audience is not certain it has a core; the two men live in the wings of life, suspended in unresolved doubt as to their existence; when not wanted, briefly, on stage, they never know what is happening, who is who, or whether they are people or characters. The setting is realistic, but there is no true reality since facts and information slip away, like smooth objects on a polished floor. In *Travesties* there is also a pseudo-realistic setting, since Tristan Tzara, Joyce and Lenin were all together in Zurich in 1917, though not (so far as we know) in contact. But the title reveals the fact that the whole play is an elaborate exercise in truth-bending and symmetrical confusion; indeed, it may in fact be about another play, *The Importance of Being Earnest*, just as *Rosencrantz and Guildenstern are Dead* may be about *Hamlet*. These plays do not terrify, like Pinter's; on the contrary, they are immensely exhilarating and entertaining; but, like Pinter's, they reinforce the view that reality is an illusion, or at best an uncertain or relative state, and that certitudes are not to be expected in life.

The reality most firmly presented, by western writers moving into the last decade of the century, is the hyper-reality or horror-reality of monsters, freaks and savages – the sort of creatures who hovered around the fringes of stories by Dickens, Balzac, Tolstoy and Conrad, but who have now taken over central roles. The point is cumulatively established that the frenzied edges of humanity are not only the proper, but the principal, concern of the artist, and that they constitute the normal core of society, if such a concept can be said to exist. Perhaps Bacon's pope (or cardinal) is screaming because he is just an ordinary human being, an intolerable thing to be; or perhaps Laing is right to imply that only the mad are sane – these assumptions run through so much contemporary writing that they must affect our vision of the reality which exists outside the theatre of imagination.

A very characteristic creation of our time is 'Crow', who appears in a series of poems published in 1970 by Ted Hughes, the most interesting of the post-war poets writing in English. These poems concentrate on the world of predatory animals and of primitive violence ruled not by reason but by unfathomable instinct. Crow is literally ferocious, and much of his destruction appears to be arbitrary or even pointless. Crow is brutal, funny in a grotesque way, greedy, selfish, violent and gruesome. It is not quite clear who or what he is; or what is his relation to the moral world, since he sometimes works in alliance with God and sometimes against him. In 'Crow's Theology', one of the poems, Hughes tells us:

> Crow realised there were two Gods –
> One of them much bigger than the other
> Loving his enemies
> And having all the weapons.

We do not know whether to be on Crow's side any more than we know whether we ought to sympathize with the screaming pope. There are a few key words: black, blood, smashed, stabbed and screamed. Evidently Crow is not just an animal, and it may be that he concentrates in his ferocious and blundering person all that Hughes can find worth observing about western civilization itself. Certainly Crow echoes, or rather symbolically re-enacts, the growing and featureless violence which is becoming its salient characteristic, and which we shall now examine.

CHAPTER 18

The Return of the Devils

It may seem absurd to discuss violence as essentially a contemporary problem; something new, as it were, threatening the established structure of our civilization. When was the world not violent? When did not all societies demand and exercise the right to use collective violence? Indeed, is not the right to a monopoly of violence the essential foundation of the state? All this is true. Man is an exceptionally aggressive species, has always used violence against other species and against his own; and always will, until there is a fundamental, and at present inconceivable, change in his nature. But violence is a human activity which must be judged quantitatively, and it must be judged in its context. There must be limits; and there must be rules. A civilization can accommodate itself to man's incorrigible practice of violence provided the limits are firmly set and defended, and the rules enforced.

The quantitative increase in violence of all kinds during our century is undoubtedly due in part to the rapid growth of population. There is a paranoid streak in man, and his paranoia increases as he feels the pressures on his space mount. The motivation here is not, strictly speaking, economic, and so measures to increase food production provide no solution; as with other species, violence breaks out not because there is a failure of food supplies but because rising density threatens movement-satisfaction and the sense of security. In these circumstances, when only a destruction of part of the species can afford relief, man's possession of terrifying weapons actually increases his paranoid tendencies (see Paul D. MacLean, 'The Paranoid Streak in Man', in *Beyond Reductionism: New Perspectives in the Life Sciences*).

In addition, however, since the nineteenth century there has been a philosophical reconsideration of the legitimate use of violence within and by civil society, and an attempt to relax the rules to the point, almost, where they become meaningless. Most philosophers of jurisprudence would agree with Burton Zweibach when he writes, in *Civility and Disobedience*, that '. . . violence is, and can only be, a technique of last resort – a strategy justified only when all other attempts to attain justice have failed.' This is the mainstream of western thinking, based, like most of our political grammar, on the social-contract theorists of the seventeenth century. Hobbes and Locke rightly treated violence as the antithesis of politics, a form of action characteristic of the archaic realm of the state of nature. Violence was a pre-political stage of human development. They saw politics as an attempt to create a tool to avoid barbarism and make civilization possible. Politics makes violence not only unnecessary but unnatural to civilized man.

Unfortunately, this is not the only philosophical stream in western political culture. In particular, in Germany there has been, since the early nineteenth century, an alternative tradition, which sees the exercise of violence as a necessary, natural and honourable expression of the human political spirit, what Nietzsche called 'the will to power'. This tradition has crossed frontiers. It found expression, for instance, in the Communist-Anarchist, later Fascist, violence-preaching of Sorel, and in the bombast of Mussolini: 'War ennobles those who dare to undertake it.' But its connection with Germany has remained close. Hitler was an activist in the Nietzschean tradition: 'Force is the first law. . . . Struggle is the father of all things. Virtue lies in blood.' The tradition was transmitted through the German philosophy schools in the universities, particularly in Berlin; and, above all, by Heidegger and his pupils. Thus it has, over the last few generations, found a number of sophisticated, even illustrious, converts, who have furnished themselves with arguments to justify force in securing desirable (to them) objectives.

Existentialism, as we have noted, is not a French philosophy but a German one. It has been widely employed, above all by Paul Tillich, to justify drastic change within a Christian theological framework, to demolish western civilization itself. Of course, violence has always played a significant part in Judaeo-Christian affairs, ever since Moses, on the instructions of the Deity, instructed his captains to revenge Israel on the Midianites: 'Now therefore kill every male among the little ones, and kill every woman that hath known man by lying with him. But all the women children who have not known a man by lying with him, keep alive for yourselves' (*Numbers*, 31:17–18). But Christian theology has rarely incited men to destroy existing society as a moral act. According to Tillich, 'all philosophies of Existence' oppose what he calls 'the "rational" system of thought and life developed by western industrial society and its philosophic representatives'. Rationality is a 'logical or naturalistic mechanism which seems to destroy individual freedom, personal decision and organic community'. It denies 'the vital forces of life' and transforms everything, including man 'into an object of calculation and control'; a secularized humanism which cuts man and the world off 'from the creative source and the ultimate mystery of existence'.

This essay by Tillich on 'Existential Philosophy' was published in the *Journal of the History of Ideas* in January 1944, before Sartre had publicized existentialism as a French contribution to the post-war philosophy of the revolutionary Left. Tillich was born in Prussia, and his formation was entirely Germanic. But then so, to a great extent, was Sartre's. He is half-Alsatian (Albert Schweizer was his cousin), and he was brought up in the house of his grandfather, Karl Schweizer, an Alsatian Protestant; his culture is as much German as French, and his major training was in the Berlin philosophy school – hence the influence of Heidegger and Kierkegaard. During the 'phoney war', 1939–40, Sartre was a meteorological clerk in the Maginot Line, where he performed the dialectically symbolic role of releasing hot-air balloons to test the wind. Sartre has found the wind increasingly favourable for his emphasis on violence, always a very marked characteristic of his work and opinions. He sees man as essentially horrible: 'Nothing indeed, neither wild beasts nor microbes, could be more terrible for man than this intelligent, flesh-eating, cruel species, which knows how to hunt and outwit the human intelligence, and whose precise aim is the destruction of man. This species is manifestly our own, as each of us sees it, in the Other, in the context of scarcity.'

Thus Sartre's theory of the state is basically the same as Hobbes's, in the first instance, though he uses the concept of 'terror', and a theory of scarcity derived from Hume. But unlike Hobbes he does not reject violence as the enemy; on the contrary he is a philosopher of great violence. In his novels, many of his characters achieved 'freedom' by gross acts of violence – for instance, Mathieu in *La Mort dans l'âme*, the third volume of his story *Les Chemins de la liberté*. Nor does he scruple to advocate, indeed enthuse over, violence in situations outside fiction. His prize pupil was Franz Fanon (whom we will examine in the next chapter), and the preface he wrote to Fanon's violent bible, *Les Damnés de la terre* is even more bloodthirsty than the text itself, which is based on the Sartrean doctrine of liberation through killing. For a black man, writes Sartre, 'to shoot down a European is to kill two birds with one stone, to destroy an oppressor and the man he oppresses at the same time'. It was Sartre who adapted the linguistic technique, common in German philosophy, of identifying certain political situations as the equivalent of violence, thus justifying violent correctives (or responses). So he told an interviewer from *France-Observateur*, 1 February 1962: 'For me the essential problem is to reject the theory according to which the Left ought not to answer violence with violence.' Not, we should note, *a* problem but the 'essential' problem. Sartre does not have much regard for the sanctity of human life, and in 1966 he publicly begged the Soviet Union to intervene in Vietnam even at the risk of starting a thermonuclear war.

Sartre, however, at least claims to justify violence by his professed pursuit of freedom; though his definition of freedom would not necessarily coincide with that of a sensible and civilized Anglo-Saxon. But Marcuse, another product of the German school of violence, does not seem to regard individual freedom, or the various liberties of which it is commonly supposed to consist, as even the ostensible object of his planned violent overthrow of society. In his *Essay on Liberation* (1969) Marcuse thought this overthrow might be imminent, because an active minority, which had somehow escaped cultural and political 'control', had begun to emerge, and had therefore acquired a moral duty to speak, think and act on behalf of the brain-washed majority. This group would consist of students, Chinese cultural revolutionaries, the NLF in Vietnam, the Cuban revolutionaries, and the urban, working-class blacks of America. The Marcuse diagnosis is weak because the only thing these various disparate groups have in common is their conflict with the established order in advanced western societies, and even that is a negotiable point in the case of the Chinese, who alone in Marcuse's list have significant military power. In fact, the Marcuse combination is an alliance between two categories Marx particularly hated, petty-bourgeois Bohemia and the lumpenproletariat; what Lenin later denounced as 'Left-wing Communism', 'an infantile disease'. The alliance has not come to pass; and hence has accomplished none of the things Marcuse said it would.

This is just as well, since in his essay 'Repressive Tolerance', published

in *A Critique of Pure Tolerance* written with R. P. Wolff and Barrington
Moore Jr, Marcuse made it clear that the 'active minority' of his alliance
would not expect to defer to the wishes of the brain-washed majority in any
shape or form. He argued that to allow freedom of speech in the present
society is to assist in the propagation of error, an argument already
familiar to St Augustine in the early fifth century. The truth is an
exclusive possession of the revolutionary minorities and their intellectual
spokesmen (Marcuse); and the majority have to be 're-educated' by this
minority, who are morally entitled to suppress rival and therefore
harmful opinions. Indeed, tolerance is precisely the basis on which the
wicked present system rests:

> The tolerance of the systematic moronisation of children and adults alike
> by publicity and propaganda, the release of destructiveness in driving, the
> recruitment for and training of special forces, the impotent and benevolent
> tolerance towards outright deception in merchandising, waste and planned
> obsolescence, are not distortions and aberrations, they are the essence of a
> system which fosters tolerance as a means for perpetuating the struggle for
> existence and suppressing the alternatives.

Hence impartial or non-partisan tolerance simply 'protects the already
established system'. Tolerance cannot be 'indiscriminate' or 'protect
false words and wrong deeds' which 'contradict and counteract the
possibilities of liberation'. He concedes that 'indiscriminate tolerance'
is 'justified in harmless debates, in conversation, in academic discussion;
it is indispensable in scientific enterprise, in private religion'. But
'society cannot be indiscriminate' where 'freedom and happiness themselves are at stake'. In this field – it is not more closely defined – 'certain
things cannot be said, certain ideas cannot be expressed, certain policies
cannot be proposed, certain behaviour cannot be permitted without
making tolerance an instrument for the continuation of servitude.'

Marcuse nowhere explains how 'freedom and happiness' are compatible with political censorship, or how it is possible to exercise such
control while leaving 'academic discussion' and 'scientific enterprise'
unfettered – a problem no totalitarian state has ever solved; and indeed,
in such states, no 'debate' can be 'harmless'. In any event, Marcuse does
not merely advocate suppression but positive indoctrination, which
must imply in practice complete control over academia. This is needed
to free men from the prevailing indoctrination: 'the trend would have to
be reversed; they would have to get their information slanted in the
opposite direction.' Thus, and here the legerdemain becomes so

clumsy as to be ridiculous, 'the restoration of freedom of thought may necessitate new and rigid restrictions on teaching and practices in the educational institutions which, by their very methods and concepts, serve to enclose the mind within the established universe of discourse and behaviour'. Maurice Cranston, in his analysis of Marcuse's doctrine (published in *The Mask of Politics and other essays*), comments: 'What is perhaps the most ruinous defect of Marcuse's whole anarcho-Marxist theory is that it combines the worst features of both anarchism and Marxism, with few of the merits of either.' Marcuse does not offer the majority any independent choice: they either continue to be ruled by the repressive elite of the present, or they submit to rule by the new liberating and enlightened elite – that is, in time, to the establishment of a Stalinist police-terror.

Marcuse has invented the concept of 'oppressive permissiveness' to explain the failure of his coalition of the discontented to take over society: capitalist permissiveness is oppressive because it acts as a safety-valve, and allows the pent-up outrage within society to escape harmlessly. What he had in mind was the kind of undirected anarchy preached, for instance, by Jerry Rubin: 'What we need is a generation of nuisances who are freaky, crazy, irrational, sexy, angry, irreligious, childish and mad!' Marcuse was disturbed at the thought of all that valuable, youthful violence going to ideological waste! On the other hand, Rubin's activism was not very far removed from the anti-social violence advocated and indeed practised by the black militants who constituted perhaps the one truly revolutionary element in Marcuse's coalition. In their own way, Stokely Carmichael, H. Rap Brown, Eldridge Cleaver and others sought their freedom within oppressive society precisely by the existential acts of violence Sartre had commended. Cleaver confessed, or boasted, after serving a prison sentence for a drugs offence: 'I set myself mentally free – a law unto myself. . . . I became a rapist. Rape was an insurrectionary act.' In *Soul on Ice*, Cleaver calls violence 'the revolutionary sickness'. Too much significance should not be attached to such remarks. Cleaver, for instance, has since abandoned his radicalism. They are quoted simply as examples of the characteristic verbal graffiti of our times.

But there is also a certain element of crude Marxist-egalitarian analysis in the black power movement, which reflects the use made of the confusion of categories and the inversions of terms worked out by social scientists like Laing, Lévi-Strauss and others we have mentioned. It is noteworthy that Stokely Carmichael's essay, 'Black Power', appears in a collection called *The Dialectics of Liberation*, edited by the eccentric psychiatrist D. Cooper. For Carmichael the world will be reordered by a violent reversal of definitions:

> You see, because you've been able to lie about terms, you've been able to call people like Cecil Rhodes a philanthropist, when in fact he was a murderer, a rapist, a plunderer and a thief. But you call Cecil Rhodes a philanthropist because what he did was that after he stole our diamonds and our gold, he gave us some crumbs so that we can go to school and become just like you. And that was called philanthropy. But we are renaming it: the place is no longer called Rhodesia, it is called Zimbabwe, that's its proper name.

The point is made another way by Angela Davis, the don-turned-terrorist: 'The real criminals in this society are not all the people who populate the prisons across the state, but those people who have stolen the wealth of the world from the people.'

It is disappointing that the academics who have joined the active revolutionary movements have failed to give them the sharper formulation, and the greater clarity of analysis and objective, they so plainly need. What people have stolen which wealth from what people? And is there, then, no such thing as a non-political crime? Another ferocious academic, Ulrika Meinhof, who left teaching to become a political bank-robber, and hanged herself in prison in 1976 while awaiting trial for multiple murder, became the ideological leader of the German Baader-Meinhof gang of ultra-Left terrorists, but she does not seem to have provided them with a programme beyond the rag-bag object of 'overturning society'. Political violence has been much discussed in the universities recently, and it is now beginning to be the subject of an extensive literature; but students do not receive much guidance, or even illumination, from social-science teachers. The Marxists and sub-Marxists among them teach the legitimacy of terrorism in certain circumstances; other sociologists remain ambivalent or even silent. Thus there is no entry on 'terrorism' in the 1968 edition of the *International Encyclopaedia of the Social Sciences*. There is a very general reluctance to condemn the phenomenon on ethical grounds. Martha C. Hutchinson, writing on 'The Concept of Revolutionary Terrorism' in the *Journal of Conflict Resolution*, September 1972, feels it necessary to say 'In this writer's opinion', terrorism is 'socially as well as politically unacceptable' because of its 'arbitrariness'; but she does not say, and we are entitled to ask, whether she would accept killing provided it were based on some system of selection.

International terrorism is comparatively new as a mass-phenomenon. The hijacking of aircraft began on a large scale only in 1968–9, when the numbers rose from about seven a year to over fifty and to over seventy in 1972 (figures compiled by the *Journal of Air Law and Commerce*). Again, political killings were infrequent until 1967–8: the United Kingdom and Ireland had none at all in the twenty years 1948–67. (There is a table, 'Frequencies of Assassination, 1948–67' in K. and R. Feierabend and Betty A. Nesvold: 'The Comparative Study of Revolution and Violence' in *Comparative Politics*, April 1973.) The impetus which created the political terrorism of the 1970s was undoubtedly provided by the Arab defeat in the 1967 Six Day war, and their consequent adoption of terrorism as a prime weapon thereafter. Terrorism, of course, has always been a feature of the Muslim world. The first organized group systematically employing murder for a cause were the Assassins (possibly derived from *hashishi*, drugged), who were Shia Muslims, an offshoot of the Ismaili sect. They followed the teachings of Hasan-i Sabbah, and developed a religious justification for murder, which they saw as a sacramental duty. They were truly a prototype terrorist movement of the modern kind, politico-religious missionaries, with their heavy emphasis on popular agitation and secrecy, their multi-class formation and nationalistic appeal, and their seizure and occupation of fortresses. Thanks to their use of terror, they often controlled local authorities, and forced governments into compliance or impotence. The various Arab terror movements now operating from the Lebanon, Syria, Libya and Algeria would have had little to teach them.

But if the Arabs were the first terrorists, the modern historical pedigree is essentially Russian, as is the debate about the selectivity of terror. The *Revolutionary Catechism*, drawn up by Bakunin and Nechaeyev in 1869, insisted that terror had to be selective: 'The first we destroy must be those men who most endanger the revolutionary organization – those whose sudden and violent deaths would most frighten the government and weaken its power by depriving it of energetic, intelligent officials.' This seemed to have been the operative principle of the first specialist terror group, the *Zemlya Volya* (Society of Land and Liberty), formed in 1876 to liquidate traitors and police-spies. But terrorists have always faced the problem that those they most wish to kill are also the best defended; and there have always been internal conflicts within such groups between the intellectuals, who argue for a high degree of selectivity and political motivation, and the anti-intellectuals, who favour indiscriminate terror, and who tend to get the upper hand as the campaign proceeds, the original catalytic figures are picked off by the police, and the calibre and morale of the group declines. In the Russia of the 1870s and 1880s, the anti-intellectual group, the *Neznavhalie* ('without authority') favoured what they termed 'motiveless terror' and regarded any murder as 'a progressive action'. Both the Arab and the Irish terror groups of the 1970s have drifted into this direction. Once indiscriminate terror is adopted, the group rapidly suffers moral disintegration; indeed, the abandonment of any system of moral criteria becomes an essential element in its training. The point is made with great brilliance in Dosto-yevsky's great anti-terrorist novel, *The Devils*, when the discriminating, intellectualized terrorism of Verkhovensky, modelled on Nechaeyev himself, is overshadowed by the diabolism of Stavrogin, who preaches the doctrine that the terror-group can only be united by fear and moral depravity. As he says to Verkhovensky: 'Persuade four members of the circle to murder a fifth, on the excuse that he is an informer, and you will at once tie them all up in one knot by the blood you have shed. They will be your slaves.' This technique is undoubtedly used in the Arab Black September and Palestine Liberation Army groups, and in the Provisional IRA. In both, too, women recruits are subjected to repeated rapes and are forced to take part in communal acts of sexual depravity, to anaesthetize moral reflexes and to prepare them for the gross travestying of their natures their future work entails. The theory is based on the assumption that neither man nor woman can be an effective terrorist so long as he or she retains the elements of a human personality.

The creation of these monsters is undoubtedly a consequence of the theories of justified violence and moral confusion we have examined in this and in earlier chapters. Once a person is wholly disorientated, he is relocated with comparative ease in a system of belief which runs counter to all his deepest moral instincts. It is no coincidence that a very high proportion of the most ruthless terrorists, who seem to regard human life itself as a positive affront to their sensibilities, are students of one kind or another; for the process of disorientation is carried out most effectively at universities. The same phenomena could be observed in nineteenth-century Russia, where the enlarged universities were the nurseries of terrorism, and similar efforts were being made, then as now, to undermine the concepts of madness and crime. As

Verkhovensky puts it in *The Devils*: 'When I went abroad, Littré's theory that crime is insanity was the vogue. When I returned, crime was no longer insanity but common sense, indeed almost a duty, and at any rate a noble protest.' The theoretical justification of violence in the name of social justice drew from Tolstoy his last indignant protest against the prostitution of the human intellect in the real or imagined cause of progress – his *The Law of Love and the Law of Violence*, part of which was published in Russian in 1909, but which was not made available in English until 1970. Quoting *John* 3: 19–21: 'For every one that doeth evil hateth the light, and cometh not to the light, lest his works should be reproved', Tolstoy called the organization of rule by a self-appointed, supposedly enlightened minority 'the axiom by which the greatest crimes are committed'. He added: 'Know this, all of you, especially the young, that to try to impose on others by violent means a regime which exists only in your imaginations is not only an enormous folly, but a crime. Such work, far from benefiting humanity, is a lie, an act of almost transparent hypocrisy, hiding the lowest passions we possess.' These were almost the last words he wrote. Unfortunately they were not heeded then or today; indeed, violence is now a principle of action not just of desperate gangs of political criminals, but of legitimized governments, which are accorded all the international attributes of sovereignty, and the privileges of assured status in the world community.

CHAPTER 19

Heart of Darkness

To the thirty-eighth chapter of his *Decline and Fall of the Roman Empire*, Edward Gibbon added an Appendix, entitled 'General Observations on the Fall of the Roman Empire in the West', and asked: 'The savage nations of the globe are the common enemies of civilised society, and we may well inquire with anxious curiosity whether Europe is still threatened with a repetition of those calamities which formerly oppressed the arms and institutions of Rome.' Writing in the 1780s, Gibbon thought he could answer his own question with a reasonably confident negative, for he estimated the strength of the civilized world to be increasing, and he believed that the scientific and rational principles on which that strength was based were becoming more firmly established with every year that passed. Now, nearly two hundred years later, we cannot be so confident. The principles of objective science and human reason are under growing and purposeful challenge, and the forces of savagery and violence which constitute this challenge become steadily bolder, more numerous and better armed.

Ironically, one principal reason why western civilization is more vulnerable than in Gibbon's day is the virtual collapse of the Christian predominance which he believed had contributed so strikingly to Rome's fall. Gibbon saw Christianity as an irrational, and therefore destructive, force; he would not accept that it had, by his own day, become a central pillar of the civilized arch of the West. For Christianity, as Pascal observed, provided the only theodicy which large numbers of civilized people were prepared to accept; and a convincing theodicy is a prerequisite of stability and a dependable barrier against violent change. The problem of theodicy, after all, is just as important to the non-

Christian as to the Christian. Peter Berger, in *The Social Reality of Religion*, notes that the Second World War, unlike the Great War, did not provoke a passionate discussion of Christian theodicy; indeed it did not even become a talking-point, presumably because it no longer seemed even remotely plausible. But the eclipse of Christian theodicy is certain to lead to more revolution and violence. For if the Christian theory of the world, and its explanation of the miseries all of us undergo, no longer holds, then the Christian legitimation of social order, law and communal self-restraint cannot be maintained very long either, and the violent revolution, from being an aberrant interruption of customary stability, becomes the normal feature of life. As Albert Camus puts it in *The Rebel*, 'man now launches the essential undertaking of rebellion, which is that of replacing the reign of grace by the reign of justice' – an even more futile undertaking, one might suppose.

In fact many radical Christians today challenge Camus's contrast, and argue that the Christian reign of grace must be made identical with the reign of 'justice' by throwing the weight not merely of Christian teaching but of Christian action behind revolutionary violence. Following the line of argument laid down by the Christian existentialist Paul Tillich, but pursuing it much further, many Christian clerics, including leading theologians, argue that the continued oppression of the coloured races must justify violence as a Christian institution, and indeed as a Christian duty. The arguments are not impressive, exploiting, as they do, some of the linguistic tricks we have already examined. The phrase 'systemic violence', for instance, meaning not violence at all but the operation of a particular political and social system, is used to justify breaking the Fifth Commandment. Here is the Rev. James Cone, in *Black Theology and Black Power*:

> The Christian does not decide between violence and non-violence, between evil and good. He decides between the lesser and the greater evil. He must ponder whether revolutionary violence is more detrimental to man in the long run than systemic violence. But if the system is evil, then revolutionary violence is both justified and necessary.

It should be noted that the 'evil system' Cone appears to be discussing is not that of a totalitarian police-terror, but United States republican democracy. In *The Transfiguration of Politics* by Paul Lehmann, based on the William Belden Noble Lectures he gave at Harvard in 1968 (lectures endowed, incidentally, 'to extend the influence of Jesus as the

Way, the Truth and the Life'), the way in which words are manipulated to defend murder is set out in all its crude simplicity: 'There is *systemic* violence and there is a *counterviolence*; and in the dynamics of the relation between power and violence, *counterviolence* is *revolutionary* violence and *systemic* violence is *counterrevolutionary*.' Moreover, 'violence' is given an extended definition (as with the word 'obscene') to cover a multitude of activities. Jacques Ellul, in *Violence*, writes of 'the violation of the humanity of my neighbour, by whatever means – military, psychological, moral, medical, institutional, religious'. The argument goes that once you have 'proved' your enemy has used violence, thus defined, you can then legitimately use real, physical violence against him in retaliation. This justified violence is often presented as God-given. Ruben Alves, in *A Theology of Human Hope*, argues that use of revolutionary violence is a kind of embodiment of God's will:

The power of God destroys what makes the world unfree. The use of power looks like violence because it destroys the equilibrium and peace of the system of domination. But . . . what looks like the violence of the lion is really the power of counter-violence, that is, power used against those who generate, support, and defend the violence of a world of masters and slaves. Violence is power that oppresses, and makes man unfree. Counter-violence is power that breaks the old which enslaves, in order to make man free.

The working out of a theology of violence, this time at a secular level, can be seen in its most complete and gruesome form in the life and works of Franz Fanon, who has some claims to be considered the founder of modern black racism. Fanon, who was born in 1925, was a French-educated black *evolué* from the Antilles, a splendid example of France's prideful system of turning blacks or Arabs from their colonies and protectorates into dark-skinned Parisian intellectuals. Fanon took a degree in medicine at Lyon, and in 1953 was made head of the Psychiatric Department at the state hospital in Blida, Algeria. He married a Frenchwoman, and in his earlier work he expresses his strong belief in a civilized French humanism and in racial education on the basis of equality – views reflected in his best book, *Peau Noire, Masques Blancs*, a study of racial tension in the Antilles. Indeed, he specifically warns of the dangers of extremism on the subject of race: 'I do not trust fervour. Every time it has burst out somewhere, it has brought fire, famine and misery. . . . And contempt for man.' Moreover, his own professional case-work at Blida made him aware of the terrible, destructive effect of violence on its perpetrators (as well as its victims).

Fanon appears to have been corrupted partly by existentialist writing on violence, chiefly Sartre's and Camus's, but also Maurice Merleau-Ponty's *Humanisme et Terreur*, and partly by the experience of the Algerian war, in which he became a participant. In 1956, Fanon resigned his job and became a black activist. In 1960 he was appointed ambassador of the Algerian Provisional Government to Ghana. The next year, having completed his best-known work, *Les Damnés de la Terre*, he died in Washington; his other writings, such as *Pour la Révolution africaine* (1964) were published posthumously. These works show a progressive intellectual degeneration: indeed, the last few years of his life might be termed 'The Making of a Savage'. During the Algerian war, Fanon learnt to hate the French. He lost faith both in the French proletariat, largely Communist, and in the Algerian white working class; he realized he was taking part in a race-war, as well as a class-war. He argued that French Left-wing intellectuals deplored the use by their government of torture against Algerian guerrillas because they thought it turned young Frenchmen into sadists, not because they cared for the victims. Simone de Beauvoir wrote that Fanon 'could not forget that Sartre was French, and blamed him for not having expiated that crime sufficiently'. He quarrelled with Sartre when the latter refused to respond to the suggestion – for Sartre an intolerable deprivation! – that he should not write another word until the Algerian war ended!

From this newly discovered racism within himself, Fanon worked out his theory, set out in *Les Damnés*, that the exploited blacks had replaced the white Marxist working class as the true proletariat. This ultra-exploited class has the historical role of overthrowing by violence the colonial conditions which cause exploitation. So when this class becomes conscious of itself, it embodies historical truth: 'Now the *fellah*, the unemployed man, the starving native do not lay a claim to the truth; they do *say* that they represent the truth, for they *are* the truth.' Hence, from urging the path of reason and reconciliation in *Peau Noire, Masques Blancs*, Fanon came to believe that violence was not just a means by which the oppressed could get their freedom from colonial rule but a necessary form of social and moral regeneration for them. The thesis is set out in *Les Damnés*, with much sociological jargon, not much argument, and tremendous passion. A good deal of it consists of massive generalizations, asserted largely without evidence. He has virtually nothing to say about Asia, still less of the (then) large Asian communities in black Africa. Indeed, he hated Gandhi, a pacifist and an advocate of non-violent methods. He also hated the native bourgeoisie and the old-style black nationalists; in fact, just as he condemned the white working class as the enemies of the blacks, he attacked the black industrial workers as privileged and useless, and likely to give their support to bourgeois black nationalists who believed in peaceful political solutions. There is, he says, only one authentic revolutionary class in the Third World – the poor peasantry, the victims of absolute poverty, who (unlike the black industrial workers) nevertheless retain their sense of community, 'a coherent people who go on living, as it were, statically, but who keep their moral values and their devotion to the nation intact'. Fanon argues that, by struggle and violence, these historic communities of the oppressed will make themselves into the genuine African nation.

This theme, however, is more an assertion than an argument. Fanon does not distinguish between what actually happens, and what he thinks ought to happen. In a way, his Algerian experience, though real, was irrelevant to the problems of black Africa, and his description of how an African revolution takes place is not based on any evidence, or even on much knowledge. He thinks, for instance, that in under-developed countries the bourgeoisie must be prevented either from 'existing or growing'. But how can living standards be raised without some kind of middle class? He does not say. He deplores 'the absence of ideology' in Africa. But his own ideology, such as it is, is not worked out in detailed African terms. He talks in the categories of western sociologists. He ignores, probably because he was largely unaware of them, the enormous cultural and economic and racial differences between the various regions of black Africa. He ignores tribalism almost completely, and the equally important problem of the internal colonization by one black African group of another. He talks of the African nation, but does not define it. Are the African states to continue to reflect the arbitrary divisions of the colonial age? Are they to be based on tribal groupings? Or is there to be a huge African super-nation, based only on colour, but with immense racial differences within it? Perhaps he means the last, since he refers to 'the re-establishment of the nation . . . in the strictly biological sense of the phrase'. But this is completely unhistorical, since no such nation ever existed. And the statement is purely racialistic.

Where Fanon makes some kind of sense is in linking this continental racialism with violence. For clearly the only object all the blacks of Africa will unite to secure is the expulsion of the whites. And indeed this dreadful purpose seems to be the one towards which Fanon turns: 'Violence alone, violence committed by the people, violence organized and educated by its leaders, makes it possible for the masses to understand social truths and gives the key to them.' Again: 'At the level of individuals, violence is a cleansing force. It frees the native from his inferiority complex and from his despair and inaction.' Fanon urges that this truly Hitlerian sentiment should be adopted by the African communities as a matter of state policy: 'The nation which decides to put the programme into practice, and to become its moving force, is ready for violence at all times. From birth it is clear to him [the intelligent black] that this narrow world, strewn with prohibitions, can only be called in question by absolute violence!'

The case of Fanon, the black French intellectual who turned into a savage, recalls Joseph Conrad's fearsome story *Heart of Darkness*, set in the Congo of King Leopold, about Kurtz, the intelligent and civilized man corrupted by the horrific temptations of the primitive jungle. Conrad writes of Kurtz's 'exalted and incredible degradation' and of 'the heavy, mute spell of the wilderness, that seemed to draw him to its pitiless breast by the awakening of forgotten and brutal instincts, by the memory of gratified and monstrous passions'. The wilderness, says Conrad – and one cannot avoid the comparison between Kurtz and Fanon – 'had whispered to him things about himself which he did not know, things of which he had no conception till he took counsel with this great solitude – and the whisper had proved irresistibly fascinating'.

Unfortunately, the whisper has also proved irresistibly fascinating to a whole generation of prominent Africans, who have used Fanon's frenzied justification of racial violence to give intellectual cover to a reversion to more primitive patterns of behaviour. Fanon, unlike Kurtz, did not die screaming 'The horror, the horror!' But before he did die, of pneumonia, his Washington hospital, in an effort to save him, changed every drop of blood in his body; so that, by a weird paradox, the psychiatrist who turned into a witchdoctor, the architect of coloured racism, went to eternity without knowing whether he had the blood of black or white men in his veins. His books, alas, have lived on; have become, in fact, the *Mein Kampf* of the campaign of the Third World against the West. For it was Fanon who instilled into the minds of the Third World leaders, especially in Africa, the idea that the civilized

West owed them an enormous and continuing recompense for past injuries and exploitation:

Europe has stuffed herself inordinately with the gold and raw materials of the colonial countries. . . . Europe is literally the creation of the Third World. . . . We will not acquiesce in the help for underdeveloped countries being a programme of 'sisters of charity'. This help should be a ratification of a double realisation by the colonial people that *it is their due*, and the realisation by the capitalist powers that in fact *they must pay*.

Hence it is Fanon's ideas which have led to the increasingly violent campaign against the dominant white racial minorities in Rhodesia and South Africa; to the creation of international terrorist bases in Libya and Algeria for action against white states branded as 'imperialist'; and to the use by the principal oil-exporting powers of embargoes and price-increases against the white West. Fanon's writings have also been used to provide some kind of theoretical doctrine for the introduction of official racialism in most of the Afro-Asian states. Hence, for instance, Indonesia, Thailand and Burma discriminate against or expel their Chinese minorities; virtually all black African states have expelled, or are in process of expelling, their Asian minorities; the Arab states discriminate against Jews, who are not admitted (the original Jewish communities were expelled in the 1950s and 1960s) and one Arab state, the Sudan, discriminates against blacks as well; virtually all Afro-Asian states discriminate against whites. The colonial epoch produced a great movement and mingling of races all over the world, as trade expanded and men were allowed to sell their labour almost anywhere under free market conditions. This 'problem' of colonial days is now being 'solved' by the application of Fanonist principles of racist violence.

But Fanon's idea that the West should somehow recompense the Third World by helping it to industrialize has proved much more difficult to put into practice, despite the fact that some people in the West, including a number in high positions, affect to agree with him. No one disputes the enormous differences that exist between incomes in the civilized West and in the underdeveloped countries. Thus average incomes in India, for instance, are about one-tenth of the figures used to establish the 'poverty line' in the United States. In 1970, to put it another way, per capita income in the United States was fifty times that of Tanzania – five times as great, that is, as the difference between a prime minister's salary, and that of the average worker, in the United Kingdom. To reduce these huge gaps, in 1969 the Lester Pearson Commission on International Development recommended that the rich countries should provide 1% of their Gross National Product by 1975, of which 0·7% should be official aid; the UN calculated that this would add 'about 10 per cent to the incomes of the underdeveloped countries, and about 100 per cent to their capital formation'. Hence the Pearson target would not have made a substantial contribution to the narrowing of the gap between current living standards in rich and poor countries; nor would it even offer hope of rapid progress in this direction in the future. In any case, the Pearson target has not been met; aid has varied from 0·4% of the GNP from Britain to 0·3 (United States and West Germany) and 0·2 (Japan). And aid per capita has varied for a great variety of reasons.

During the 1970s, moreover, the advocates in the West of aid on the moral basis of past guilt lost ground steadily. The oil-price revolution by the OPEC states, who classify themselves as part of the Third World, hit western economies badly, and destroyed the popular basis for such aid, which had never been a particularly firm one. There has been a growing realization among economists and administrators that the success or failure of aid programmes varies not so much according to the total given, as to other factors, often beyond the power of the donor country to control. Aid often fails to provide help to the poorest countries, and especially to help the poorest groups within those countries. And it tends to be redistribution between governments, as opposed to persons. P. T. Bauer, in a savage critique of development aid, *Dissent on Development*, wrote: 'Foreign aid is a process by which poor people in rich countries help rich people in poor countries.' There is, as he points out, a tendency for comparatively poorly paid workers in the United States to be taxed to help comparatively wealthy mine-workers in Zambia or prosperous businessmen in Liberia. And this difficulty would, of course, arise in any proposal for an international negative income-tax scheme.

In any case, it is now pointed out, a prerequisite for any kind of take-off is a very high rate of internal saving. With populations expanding, this would amount in the underdeveloped countries to at least 10% of national income. We now realize that the tropical countries, at least, did not do too badly under colonial rule. Arthur Lewis, in *Tropical Development 1880–1913*, shows that the colonial governments laid down the foundations of a social and economic infrastructure, allowed a professional and middle class to grow, improved the economic, legal and political institutions, and enhanced the overall productive capacity. In short, far from plundering these countries, colonial rule often created a political and economic situation in which high rates of saving could and would be achieved, and so a take-off made possible some time this century, in many cases. Unfortunately, with few exceptions, the under-developed countries, as sovereign states, have tended to conform to authoritarian types, with huge administrative machines and armed forces; and with Caesarian links between the governing elites and the politically passive mass of the citizens. Such regimes are unstable, and the army, as the mediator, tends to absorb an undue proportion of the national income. The absence of the rule of law means that property is constantly at risk, and the lack of political and economic freedom means that the middle class remains vulnerable and small. In these circumstances, high rates of savings, either by governments or individuals, are virtually impossible, and take-off therefore ruled out.

Moreover, the cost of the take-off is constantly increasing. If we take capital formation as the key factor (and it probably is), we get some idea of the really terrifying difficulties which now face the non-industrialized states. In most industries, capital requirements for a production unit of optimum size are enormously larger than they were a century or two ago. As long ago as 1963, the French economist Paul Bairoch, in *Revolution industrielle et sous-development*, showed that in England during the Industrial Revolution, capital, including stocks, needed per head of the industrial labour force was equal to about four months' wages. By the early nineteenth century, when France was beginning to industrialize, it had risen to six-to-eight months' wages. In the United States, in 1953, despite infinitely higher wage-rates, it had risen to twenty-nine months' wages. For a typical underdeveloped country of the late 1970s, the level of capital per worker needed to produce the investment requirement of the United States even at the 1950 standard would be the equivalent of about four years' wages. That figure gives some indication of the sort of savings rates which would need to be produced, either by private incentives, or government enforcement, to achieve a real breakthrough into self-sustaining growth.

Moreover, this is not the only intrinsic difficulty. In the early nineteenth century, Britain was able to export the Industrial Revolution comparatively easily to Europe and the United States. The French and Belgians, for instance, built their first factories under supervision of trained British workmen, often with British machine-tools and British capital. But it is now much harder for the underdeveloped countries to build their own factories under supervision. Growth, therefore, involves import restraints as well as savings restraints, and countries importing the bulk of their machinery do not get the same opportunity of developing their engineering skills. The technological and economic environment for 'late starters' is constantly changing, and in most respects to their disadvantage. Among the so-called underdeveloped countries, the group most likely to carry through industrialization are those which have profited from the 'energy crisis', which has given them truly gigantic quantities of investment capital. But the oil-price increases which raised this capital have inflicted great and lasting damage on the Third World countries without energy resources, whose chances of achieving take-off must be regarded, as things stand, as quite hopeless. Hence the application of Fanonist tactics has ended merely by setting one group of coloured countries against another, and by introducing another form of international 'plundering'.

The cult of violence in the Third World, taken in conjunction with the mounting frustrations produced by real and inescapable economic obstacles to advancement, constitute a permanent menace to western civilization, for whatever the true explanations of their predicament, the Third World countries blame no one but the West. Indeed, they have no one else to blame, except themselves and their leaders. For violence, preached as a form of righteousness, requires villains. And if the villains do not exist, they must be invented. Hence the United Nations, which in a non-violent world might be a useful forum in which genuine difficulties could be resolved by argument and negotiation, has become a kind of Roman arena, in which the advanced nations of the West are hunted, in the expiation of largely imaginary crimes, past, present and to come. Or, to vary the metaphor, we can use the expression of the former American ambassador to the UN, Daniel Moynihan: 'The inmates have taken over the lunatic asylum.' In a world where real distinctions are being deliberately eroded or inverted by pseudo-science, where reason is derided, knowledge assassinated and the most fundamental principles of civilization assaulted, we must not be surprised to find that the United Nations, the fount of international authority – such as it is – should have become the World Theatre of the Absurd, a global madhouse where lunatic falsehood reigns and the voices of the sane can scarcely be heard above the revolutionary and racist din. Heart of Darkness, indeed!

CHAPTER 20

A New Deuteronomy

On the last day of 1911, Wilfred Scawen Blunt, the poet and propagandist for the subject peoples – the first of the modern anti-colonialists – made a despondent entry in his diary:

> Today a sad year ends, the worst politically I can remember since the 1880s, bloodshed, massacre and destruction everywhere, and all accepted in England with cynical approval, our Foreign Office being accomplice with the evil-doers, and Grey [Foreign Secretary] their apologist. It has been a losing battle in which I have fought long, but with no result of good. I am old, and weary, and discouraged, and would if I could slink out of the fight. I am useless in face of an entirely hostile world.

At the end of the 1970s, virtually everything that Blunt campaigned for, in what he then thought a hopeless struggle, has been triumphantly accomplished. The British empire he hated, which he regarded as an evil conspiracy against the weak and innocent coloured peoples of the world, is now 'at one with Nineveh and Tyre'. Africa has been unscrambled, Asia 'liberated', sovereignty awarded to more than a hundred nations which, in Blunt's day, were administered by European officials. The world he knew and deplored has been erased from the map, in the greatest transfer of power in human history; and almost all the dominant values and assumptions of 1911 have been cast aside or inverted. The 'hostile world' has dissolved as if it had never been, and Blunt's views have become the prevailing wisdom of our planet.

Yet it is difficult to argue that civilization is any richer, or more secure, than it was then. 'Bloodshed, massacre and destruction everywhere': the phrase applies as well, or better, to our times, as to his. New tyrannies have replaced old ones, and fresh injustices have been generously heaped on the heads of countless innocents in every quarter of the earth. Few sensitive souls can look around the world today with feelings of satisfaction, or optimism. This is not to say that the revolution through which we have passed could and should have been prevented; on the contrary, it was both just and inevitable. But the events of this century should remind us that the hopes of mankind almost always prove illusory, and that we have only a limited ability to devise permanent and equitable solutions to problems which spring from human nature. Violence, shortage amid plenty, tyranny and the cruelty it breeds, the gross stupidities of the powerful, the indifference of the well-to-do, the divisions of the intelligent and well-meaning, the apathy of the wretched multitude – these things will be with us to the end of the race.

Hence civilization will always be at risk, and every age is prudent to regard the threats to it with unique seriousness. All good societies breed enemies whose combined hostility can prove fatal. There is no easy defensive formula, and the most effective strategy is to identify the malign forces quickly, as and when they appear. That has been the chief purpose of this book. At the same time, there are certain salient principles, valid always but of especial relevance today, which we should take particular care to uphold. They are the Ten Pillars of our Civilization; or, to put it another way, a new and secular Ten Commandments, designed not, indeed, to replace the old, but rather to update and reinforce their social message.

The first, and perhaps the most important, is to reassert our belief in moral absolutes. It is not true that all codes of human conduct are relative, and reflect cultural assumptions and economic arrangements which do not necessarily possess any authority. It is not true that there is no such thing as absolute right, and absolute wrong. It is not true that our behaviour is wholly determined by environment. Nor is it true that to seek to impose moral norms is an arrogant and unwarrantable assumption of infallibility; on the contrary, in the long run it is a necessary condition of human happiness, and even of human survival. What *is* true is that every rational human being is in a moral sense free, capable of reacting to moral absolutes, and of opting for good or evil.

It follows from this that certain acts are intrinsically, always and everywhere wrong. Murder is always wrong. Thus anyone who tries to justify political violence, the greatest single evil of our age, must automatically be suspect as an enemy of our society. In fact the theories which attempt to legitimize killing in the pursuit of political objectives are, without exception, founded on false premises, illogical or rest on deliberate linguistic conjuring. Hence there is a natural presumption that anyone seeking to circumvent the common opinion that violence is wicked is an intellectual crook; as John Rawle puts it in *A Theory of Justice*: 'On a subject as ancient and much discussed . . . we may probably assume that a novel, and hence interesting, view of violence is likely to be false.' Moreover, a propagandist or pedagogue who is wrong about violence is almost certainly wrong about all his other claims to truth. The virtue we should cherish most is the courage to resist violence, especially if this involves flying in the face of a public opinion which, in its fear, and in its anxiety for peace, is willing to appease the violators. Above all, violence should never be allowed to pay, or be seen to pay.

The third moral axiom is that democracy is the least evil, and on the whole the most effective, form of government. Democracy is an important factor in the material success of a society, and especially in its economic success; it should, other things being equal, produce rising living-standards. But of course the essence of democracy is not one-man-one-vote, which does not necessarily have anything to do with individual freedom, or democratic control. The exaltation of 'majority rule' on the basis of universal suffrage is the most strident political fallacy of the twentieth century. True democracy means the ability to remove a government without violence, to punish political failure or misjudgement by votes alone. A democracy is a utilitarian instrument of social control; it is valuable in so far as it works. Its object is to promote human content; but perhaps this is more likely to be secured if the aim is rephrased. As Karl Popper says, the art of politics is the minimization of unhappiness, or of avoidable suffering. The identification of the cause and scale of suffering draws attention to, and defines, problems in society; and, since man is a problem-solving creature, eventually gets something done about them. The process of avoiding suffering is greatly assisted by the existence of free institutions. The greater their number, variety and intrinsic strength, and the greater their individual independence, the more effective the democracy which harbours them will be. All such institutions should be treated like fortresses: that is, soundly constructed and continually manned.

Free institutions will only survive where there is the rule of law. This is an absolute on which there can be no compromise: the subjection of everyone and everything to the final arbitration of the law is more fundamental to human freedom and happiness than democracy itself.

Most of the post-war democratic creations have foundered because the rule of law was broken and governments placed themselves above the courts. Once the law is humbled, all else that is valuable in a civilized society will vanish, usually with terrifying speed. On the other hand, provided the rule of law is maintained intact, the evil forces in society, however powerful, will be brought to book in the end – as witness the downfall of the Nixon administration. The United Nations has proved not merely a failure, but a positive obstacle to peace and justice, because it has put the principle of one-nation-one-vote above the rule of the law, including its own. But the rule of law is essential, not merely to preserve liberty, but to increase wealth. A law which is supreme, impartial and accessible to all is the only guarantee that property, corporate or personal, will be safe; and therefore a necessary incentive to saving and investment.

The fifth salient rule is always, and in all situations, to stress the importance of the individual. Where individual and corporate rights conflict, the political balance should usually be weighted in favour of the individual; for civilizations are created, and maintained, not by corporations, however benign, but by multitudes of individuals operating independently. We have seen how, under the Roman empire, political and economic freedom declined, *pari passu*, with the growth of the corporations, and their organization by the state. The Roman concept of the *collegia* survived; it was built into the Christian church, and so was carried over into the Dark-Age towns and into the guilds of medieval and early modern society. Guild-forms were eventually transmuted into trade unions. The liberal epoch, which occurred after the powers of the guilds had been effectively curbed, and before the powers of the unions had been established, was thus a blessed and fruitful interval between two tyrannies – fruitful, indeed, because it produced the Industrial Revolution, the first economic take-off, and thus taught the world how to achieve self-sustaining economic growth. The trade union is now increasing its economic power and its political influence faster than any other institutions in western society. It is not wholly malevolent, but it has certain increasingly reprehensible characteristics. One is that it claims, and gets, legal privilege; it thus breaks our fourth commandment, the rule of law. Another is that it curbs the elitist urge in man, the very essence of civilization, and quite deliberately and exultantly reinforces the average. As Ortega Y Gasset puts it, in *The Revolt of the Masses*, 'The chief characteristic of our time is that the mediocre mind, aware of its own mediocrity, has the boldness to assert the rights of mediocrity and to impose them everywhere.' Such an actual or potential menace to our culture can be contained, provided we keep this commandment strictly, and protect the individual against corporatism.

The sixth of our rules is that there is nothing morally unhealthy about the existence of a middle class in society. No one need feel ashamed of being *bourgeois*, of pursuing a *bourgeois* way of life, or of adhering to *bourgeois* cultural and moral standards. That it should be necessary to assert such a proposition is a curious commentary on our age, and in particular its mania for the lowest common denominator of social uniformity. Throughout history all intelligent observers of society have welcomed the emergence of a flourishing middle class, which they have rightly associated with economic prosperity, political stability, the growth of individual freedom and the raising of moral and cultural standards. The middle class, stretching from the self-employed skilled craftsman to the leaders of the learned professions, has produced the overwhelming majority of the painters, architects, writers and musicians, as well as the administrators, technologists and scientists, on which the quality and strength of a culture principally rest. The health of the middle class is probably the best index of the health of society as a whole; and any political system which persecutes its middle class systematically is unlikely to remain either free or prosperous for long.

We have seen that there is a close connection between the rise of a middle class, and the growth of political and economic freedom. But it is not true, as Lenin contemptuously asserted, that 'freedom is a *bourgeois* prejudice'. Freedom is a good which any rational man knows how to value, whatever his social origins, occupation or economic prospects. Throughout history, the attachment of even the humblest people to their freedom, above all their freedom to earn their livings how and where they please, has come as an unpleasant shock to condescending ideologues. We need not suppose that the exercise of freedom is bought at the expense of any deserving class or interest – only of those with the itch to tyrannize. So the seventh commandment is that, when the claims of freedom conflict with the pursuit of other desirable objects of public policy, freedom should normally prevail; society should have a rational and an emotional predisposition in its favour. In our times, liberty's chief conflict has been with equality. But absolute equality is not a good at all; it is a chimera, and if it existed would prove as fearful and destructive a monster as that grotesque creature Bellerophon killed. And the unregarding and indiscriminate pursuit of relative equality, itself desirable, has led to many unwarrantable restrictions on human freedom without attaining its object. In short, for many years the bias has been in the wrong direction, and it is now necessary to strike a new balance of moral good by redressing it. Where there is genuine doubt between the legitimate claims of liberty and equality, the decision taken should be the one most easily reversed if it proves mistaken.

When we are dealing with concepts like freedom and equality, it is essential to use words accurately and in good faith. So the eighth commandment is: beware of those who seek to win an argument at the expense of the language. For the fact that they do so is proof positive that their argument is false, and proof presumptive that they know it is. A man who deliberately inflicts violence on the language will almost certainly inflict violence on human beings if he acquires the power. Those who treasure the meaning of words will treasure truth, and those who bend words to their purposes are very likely in pursuit of anti-social ones. The correct and honourable use of words is the first and natural credential of civilized status.

Of course using words in their true sense is one element in precision of thought. And trained skill in thinking precisely to advance knowledge is what we mean by science. So the ninth commandment is: trust science. By this we mean a true science, based on objectively established and agreed foundations, with a rational methodology and mature criteria of proof – not the multitude of pseudo-sciences which, as we have seen, have marked characteristics which can be readily detected and exposed. Science, properly defined, is an essential part of civilization. To be anti-science is not the mark of a civilized human being, or of a friend of humanity. Given the right safeguards and standards, the progress of science constitutes our best hope for the future, and anyone who denies this proposition is an enemy of society.

The last of our laws follows from the ninth, and in a sense embraces all of them. It is this: no consideration should ever deflect us from the pursuit and recognition of truth, for that essentially is what constitutes civilization itself. There are many around today who will concede, in theory, that truth is indivisible; but then insist, in practice, that some truths are more divisible than others. If we want to identify a social enemy we need go no further than examine his attitude to truth: it will always give him away; for, as Pascal says, 'The worst thing of all is when man begins to fear the truth, lest it denounce him.' But truth is

much more than a means to expose the malevolent. It is the great creative force of civilization. For truth is knowledge; and a civilized man is
one who, in Hobbes's words, has 'a perseverance of delight in the continual and indefatigable generation of knowledge'. Hobbes also writes:
'Joy, arising from imagination of a man's own power and ability, is that
exaltation of mind called glorying.' And so it is; for the pursuit of truth
is our civilization's glory, and the joy we obtain from it is the nearest we
shall approach to happiness, at least on this side of the grave. If we are
steadfast in this aim, we need not fear the enemies of society.

Bibliography

Andrew Alfold: *A Conflict of Ideas in the Late Roman Empire* (trns., Oxford 1952)

Lawrence Alloway: *Francis Bacon* (New York 1963)

Louis Althusser: *Lenin and Philosophy, and Other Essays* (trns., London 1971)

Ruben Alves: *A Theology of Human Hope* (Cleveland 1969)

Margaret Scotford Archer: *Students, University and Society: A Comparative Sociological Review* (London 1972)

Robert Ardrey: *The Social Contract* (London 1972)

Hannah Arendt: *On Violence* (New York 1970)

A. B. Atkinson: *The Economics of Inequality* (Oxford 1975)

T. S. Ashton: 'Some Statistics on the Industrial Revolution', in E. M. Carus-Wilson (ed.): *Essays in Economic History*, 3 (London 1962)

Paul Avrich: *The Russian Anarchists* (Princeton 1967)

Jean Baechler: *The Origins of Capitalism* (trns., Oxford 1975)

Sydney D. Bailey: *The Procedure of the UN Security Council* (Oxford 1975)

G. S. Bain: *The Growth of White-Collar Unionism* (Oxford 1970)

John H. Barnsley: *The Social Reality of Ethics: The Comparative Analysis of Moral Codes* (London 1972)

Jacques Barzun: *Science: The Glorious Entertainment* (London 1964)

B. H. Slicher von Bath: *The Agrarian History of Western Europe, 500–1850* (Oxford 1963)

Lee Baxendall: *Radical Perspectives in the Arts* (London 1972)

Wilfred Beckerman: *In Defence of Economic Growth* (London 1974)

R. Bendix: *Max Weber: An Intellectual Portrait* (London 1960)

Peter L. Berger: *The Social Reality of Religion* (London 1969)

Marc Bloch: 'Comment et pourquoi finit l'esclavage antique?' *Annales*, 1947

E. R. Boak: *Manpower Shortage and the Fall of the Roman Empire in the West* (Ann Arbor 1955)

Robert Bocock: *Ritual in Industrial Society* (London 1974)

M. Bornstein (ed.): *Comparative Economic Systems* (2nd ed., New York 1969)

Jacob Bronowski: *Science and Human Values* (New York 1956)

J. Buchanan and G. Tullock: *The Calculus of Consent* (Michigan 1962)

M. S. Bunim: *Space in Medieval Painting and the Forerunners of Perspective* (New York 1940)

Andrew Boyd: *Fifteen Men on a Powder Keg* (London 1971)
John M. Blair (ed.): *The Roots of Inflation* (London 1976)
John Cage: *Silence* (London 1968)
—— *Notations* (New York 1969)
Peter Calvert: *A Study of Revolution* (Oxford 1970)
L. Casson: *The Ancient Mariners* (London 1954)
David Caute: *Fanon* (London 1970)
Noam Chomsky: *Language and Mind* (2nd ed., New York 1972)
Carlo M. Cipolla: *The Economic History of World Population* (London 1962)
Alexander Cockburn and Robin Blackburn (eds.): *Student Power* (London 1969)
John Stewart Collis: *Paths of Light* (London 1959)
Barry Commoner: *Science and Survival* (New York 1966)
James H. Cone: *A Black Theology of Liberation* (New York 1970)
David Craig: *The Real Foundations: Literature and Social Change* (London 1973)
Maurice Cranston: *The Mask of Politics and Other Essays* (London 1973)
Brian Crozier: *A Theory of Conflict* (London 1974)
Alexander Dallin and George W. Breslauer: *Political Terror in Communist Systems* (Stanford, California 1970)
D. B. Davis: *The Problem of Slavery in Western Culture* (Cornell 1966)
Phyllis Deane and W. A. Cole: *British Economic Growth, 1688–1959: Trends and Structures* (2nd ed., Cambridge 1967)
Régis Debray: *Revolution in the Revolution* (London 1968)
Kenneth Denbigh: *Science, Industry and Social Policy* (New York 1963)
Anthony Downs: *An Economic Theory of Democracy* (New York 1957)
Paul R. Durbin: *Philosophy of Science: An Introduction* (New York 1968)
T. Eagleton: *The New Left Church* (London 1966)
J. W. Eaton and R. J. Weil: *Culture and Mental Disorders* (Glencoe 1955)
John Elliot: 'The Decline of Spain', *Past and Present*, November 1961
Jacques Ellul: *Violence* (trns., New York 1969)
William Empson: *The Structure of Complex Words* (London 1951)
Martin Esslin: *The Theatre of the Absurd* (London 1968)
Hans Eysenck: *Crime and Personality* (rev. ed., London 1970)
K. T. Fann: *Wittgenstein's Concept of Philosophy* (Oxford 1969)
Franz Fanon: *Les Damnés de la Terre* (Paris 1961)
M. Farren, E. Barker, etc.: *Watch Out, Kids!* (London 1972)
B. Farrington: *Greek Science* (London 1963)
I. K. and R. Feirabend and Betty A. Newvold: 'The Comparative Study of Revolution and Violence', *Comparative Politics*, April 1973
Lewis Feuer: *The Conflict of Generations* (London 1969)
M. I. Finley (ed.): *Slavery in Classical Antiquity: Views and Controversies* (Cambridge 1968)
P. H. Fontaine: *Basic Formal Structures* (New York 1967)
Brian Foster: *The Changing English Language* (London 1968)
Michel Foucault: *Madness and Civilisation* (trns., London 1967)
—— *The Order of Things: an Archaeology of the Human Sciences* (trns., London 1972)
Bruce Fraser (ed.): *Ernest Gower's Complete Plain Words* (London 1973)
Milton Friedman: *Capitalism and Freedom* (Chicago 1962)
J. K. Galbraith: *Economics and the Public Purpose* (London 1974)
Peter Garview (ed.): *Music and Western Man* (London 1958)

Roland Gaucher: *The Terrorists: from Tsarist Russia to the OAS* (trans., London 1968)

Graham George: *Tonality and Musical Structure* (London 1970)

A. H. Georghegan: *The Attitude towards Labour in Early Christianity and Ancient Culture* (Washington 1945)

James J. Gibson: *The Perception of the Visual World* (Boston 1950)

—— *The Senses Considered as Perceptual Systems* (London 1968)

E. H. Gombrich: *Art and Illusion: a Study in the Psychology of Pictorial Representation* (London 1960)

Marcus C. Goodall: *Science, Logic and Political Action* (Cambridge, Mass., 1970)

P. Goodman: *Compulsory Mis-education and the Community of Scholars* (New York 1966)

Margaret Gowing: *Britain and Atomic Energy, 1939–45* (London 1964)

J. D. Gould: *Economic Growth in History* (London 1972)

Loren H. Graham: *Science and Philosophy in the Soviet Union* (London 1973)

D. M. Green: *Form in Tonal Music* (New York 1965)

P. Green: 'The First Sicilian Slave War', *Past and Present*, 1961

H. J. Habbakuk: *American and British Technology in the 19th Century* (Cambridge 1962)

R. Harre: *The Philosophy of Science* (Oxford 1972)

Alan Harrington: *Psychopaths* (New York 1972)

R. M. Hartwell (ed.): *The Causes of the Industrial Revolution in England* (London 1967)

E. F. Hechscher: *Mercantilism*, 2 vols (2nd ed., London 1956)

Robert L. Heilbroner: *The Worldly Philosophers* (New York 1961)

John Hicks: *A Theory of Economic History* (Oxford 1969)

Julian E. Hochberg: *Perception* (New York 1964)

Samuel Hollander: *The Economics of Adam Smith* (London 1973)

Sidney Hook (ed.): *Human Values and Economic Policy* (New York 1967)

Martha C. Hutchinson: 'The Concept of Revolutionary Terrorism', *Journal of Conflict Resolution*, September 1972

Ivan D. Illich: *Deschooling Society* (London 1971)

International Bank for Reconstruction and Development: *Report on the Limits to Growth* (Washington 1972)

D. Jackson, H. A. Turner and F. Wilkinson: *Do Trade Unions Cause Inflation?* (2nd ed., Cambridge 1975)

Paul Jacobs and Saul Landau: *The New Radicals* (London 1966)

Eric John: 'Agriculture and Economic Growth in England, 1660–1750', *Journal of Economic History*, 1965

A. H. M. Jones: *The Later Roman Empire, 284–602: a Social, Economic and Administrative Survey*, 3 vols (Oxford 1964)

O. K. Jones (ed.): *The Private Language Argument* (New York 1969)

D. Kagan: *Decline and Fall of the Roman Empire* (Boston 1962)

William Kay: *Moral Education: A Sociological Study of the Influence of Society, Home and School* (London 1975)

Andrew K. Kennedy: *Six Dramatists in Search of a Language* (Cambridge 1975)

Edwin C. Kilbourne and Wilson G. Smillier (eds.): *Human Ecology and Public Health* (New York 1970)

Frank Kitson: *Low Intensity Operations: Subversion, Insurgency and Peace-Keeping* (London 1971)

T. S. S. Kuhn: *The Structure of Scientific Revolutions* (Chicago 1962)
S. S. Kuznets: *Capital in the American Economy: its Formation and Financing* (Princeton 1961)
R. D. Laing: *The Divided Self: a Study of Sanity and Madness* (London 1960)
—— *The Politics of the Family and Other Essays* (London 1971)
R. D. Laing and D. G. Cooper: *Reason and Violence: A Decade of Sartre's Philosophy, 1950–60* (London 1964)
H. T. Lambrich (ed. and trns.): *The Terrorist* (London 1972)
Gabriel Le Bras: *Études de sociologie religieuse* (Paris 1955)
Paul Lehmann: *The Transfiguration of Politics* (London 1975)
Edmund Leach: *Lévi-Strauss* (London 1970)
—— *A Runaway World?* (London 1968)
Carl Leider and Karl M. Schmitt: *The Politics of Violence* (New Jersey 1968)
M. Leivis: *Francis Bacon* (London 1967)
Claude Lévi-Strauss: *The Savage Mind* (trns., London 1966)
Arthur Lewis: *Tropical Development 1880–1913* (London 1970)
Bernard Lewis: *The Assassins: A Radical Sect in Islam* (London 1967)
Edward Lucie-Smith: *Movements in Art Since 1945* (London 1969)
John Lyons: *Introduction to Theoretical Linguistics* (Cambridge 1968)
—— *Chomsky* (London 1970)
H. F. Lydall: *The Structure of Earnings* (Oxford 1967)
A. MacIntyre: *Secularisation and Moral Change* (Oxford 1967)
Roy McMullen: *Art, Affluence and Alienation* (London 1968)
Edward McWhinney: *The Illegal Diversion of Aircraft and International Law* (The Hague 1973)
C. A. Mace (ed.): *British Philosophy in Mid-century* (2nd ed., London 1966)
Angus Maddison: *Economic Growth in the West* (London 1964)
Bryan Magee: *Modern British Philosophy* (London 1971)
—— *Popper* (London 1974)
Thomas Mathieson: *Beyond the Boundaries of Organisations* (California 1972)
K. Mellandy: 'Biological Effects of Polution: an Ecological Problem', *Presidential Address to the Zoology Section of the British Association for the Advancement of Science*, September 1972
Wilfred Mellers: *The Sonata Principle* (London 1957)
P. B. Medawar: *The Art of the Soluble* (London 1967)
—— *The Hope of Progress* (London 1972)
Robert K. Merton: *Social Theory and Social Structure* (3rd ed., London 1968)
E. J. Mishan: *The Costs of Economic Growth* (London 1967)
—— 'Economic Growth: the Need for Scepticism', *Lloyds Bank Review*, October 1972
Dennis Meadows, Donella Meadows, J. Randers and W. W. Behrens: *The Limits to Growth* (New York 1972)
John Morton (ed.): *Biological and Social Factors in Psycholinguistics* (London 1971)
H. Morlick: *Wittgenstein and the Problem of Other Minds* (New York 1967)
Jonathan Miller: *McLuhan* (London 1971)
Robert Moss: *Urban Guerillas* (London 1972)
H. J. Muller: *Uses of the Past* (Oxford 1952)
H. Myint: *The Economics of the Developing Countries* (London 1965)
J. Needleman: *The New Religions* (New York 1970)

R. A. Nisbett: *The Sociological Tradition* (New York 1966)

Douglas C. North and Robert Paul Thomas: *The Rise of the Western World: A New Economic History* (Cambridge 1973)

G. W. Nutter and H. A. Einhorn: *Enterprise Monopoly in the US, 1899–1958* (Colombia 1969)

John O'Dea: *The Social History of Lighting* (London 1958)

F. Parkin: *Class Inequality and Political Order* (London 1971)

Mario Pei: *Words in Sheep's Clothing* (London 1970)

A. Piganiol: *L'Empire chrétien* (Paris 1957)

Karl Polanyi (ed.): *Trade and Market in the Early Empires* (New York 1957)

Karl Popper: *The Open Society and Its Enemies* (rev. ed., London 1966)

—— *The Poverty of Historicism* (London 1957)

—— *The Logic of Scientific Discovery* (London 1959)

—— *Objective Knowledge: An Evolutionary Approach* (London 1972)

Simeon Potter: *Changing English* (London 1969)

Gerald Priestland: *The Future of Violence* (London 1974)

Moody E. Prior: *Science and the Humanities* (Evanston 1962)

William Ramsay and Claude Anderson: *Managing the Environment* (London 1972)

Jerome R. Ravetz: *Scientific Knowledge and its Social Problems* (Oxford 1971)

John Rawls: *A Theory of Justice* (Harvard 1971)

John Raynor: *The Middle Classes* (London 1969)

G. Revesz: *Introduction to the Psychology of Music* (trns., London 1953)

A. Reymond: *Histoire des sciences exactes dans l'antiquité gréco-romaine* (2nd ed., Paris 1955)

Ian Robinson: *The Survival of English* (Cambridge 1973)

—— *The New Grammarian's Funeral: a Critique of Noam Chomsky's Linguistics* (Cambridge 1975)

George Rosen: *Madness in Society: Chapters in the Historical Sociology of Mental Illness* (London 1968)

Harold Rosenberg: *The Tradition of the New* (London 1962)

M. I. Rostovtzeff: *Social and Economic History of the Hellenistic World*, 3 vols (Oxford 1941)

—— *Social and Economic History of the Roman Empire*, 2 vols (rev. ed., Oxford 1957)

W. W. Rostow (ed.): *The Economics of Take-off to Sustained Growth* (London 1963)

T. Roszak: *The Making of a Counter-culture* (London 1968)

J. Rothenstein and R. Alley: *Francis Bacon* (London 1964)

G. Routh: *Occupation and Pay in Great Britain, 1906–1960* (Cambridge 1965)

Jerry Rubin: *Do It! Scenarios of the Revolution* (New York 1970)

C. Sachs: *The Rise of Music in the Ancient World* (New York 1943)

Ignacy Sachs (ed.): *Political Economy of the Environment: Problems of Method* (The Hague 1972)

W. E. G. Salter: *Productivity and Technical Change* (Cambridge 1960)

Jacob Schmorkler: *Invention and Economic Growth* (Cambridge, Mass., 1966)

Louis Schneider and Sanford M. Dornbusch: *Popular Religion: Inspirational Books in America* (Chicago 1958)

Arnold Schoenberg: *Structural Functions of Harmony* (New York 1954)

Andrew Schonfield: *Modern Capitalism: the Changing Balance of Public and Private Power* (Oxford 1965)

John Searl: *The Campus War* (London 1972)

D. V. Segre and J. H. Adler: 'The Ecology of Terrorism', *Encounter*, February 1973

E. B. Sheldon and W. E. Moore (eds.): *Indicators of Social Change: Concepts and Measurement* (New York 1968)

C. Singer and E. J. Holmyard: *A History of Technology* (Oxford, 1954–   )

Ninian Smart: *The Philosophy of Religion* (London 1970)

W. B. Smerud: *Can there be a Private Language?* (The Hague 1970)

L. Sprague de Camp: *The Ancient Engineers* (New York 1964)

P. Stanworth and A. Giddens (eds.): *Elites and Power in British Society* (Cambridge 1974)

W. Stark: *The Ideal Foundations of Economic Thought* (London 1943)

Werner Stark: *The Sociology of Religion: a Study of Christendom, vol. 5: Types of Religious Structure* (London 1972)

George Steiner: *After Babel* (Oxford 1975)

Stephen P. Stich: 'What Every Speaker Knows', *Philosophical Review*, 80, 1971

P. F. Strawson: *Individuals* (2nd ed., Oxford 1965)

Sussex University Policy Research Unit: *Futures* (Sussex 1973)

R. Swinburne: *Space and Time* (London 1968)

Ian Taylor, Paul Walton and Jock Young: *The New Criminology: for a Social Theory of Deviance* (London 1973)

John Russell Taylor: *The Second Wave: British Drama for the Seventies* (London 1971)

Victorino Tejera: *Art and Human Intelligence* (London 1966)

Hugh Thomas: *Goya: 'The Third of May 1808'* (London 1972)

E. A. Thompson: 'Peasant Revolts in Late Roman Gaul and Spain', *Past and Present*, 1952

—— 'Slavery in Early Germany', *Hermanethena*, 1957

Lionel Tiger and Robin Fox: *The Imperial Animal* (London 1972)

Leo Tolstoy: *The Law of Love and the Law of Violence* (trns., London 1970)

S. Toulmin: *The Philosophy of Science* (London 1967)

Stephan Viljoen: *Economic Systems in World History* (London 1974)

Joseph Vogt: *The Decline of Rome* (trns., London, 1967)

Geoffrey Wagner: *On the Wisdom of Words* (London 1968)

F. W. Walbank: *The Awful Revolution: the Decline of the Roman Empire in the West* (Liverpool 1969)

Immanuel Wallerstein: *The Modern World System: Capitalist Agriculture and the Origins of the European World-economy in the 16th century* (New York 1974)

Eugene V. Walter: *Terror and Resistance: a Study of Political Violence* (Oxford 1969)

G. L. Warnock: *Contemporary Moral Philosophy* (Oxford 1967)

John White: *The Birth and Re-birth of Pictorial Space* (London 1967)

Lynn White Jr.: *Medieval Technology and Social Change* (Oxford 1966)

A. N. Whitehead: *The Functions of Reason* (Boston 1959)

W. F. Willcox: *International Migrations*, 2 vols (New York 1969)

Paul Wilkinson: *Political Terrorism* (London 1974)

Charles Wilson: *Economic History and the Historians* (London 1969)

Ludwig Wittgenstein: *Tractatus Logico-Philosophicus* (3rd imp., Cambridge 1966)

—— *Philosophical Investigations* (2nd ed., London 1958)

Donald Winch: *Economics and Policy: a Historical Study* (London 1969)

Gerald Woods, Philip Thompson and John Williams (eds.): *Art Without Boundaries, 1950–70* (London 1972)

Barbara Wooton: *Social Foundations of Wage Policy* (2nd ed., London 1962)

Robert Young: 'The Historiographic and Ideological Contexts of the 19th-century Debate on Man's Place in Nature', in Michulas Teich and Robert Young (eds.): *Changing Perspectives in the History of Science: Essays in Honour of Joseph Needham* (London 1973)

Burton Zwiebach: *Civility and Disobedience* (Cambridge 1975)

Index

PAUL JOHNSON

From 1965-1970 Paul Johnson was editor of the influential English weekly, *The New Statesman*. His previous books include the widely praised *A History of Christianity* (1976), *Elizabeth I: A Study in Power and Intellect* (1974), *The Offshore Islanders: From Roman Occupation to European Entry* (1972) and *Pope John 23rd* (1974).

We admit that all
knowledge is permanently
provisionary